Yankee Moderns

Yankee Moderns

Folk Regional Identity in the Sawmill Valley of Western Massachusetts, 1890–1920

Michael Hoberman

The University of Tennessee Press / Knoxville

First Edition.

The paper used in this book meets the minimum requirements of ANSI/NISO Z39.48-1992 (R 1997) (Permanence of Paper). The binding materials have been chosen for strength and durability. Printed on recycled paper.

Frontis.: Robert Ripley, 1990. Photograph by Paul Frantz, *Greenfield Recorder.*

Library of Congress Cataloging-in-Publication Data

Hoberman, Michael.
Yankee moderns : folk regional identity in the Sawmill Valley of Western Massachusetts, 1890–1920 / Michael Hoberman.— 1st ed.
p. cm.
Includes bibliographical references and index.
ISBN 1-57233-087-2 (cl.: alk. paper)
1. Oral tradition—Massachusetts—Sawmill River Valley. 2. Folklore—Massachusetts—Sawmill River Valley. 3. Sawmill River Valley (Mass.)—Social life and customs. 4. Group identity—Massachusetts—Sawmill River Valley. 5. Regionalism—Massachusetts—Sawmill River Valley. I. Title.
GR110.M4 H63 2000
974.4'22—dc21 00-008138

This book is dedicated to Mrs. Loyce Glazier Dunbar of Leverett, Massachusetts—my dear friend and teacher

This book is dedicated to Mrs. Loyce Glazier Dunbar
of Leverett, Massachusetts—my dear friend and teacher

Contents

Figures

Maps

Preface

Popular and academic authors routinely have portrayed post–Civil War rural New England as a region in decline. At worst, the area's inhabitants have been cast as backward-looking and dangerously homogeneous in their cultural makeup. Even writers who have sought to emphasize what they have marked as the region's more laudable qualities—its residents' stalwart independence, for instance, or their hard-headed "Yankee ingenuity"—have offered rural New England up as a crotchety exception to modernity's nearly worldwide sway—the home of "America's hobbits," as historian Stephen Nissenbaum wryly puts it (38). In this book I have sought to challenge this account on several fronts. The narratives I collected in the course of my field study of oral traditions in western Massachusetts' Sawmill Valley have led me to believe that, if anything, rural New England was as profoundly *modern* as any city in the turn-of-the-century period. The men and women who lived in this valley between 1890 and 1920 may have been motivated by agrarian, or premodern, *ideals,* but in actuality they inhabited—and coped quite competently with—a remarkably unstable world. To begin with, the late-industrial-era economic conditions under which they lived precluded self-sufficiency. Moreover, the region's culture, which once had been singularly Anglo, expanded to encompass (or at least to acknowledge the presence of) Polish and French Canadian immigrants, among others, and cultural homogeneity became a matter of distant memory. Residents of the Sawmill Valley recognized these facts and adapted quite competently to the changing conditions of their lives.

Based in part on what I learned in the course of my interviews in the Sawmill Valley, I also argue in this book that the folklore of a given region is, by definition, a dynamic or *permeable* entity. Dating at least as far back as the birth of folklore as an academic discipline in the late nineteenth century, many scholars have drawn limiting maps around rural people, in effect consigning them to—or, perhaps more accurately, projecting upon them—a condition of cultural stasis and geographical isolation. In the last few decades, several folklorists have challenged this rather condescending view of "the folk," but few have done so by examining the concept of *region* itself.

This book is the result of my attempt to expand upon current trends in folklore research and to apply them to the specific group of tradition-bearers whom I met in the Sawmill Valley.

I began the project as a doctoral candidate in American Studies at the University of Massachusetts at Amherst. Having spent my first four years as a graduate student pursuing a more traditional course of study in literature, I decided at the dissertation stage to turn my attention to the sorts of cultural texts I could find in my own backyard, as it were. The Sawmill Valley was familiar to me because, at the time, I lived and worked in it and experienced its landscape on a daily basis.

Beginning in the winter of 1991–92, I conducted interviews with men and women who had been living in the valley all or most of their lives; most of my informants were between 65 and 90 years of age. In the interviews, I asked people both about their own experiences growing up in the valley around the turn of the century and about what they remembered having been told by older relatives and neighbors. The primary textual basis for this book is the transcribed record of those recorded interviews.

Acknowledgments

I could not have written this book without the help and enthusiasm of both my informants and my various advisors and readers over the years since I began my fieldwork. My greatest debt is to the men and women who participated in the interviews; this book's appendix presents a brief biography of each of them. Four people who helped lead me to my informants were Audrey Duckert, Michael Kline, Louise Minks, and Mary Wyatt. Once I reached the writing stage, I was given invaluable and devoted assistance by my dissertation advisor, Margo Culley; in fact, her helpfulness has persevered into the present. The University of Massachusetts, Amherst, supported me with a University Fellowship during the year that I was completing the dissertation; because it enabled me to lighten my teaching load, the fellowship made a significant difference. The other members of my original dissertation committee—Robert Paynter and George Carey—offered useful critiques as well. David Lovelace and Roberta Frederick have read more recent versions of the manuscript, and I owe them thanks. I also would like to thank my editors at the University of Tennessee Press, Joyce Harrison and Stan Ivester, for enthusiastically helping me see this project through to its publishable conclusion.

I also owe several debts for inspiration. First, I appreciate my family—my partner Janice Sorensen and children Della and Langston—for being their loving, inquisitive selves at every step along the way. Janice is the book's photographer; I would like to think that her artistry, technical skill, and perfectionism have made up for my own lack of those qualities. I have been consistently inspired, too, by my students at Greenfield Community College, who have helped to teach me the value of common sense and straight talk. Thanks are due as well to my Dutch friends and colleagues, Eugene Van Erven and Jaap Verheul, who twice have provided me with the opportunity both to teach a course on American Modernism and to leave my New England digs for a foreign land (and a flat one at that) from which I might better reflect on the Yankee world in which I usually am immersed. Like their counterparts in Massachusetts, my students in Utrecht helped me in several unforeseen ways, especially when it came to the difficult—some would say impossible—task of defining modernity. Like all good scholars, they forced the question and never gave up seeking and formulating responses to it.

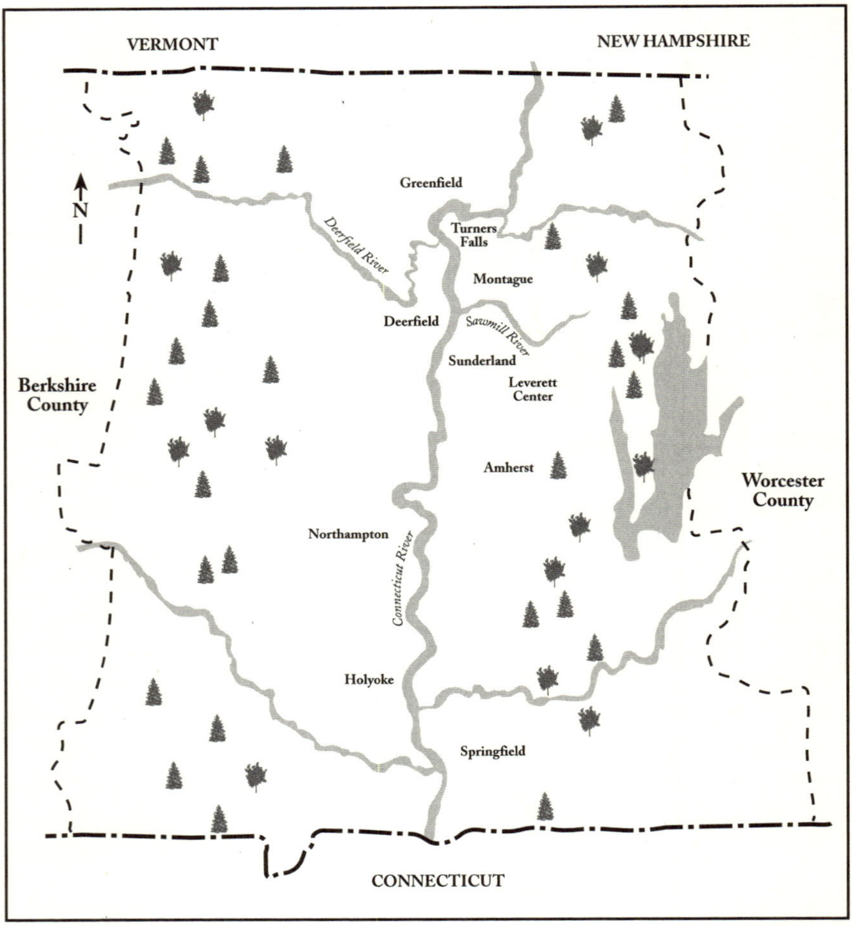

Western Massachusetts.

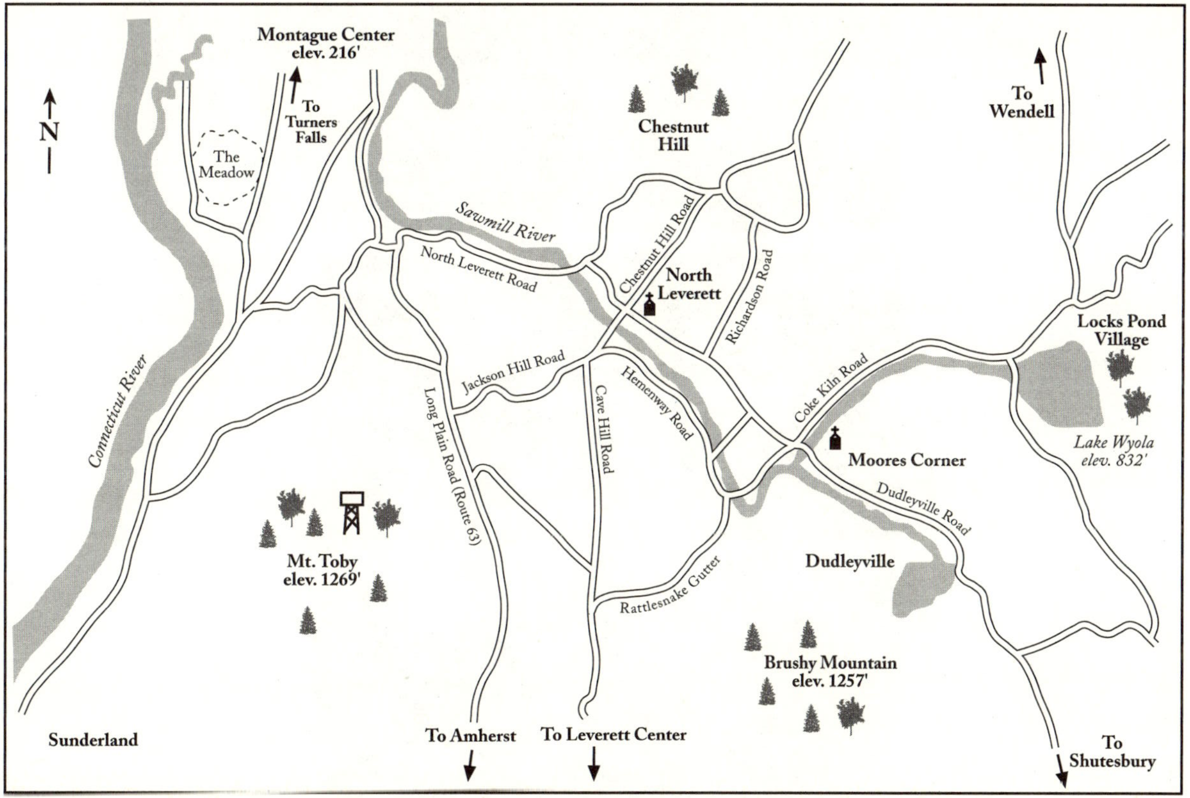

The Sawmill Valley.

Introduction

Clifford Blinn working his makeshift maple syrup evaporator, February 1999. Photograph by Janice Sorensen.

Rivers and Tributaries: An American Folk Region

"Low-ranking, Particular, Regional Knowledge": Folklore Meets Modernity

I moved to rural New England ten years ago, mostly because I was enthralled by the *idea* of it. I'd been won over by enchanting images from my past—a spruce forest on Glastonbury Mountain in Vermont, the worn wooden floor of an old bookstore in the Litchfield Hills of Connecticut. Having spent most of my childhood and young adulthood with no solid ties to any one place, I was eager to begin a new, settled life (as well as a career as a graduate student) rooted in the mossy and stone wall–strewn landscape of New England's heartland—the Connecticut River Valley of Massachusetts. I suppose now that I aspired to become a living exemplar of Thoreau's ideal: a man who would know the names of all the local ponds, spend the day tending a vegetable crop, and then devote the evening to analyzing the essays of Thomas Carlyle. My rural longings undoubtedly were inflected by a large measure of romanticism. I was quite self-conscious about my place in that long-standing tradition of idealists who, in their alienation from the sordid, complex conditions of modern life, sought solace and a sense of belonging in the "simpler" life of an enlightened agrarian America. Several of my friends, in fact, had warned me that they had known like-minded people who had moved to this "Happy Valley" and then vanished from sight; evidently, the rustic pleasures of rural life, in combination with the small-scale sophistication of area college towns such as Amherst and Northampton, had proven irresistible.

Ironically, like many of my maladjusted predecessors in the Romantic tradition, upon my arrival I felt in almost every respect as if I were an outsider in the verdant countryside to which I so sincerely wished to become indigenous. As a product of urban America, as a son of the professional class, and, perhaps most significantly, as a Diaspora Jew, I felt my cultural identity entirely circumscribed by a sense of placelessness. Whenever I passed the weather-beaten houses of my neighbors, both in my adopted village of Montague and upstream along the Sawmill River (the local, westward-flowing tributary of the Connecticut), I noted that the names on the mailboxes matched the names of the local roads. These people had been here forever. Weighed down by all my modern allegiances, I, on the other hand, never would stop being an outsider.

I realize now that, as I marked the apparent differences between myself and the locals, I was taking it for granted that native-born inhabitants of rural districts lived more "simply" than I did, that they were so firmly tied to their local hills, woods, and farm buildings that their cultural existence was an unmediated aspect of the landscape itself. Among other things, I have learned over the course of the last ten years that those farms were put there and kept up by people *who knew what they were doing.* Self-consciousness and acts of cultural invention are not the province solely of urban intellectuals and bookish Romantics; several generations of rural New Englanders have been no less self-aware and worldly than several generations of New York Jews. My neighbors' cultural identity, much like my own, was the result of their long-standing engagement with, and alienation from, what Marshall Berman refers to as the "maelstrom" of the modern world (1). Even in their relative geographical removal, residents of the Sawmill Valley, like inhabitants of other rural areas in New England and throughout North America a hundred years ago, were anything but isolated or culturally stagnant. In the early decades of the twentieth century, their lives were affected profoundly by many of the same forces that went on to shape my late-twentieth-century urban world as well. Among these forces were large-scale industrial capitalism, immigration, and the eclipse of an overarching Protestant faith. Their cultural life was an outgrowth of their encounters with, and participation in, a world very much like the one that I, for all my bucolic longings, belong to as well.

This book is about the convergence of folk regional identity—a culturally based sense of place—with the social, economic, and psychic pressures enacted by the multifarious force we have come to know as modernity. The book explores the effects of this convergence on the oral traditions of inhabitants of a tiny section of upland New England at the turn of the century, but its implications are wide-ranging and broadly relevant to the fashioning of regional identity throughout the rural United States. The Sawmill River itself is a forceful, if somewhat obscure, *tributary.* A mere six miles from its source, however, it flows into the 360-mile-long Connecticut River, which divides New England along a north-south axis from the Canadian border to Long Island Sound. Like the Hudson, Delaware, and Susquehanna rivers (among others), the Connecticut literally has shaped the course of history in the northeastern United States. In effect, I have chosen to concentrate on the particularities of a single stream's worth of human experience in order to approach larger, theoretical questions which apply to a river full of cultural existence.

Notwithstanding an ever-popular trend among scholars, as well as a more recent tendency for purveyors of bumper-stickers to admonish us to "think globally and act locally," this study's near-microscopic focus on a locale that is barely twelve square miles in extent is more than incidental. In fact, the small scale of this book derives directly from my thematic interest in *region* and *regional identity*—terms which the reader will encounter throughout its pages. Ordinarily, regions have been defined in both popular and academic contexts as slightly (or largely) amorphous subcategories of geographical and cultural (or economic or social) spaces within existing nations: New England is a region of the United States; Normandy is a region in France. But do regions have to be such large entities? Unfortunately, close attention to the last several decades of writing on the concept of "region" has led me only to the following conclusion, which I have found articulated in various places but never explained or accounted for: "Region," according to Clarence Mondale, "is understood to be an area of almost any size" (25). Existing definitions suggest that a *region* can be as small as a twelve-mile-square locale *or* as large as a six-state expanse of the United States.

In completing this study, then, I have found it necessary to build a definition of *region* from the ground up. Perhaps this should come as no surprise, given the fact that, as Patricia Nelson Limerick puts it, regional studies often have been places where generations of scholars have gone "for a nap" (84). In any case, it is my suggestion that any convergence of landscape and culture can constitute a region. A region—especially when it is as bounded and small as the Sawmill Valley was at the beginning of the twentieth century—is a place where people share a common body of narrative knowledge, some but not all of which derives from a shared geography. A region is a place whose inhabitants have inscribed a set of (often shifting) borders, both physical and psychological, and have applied those borders in order to separate those who belong in it from those who do not. And although, by definition, a region is a part of a whole, the region can also be said to be, as Etienne Juillard points out, "endowed with a certain self-sufficiency . . . in the sense that most of the functions and services of primary importance are represented there in such a way that the region is capable of satisfying . . . the needs of its inhabitants" (435). Clearly, according to such an understanding, size ought not to be a crucial factor in our determination of whether or not a given geographical entity is a region or not.

One of premises of this book is that New England and the Sawmill Valley are both regions. I would argue that their coexistence under the same rubric does not render the term *region* either meaningless or excessively broad. Rather, such a coexistence occasions a long overdue redefinition of region. An individual's sense of regional identity, understood in this way, occurs within a concentric and often overlapping array of regions which vary in size. To the extent that someone participates in a cultural milieu that derives from her or his identity as an inhabitant of North America, North America is a region. To the extent that that person belongs to a cultural group whose oral traditions derive from its settlement along a single tributary of the Connecticut River, that tributary also marks out a region.

At least two generations of folklorists have used the category "folk group" to label the sorts of communities—varying widely in size—which create, pass on, and remake traditions. Typically, folk groups are built out of preexisting vocational, ethnic, age-specific, and regional commonalties. Police officers, for example, share a body of folklore, as do Italian-Americans, children, and residents of, say, rural New England valleys. Even if, at the close of the twentieth century, folklore still is understood to be a predominantly *informal* means of communication, the existence of folk groups no longer is contingent upon face-to-face interactions. In recent years, folklorists such as Alan Dundes have devoted their attention to the ever-increasing body of lore that has emerged from any number of "cyber" contexts, not to mention the receiving trays of office copiers (Dundes and Pagter, *Work Hard).* Other studies, such as Gene Bluestein's *Poplore* (1994), have worked to dismantle or at least to critique the formerly hard and fast distinction between folklore and popular culture. Thus, it might be argued that New Englanders who trade Red Sox or Patriots trivia in Internet chat rooms devoted to such pastimes might be building upon their folk cultural identity as New Englanders, even if they never encounter one another physically. Indeed, as long ago as the turn of the twentieth century, New Englanders' collective status as Yankees already was the result of large-scale ideological and expressive endeavors—from rural schoolroom readings of John Greenleaf Whittier's poem "Snow Bound" to public observances of Revolutionary War events in Boston. Regional identity writ large, in other words, long since has outgrown its face-to-face stage of development. At least at the beginning of this century, however, in small-scale localities, regional identity still was the result of human encounters. In these places, folk traditions continued to be exchanged intergenerationally in front of the wood stove, at the sawmill, and at church socials.

Such daily exposure never has been the sole basis for the creation of folklore, of course; folklore is notorious for crossing and recrossing oceans and mountain ranges, moving quickly from one group to the next and changing in the process. But the existence of a face-to-face community *is* inherent in the fashioning of a small-scale regional folk group such as the one that lived along the Sawmill Valley during the turn-of-the-century period. This is because the body of narratives that held this group together derived from the fact that its members *did* share actual geographical reference points. Only people who lived in the Sawmill Valley could be counted upon to know certain things—the settlement history of Brushy Mountain, for instance, or who Baker Whipple was and why he lived in that shanty at the foot of Richardson Road. Valley residents, as folklorist Barbara Allen observes about regional folk groups in general, were people who "share[d] a body of folklore by virtue of living in a certain geographical area that form[ed] the basis for a shared identity" ("Regional Folklore" 619). Valley residents also were members of any number of larger folk groups; they belonged to particular ethnic groups, as well as to particular occupational and religious groups. But the one factor that all of them had in common was their collective occupation of a specific geography.

This is not to say that the valley's folklore and folklife were the exclusive inventions of local residents. Sawmill Valley people developed a vernacular culture that derived from their collective identity as residents of the Connecticut Valley, their status as New Englanders, and their American citizenship. Like storytellers and tradition-bearers in all regions, the residents of the Sawmill Valley absorbed beliefs, practices, and (in some cases) actual narrative motifs from all over the world. Where valley residents diverged from their neighbors in nearby towns, as well as from their fellow New Englanders and Americans, was in their collective acts of *regionalization*, their reinterpretation of otherwise broadly based cultural forms within a specific and relatively narrow geographical context.

The various qualifications that scholars have applied to the term *regional* appear to obscure the issue of what constitutes a region, in large part because, owing to habitual practice, so many of us are accustomed to thinking of regions not only as large entities but also as inherently amorphous. Several recent definitions of the concept, however, seem to offer insight even as they fail to indicate how big or small a region must be in order to qualify as such.

Interestingly, the most stable ingredient to be located in a region is its very *in*stability, its status as a category of the imagination rather than as a geographical or social fact. In this regard, the Annales School of historians has exerted a major, if an unintended, influence upon most recent regional studies, most of which elevate *mentalité* to a height equivalent to that of historical/social circumstance (Mondale 18). Ideas are central to the creation of regions—so central, in fact, that they seem to constitute the only consistent presence concerning which regional theorists have reached any sort of agreement. Limerick echoes several other recent and not-so-recent regionalists in her qualified assertion that, indeed, "regions . . . do not seem altogether real" (96). Geography (surely one of the world's few actual "facts") is almost incidental—"it plays a role in their definition, [but] regions are more the creations of human thought and behavior than they are products of nature" (96). Like so many other cultural devices, the region—and I would argue that this applies to both the local or small region and the larger, more conventional region—is, as Stephen Nissenbaum defines it, not only an imaginative construct but a specifically ideological one as well, something that usually "gets generated in the process of distinguishing itself from something else" (46). If nothing else, the oral traditions which occupy the core of this book make manifest both the imaginative and the ideological premises which give rise to the creation of a specifically *regional* folklore.

And here we are brought to an odd, almost unexpected convergence. Ideological concerns have been central not only to the lives of the members of regional folk groups, but also to the work of academics who have studied them. The twentieth century has seen the formation of at least two distinct regionalist movements among scholars in the humanities and social sciences. In the 1930s, as American intellectuals responded to the economic and social crises brought on by large-scale capitalism, urbanization, and the decline of nearly all forms of centralizing moral authority, an increasing number of academics and *literateurs* worked to orchestrate a rediscovery of American regions. The mid-century regionalist movement reached an almost utopian fervor at times; in certain respects, it was a last-ditch effort to restore the primacy of rural values and folkways to the forefront of American culture. Regionalists of the 1930s included New Deal enthusiasts, people like folklorist Benjamin Botkin. Thanks in part to Simon Bronner and Jerrold Hirsch, who recently have restored Botkin to academic respectability in the aftermath of Richard Dorson's debunking of him as an illegitimate popularizer of folk materials, we now can recognize this editor of several popular anthologies of American regional folklore as having offered readers a bountiful trove (indeed, the books were entitled *Treasuries*) of *common* people's heritage: folk legends, songs, proverbs, and so on, with origins in the nation's various geographical "corners."

To the extent that it ever truly existed as such, however, the Regionalist movement also included the members of the Fugitives, a group of Southern intellectuals whose collective rhetorical efforts to reinvent the Old South were published in 1930 in the book *I'll Take My Stand.* Both left-wing and right-wing regionalists, as Richard Dorman observes in the introduction to his comprehensive study of the 1930s regionalists, *Revolt of the Provinces* (1993), posed region "against . . . modern tendencies as the means towards a richer, freer, and more humane way of life" (xii). Perhaps because regions—large and small—pose a form of seemingly premodern defiance of arbitrary, politically imposed borders and other normative categories of thought, their reinvention in the New Deal era offered an increasingly alienated intelligentsia an imaginative realm in which it could base its response to modernity. And, in the increasingly leveling spirit of the age, vernacular regions in particular offered the prospect of a largely unmined cultural wealth, much of which was, theoretically at least, still predominantly in the hands of poor people.

As a nearly invisible current ties the left-wing ideology of the 1930s to the countercultural and anti-imperialist movements of the 1960s and 1970s, so too has the regionalist trend (which largely had been subsumed by the centralizing ethos of the Cold War) seen a resurgence that gradually has been gaining strength on American campuses since the 1970s. No lesser a bright light than Michel Foucault (if such a label appropriately can be applied to a man whose career rained a continuous stream of cheerless revelation and admonition down upon the academic world), at the height of his influence, pronounced the need for new areas of inquiry, to include "'low-ranking, particular, regional knowledge'" (Mondale 13–14; Miller 7). The prospect of a "new" regionalism is taken up in greater detail and with a heavy dose of ideological—indeed, moral—fervor in an influential 1979 article by Jay Mechling. As the field of American studies began to move away from the centralizing "myth and symbol" school and into (among other arenas) the realm of "low-ranking" bodies of knowledge, Mechling offered his fellow scholars the model of regional studies as a ground upon which they might effectively reconstitute the field. Like his predecessors in the 1930s, his article begins with an assertion of the moral imperative at hand. For Mechling, the study of regions (which, in my reading of the piece, may be as large as California or as small as the Sacramento Valley) offers both a serviceable and a spiritual renewal of the soul. Regionalism also serves, in his estimation, as a "mediating" bulwark against the tide of modernity, a means by which presumably "low-ranking" people have been able to resist the temptations and incursions of a synthesizing and annihilating American culture. Finally, region offers researchers a means of avoiding—or supplanting—a "uniformist" American studies, the sort of thing that, although it now may appear to be an element of the pre-1960s distant past, certainly has plenty of vocal advocates among today's conservative culture warriors ("If They Can").

Indeed, regionalism has been a dominant force in the field of American studies since the 1970s, although most of its practitioners have not been self-conscious or even ideological regionalists. It is the very elasticity of regionalism as a concept, and its inclusive appeal to both the pluralists of the 1930s and the multiculturalists of the current era, that have provided it with such a long, if often meandering, academic life. Contemporary scholars such as myself, who have an inherent interest in the modalities of race, ethnicity, class, and gender, among other categories of (invented) cultural identity, have located in the region—both in its macrocosmic role (i.e., New England, the South) *and* in its microcosmic application (i.e., the Sacramento Valley, the Sawmill Valley)—a place where, according to Peter Onuf, "discrete, though related, structures intersect and interact in particular patterns" (5). The region is a place where, theoretically at least, different sorts of people have been encountering one another for as long as they have shared the same geography. Since American studies as a discipline is largely about the process and aftermath of such encounters, a regional perspective seems particularly appropriate. Moreover, for the moralists among us, such a perspective does seem to offer a welcoming form of inclusion; regionalism is, as Onuf puts it, "more about belonging than it is about exclusion" (4). Besides, it's nice to take a nap once in a while.

Not that the nap time lasts long. Even when the regional approach is an incidental aspect of a given study, it necessitates a continual reach toward meaning and theoretical relevance. Focusing on small-scale regions or pieces of America need not be an antiquarian or trivial pursuit. The microcosmic approach, as folklorist Sandra Dolby suggests in a 1996 article, is not an excuse for escapism. On the contrary, while folklorists such as myself "do not always succeed in making the difficult leap from particular to general, from micro to macro," we are always making the attempt and have applied the "micro" approach in order to combine a need to "attend to real communities" with a theoretical interest in, among other things, the continually occurring encounters and cross-fertilizations that comprise American culture (60). Such microcosmic concentration on the local as a means of engaging wide-ranging interests is nothing new to scholarship in American studies or folklore, of course. This has been true especially in New England, where researchers have taken advantage of the Puritan legacy of abundant and painstaking recordkeeping. Historian Kenneth Lockridge's influential 1970 study of Dedham, Massachusetts, is one such book. Although his study is "geographically confined," Lockridge explains, it is "comprehensive in terms of human activity" and thus fully warranted in offering informed speculations regarding other early American towns and the colonial era as a whole (xiv). Likewise, Thomas Hubka's 1983 exploration of the New England connected farm (focusing almost entirely on a relatively small region of eastern New Hampshire and western Maine) addresses itself not only to the particulars of one kind of vernacular landscape and architecture, but also to "larger" matters, such as the decline of farming throughout New England in the latter half of the nineteenth century and local farmers' determination to stave off their own impending obsolescence.

In its overall structure, the present book reflects the historical and cultural particularities of life in the Sawmill Valley. The chapters to follow are built around folk traditions pertaining, respectively, to the hills, farms, woodlots, and villages of the region. On the other hand, each chapter is organized around my guiding theoretical interests in regionalism and modernity.

Each section of the book addresses itself to two basic questions. First, how does regional identity take shape as a response to economic and social pressures which *transcend* regional boundaries? In other words, to what extent is a region a permeable, dynamic entity, whose folklife is a direct result of its commerce with the *outside* world? Second, as they respond to these "outside" pressures, how do the members of a regional group invent a cultural life that stakes a claim to the landscapes that they inhabit? How and why does folklore—an inherently transitory and transregional entity that seldom obeys ethnic (or any other) lines of demarcation—become embedded in a specific geographical setting? To all appearances, the folk region is a primary locus for the sort of cultural admixture which folklorist Roger Abrahams marks as characteristic of the twentieth century, within which "peoples from widely different cultural traditions converge, selectively maintaining certain traditional practices, altering others to conform to new situations, and producing bold new realized synthetic forms and styles" (397).

Despite this large frame of reference, my interest in this book is not in generalizing from the particular, but rather in engaging the particular as a mode of inquiry, as a means of formulating useful questions and illustrating their application to one set of human experiences. Throughout the book, I am addressing myself not only to scholars in the fields of folklore, oral history, and American studies, but also to members of a more general audience, whose interests very well may be in the observable "facts" of cultural life in rural New England rather than in their theoretical implications. I have written a book, parts of which, I hope, might prove to be as approachable to the residents of the Sawmill Valley itself as it is to my peers in the academic arena. Although these people comprise what I would assume to be a relatively minuscule portion of an admittedly small readership, I consider myself largely answerable to them, as any conscientious neighbor—even in relatively *laissez-faire* rural New England—would be.

I am well aware that a large proportion of current humanities and social-science scholarship approaches and often enough achieves impenetrability, at least as far as the common reader is concerned. Writers of academic books usually are working within a highly competitive and specialist-oriented context. They are compelled, in other words, to write books for their colleagues in the field, rather than for a general, common-sense readership. In some senses, this book is no exception. As the foregoing discussion of regionalism should suggest, one of my main purposes in this study is to offer an innovative contribution to current scholarship in folklore and American studies. Moreover, readers who do not find the symbolic analysis of texts as thrilling as I do may deem the interpretive sections of the book less interesting than quoted bits of interview transcripts. As a community-college English instructor whose students display a patient but bemused tolerance for my interest in reading *into* literary works ("Did we just spend half an hour discussing 'My mother is a fish'?"), I am somewhat sensitive and accustomed to such protests; on a certain level, I see their validity. Nonetheless, I ask nonspecialist readers of this book to suspend their disbelief and indulge me in my interpretive impositions. Certainly, every one of the transcribed narratives contained in the book merits attention on its own terms. Folklore and oral history books featuring relatively intact texts have their value, implying as they do that the folk ought to be understood on their own terms rather than being interpreted by scholars who, more often than not, are outsiders to the communities being studied. Nonetheless, in this book I have chosen to supply a highly active interpretive voice and framework. Quite simply, I consider myself the narrator of this particular tale and willingly assume full responsibility for its failures, exaggerations, and blind spots. I have adopted this role for several reasons, not the least of which is the fact that—to the extent that this book tells a story—the story needs coherence and purpose. In effect, my thematic readings of the featured oral texts make an ordered whole out of an otherwise divergent set of orally recounted traditions.

Beyond lending coherence to the project, the interpretive framework that holds the book together also may bear a populist message. If the nonspecialist reader is willing to forgive a seemingly overwrought spirit of interpretation, she or he may find that one of the assumptions underlying such interpretation is the notion that these texts—as informal as they are—deserve the same respect and high regard as any great work of literature. When literary critics apply their deep-reading fervor to works of fiction and poetry, they usually justify such attention by pointing to the inherent complexity of such texts. But varying narrative strategies, irony, symbolism, ambivalence, and the like are hardly the sole property of works by Metaphysical Poets, Victorian-era Aesthetes, or genre-exploding postmodernists. The men and women who are the sources of the narratives included here are no less innovative, rhetorically sophisticated, or psychologically conflicted than the brightest stars in the literary firmament. My dedication to reading and juxtaposing their narratives carefully derives from my own conviction that the apparently ordinary pronouncements of apparently ordinary people are just as worthy of multilayered readings as the most finely wrought works of literature. I have been motivated, in other words, by my admiration of these people as verbal artists in their own right.

"Steep Hillsides and Stony Soil": Settlement History of the Sawmill Valley

Needless to say, my commitment to the particularities of Sawmill Valley life also owes itself to the fact that, not so long ago, I called it home. Indeed, this book is a direct result of my own experiences there, which were the actual impetus for my scholarly interest in the region's folk history. When I first came to western Massachusetts, I sought all the accouterments that I associated with a country life. Before I'd even secured a library card at the university or mapped out my course schedule, I found myself a job as a part-time milker on a goat farm situated along the Sawmill River near the village of Moores Corner, about five miles upstream from my home in Montague Center. I figured that farm work would afford me a healthy escape from my academic duties, which, for all their mental challenges, would not offer me anything in the way of physical exertion and familiarity with the soil, both of which I took to be requisite features of a rural existence. I formed an easy rapport with both the people and the animals of E.I.E.I.O. farm and reveled in the quiet surroundings. Because I was a mere farmhand, not charged with any sort of financial responsibility for the animals I was helping to steward, I was able to indulge my meditative inclinations on the job. As I hefted hay bales and carried water buckets, I often would rest for a moment in order to take stock of the Sawmill Valley's defining hills, barns, houses, and fields. I would speculate as to what they might have meant to previous generations of haulers of hay and water. I wanted the land to mean as much to me as did the books I was reading at the university.

My pauses in the farmyard, though inspiring, did not lead me to my intellectual trough. It was not until I thought to ground my speculations with some readings in local history that the connection between landscape and culture crystallized for me. If the hours I spent in the farmyard helped me to choose this book's geographical and historical scope, E. P. Pressey's chance description of a property sale in his 1910 *History of Montague* had the effect of defining my theoretical interest. I recognized the site of Asa Orcutt's mill instantly as I read the historian's description of it in his chapter on "Old Town Industries," but I was especially intrigued to read about the man to whom Orcutt had sold his mill in 1837. "Above the bridge where Federal Street meets the North Leverett Road," I read, "Asa Orcutt built a dam and a sawmill and sold [it] to Silas Lamson, a Jew, about 1837."

For years after Lamson himself had left the place, Pressey's book told me, the sawmill in question was referred to by locals as either "the Jew's mill" (207) or "the Jew place" (134). What surprised me as I read these passages was not the fact that a Jewish man had once owned and operated a sawmill in an overwhelmingly Anglo-Protestant community; I was struck by the writer's references to the cultural attributes of a given *place.* Pressey's offhand inclusion of this now-departed place-name reminded me that local spoken traditions such as this one tell us more about the people who create them than they do about the bare facts of geography. The existence of a "Jew place" within the local lexicon piqued my interest in the often proprietary oral traditions that accrue around places. The author's reference to Silas Lamson spoke to me on a personal level as well, of course. As a Jew and self-described outsider who at that time made his home in the Sawmill Valley, I had an important stake in his story.

Through spring, summer, fall, and winter of several years, I rode my bicycle past that millsite, uphill from my home near the Connecticut River, to milk those goats. As I repeated that climb and made the swift descent back home, I began really to see the valley's topography, its hardscrabble hillsides and the looping, stony river that formed its center. Only ten miles distant from the town of Amherst, with its dozen cappuccino-serving establishments and its postmodern book displays, lay this paradise of sloping pastures and gardens. Its beauty was almost otherworldly. But I wondered why eminently practical Yankees ever would have bothered to settle so thickly in such a tightly bounded, seemingly unfarmable valley.

I found the answer to my question not only in books like E. P. Pressey's but also as I bushwhacked along the thickly wooded banks of the river itself, where the moss-covered, rocky remains of several watermills still stand. Rocks and books alike tell us that the first known European settlement in the Sawmill River Valley was a gristmill on the site of the present-day Billings Mill (the former "Jew place"), near the intersection of North Leverett Road and Route 63. This mill was built in 1715, and it ground grain for the people of Sunderland (then called Swampfield), who lacked their own source of water power. In other words, from the earliest moment of permanent European presence, the Sawmill Valley was settled primarily as an industrial corridor. The writers of the Leverett Bicentennial Committee's *A History of Leverett, Massachusetts, 1774–1974,* provide a survey of the local landscape that speaks to some of the facts underlying this settlement history: "The portion of the [Sawmill] Valley from the source of the river, at Lake Wyola, to Route 63 is two or three miles wide and has a length of six miles. In this distance, the river drops a total of five-hundred and seventy-one feet. The valley runs in an east-west direction and is rimmed on the north and south by hills ranging to a elevation of twelve hundred thirty feet. The steep hillsides, stony soil and non-productive areas of tillable land have never lent themselves to agriculture. The early settlers recognized this but the potential power was not overlooked, and mills and shops began to spring up beside the waters" (39). Even as the people of the Sawmill Valley raised much of their own food in the eighteenth, nineteenth, and early twentieth centuries, they certainly did not do so to the exclusion of trading and interacting with—not to mention *thinking* about—people from other places.

When English people first came to the Sawmill Valley in the early decades of the eighteenth century, many of them probably were thinking about the more populous towns and villages of the Connecticut Valley proper—places they had left behind. Originally settled in the 1660s by a dual emigration from coastal Massachusetts and Connecticut, the Connecticut River floodplain was prone to such prosperity that it came to be known, by the early nineteenth century, as the "breadbasket" of New England. In the period following the American Revolution, the region's farms generated wealth by producing large quantities of stall-fed cattle, as well as an assortment of grains and other crops. Having put their frontier troubles (some of the fiercest battles of King Phillip's War took place along the Connecticut River) behind them by the middle 1700s, the inhabitants of such towns as Springfield, Northampton, Hadley, and Deerfield came to enjoy a cultural, religious, and social life that was quite rich by New England standards. Jonathan Edwards, the famed preacher of the Great Awakening which swept the eastern seaboard in the 1740s, had his home church in Northampton. The homes of established Connecticut Valley farmers and merchants—many of which remain inhabited to this day—often were large and ornate, and the streets that they lined bespoke an active village commerce. Men and women who chose to *leave* such places behind (or to ignore them altogether) in favor of a much more tenuous existence in the adjacent hills certainly were risk-takers. Upland regions like the Sawmill Valley offered much less in the way of economic opportunity—or cultural engagement—than their lowland counterparts.

As we view New England from our perch in the late twentieth century, it is easy to forget that it was not always the far easterly region that the rest of the nation left behind in its westward surge. The period leading up to and following the Revolutionary War saw large-scale economic *expansion* in the New England states, not to mention their famed cultural predominance. In the same fashion that coastal and southern New Englanders in the period between 1660 and 1750 found their way to the Connecticut Valley in search of new land, their descendants found their way up the big river's tributaries in the years that followed. Their initial excursions often were intended only as means of feeding people in the lowlands—as the settlement history of "the Jew place" and other mills appears to indicate. But land shortages and population growth along the Connecticut impelled settlers to travel farther and farther afield, and in most cases this meant traveling uphill and settling permanently in places like the Sawmill Valley and countless other upland communities throughout New England. Economic *disparity* was the major factor in this new settlement pattern. Indeed, when one of the largest civil uprisings of the post-Revolutionary period coalesced around the leadership of Continental Army veteran Daniel Shays (a resident of nearby Pelham, Massachusetts), upland farmers swelled the ranks. As historian Ritchie Garrison suggests in his study of western Massachusetts' vernacular landscapes, even well into the 1800s the inhabitants of upland communities were "worlds away" from their neighbors along the Connecticut (94–114).

Nevertheless, the women and men of the Sawmill Valley, like the residents of so many other apparently isolated corners of the earth, were inextricably tied, in both economic and cultural terms, to the more prosperous towns of the bountiful floodplain. By the beginning of the nineteenth century, environmental historian Carolyn Merchant writes, farmers across New England had begun to participate in a market system that had rendered self-sufficiency all but obsolete. A number of factors contributed to this change. The Napoleonic Wars created an increased demand for imported grain in Europe. At the same time, however,

New Englanders were running out of unsettled, arable land. "At this point," Merchant writes, "two broad choices became available to New Englanders that relieved the mounting tensions: westward migration to the fruitful soils of New York, or a change to intensive farming [stall-fed oxen, for example] or non-agricultural production" (188).

Given a dearth of farmable soil, the settlers of the Sawmill Valley opted for the latter strategy. Their decision to remain in New England was contingent entirely upon their choice to participate in the burgeoning *market* economy that Carolyn Merchant describes. For most of the nineteenth century, Sawmill Valley residents engaged in a lively industrial commerce with buyers downstream. The several mills founded along the Sawmill River offered an alternative means of economic sustenance for people for whom large-scale farming was an impossibility. These mills processed food, lumber, and other goods to be used not only in the Connecticut Valley towns, but also in other parts of New England. Settlers had taken full advantage of the local topography. The twenty-two sawmills that once flourished along the banks of the Sawmill River attested to an active involvement on the part of valley residents in a regional commerce that quite obviously precluded isolation.

Native-born and Foreign Yankees: French Canadian and Eastern European Immigration to the Connecticut River Valley at the Turn of the Century

Much of the clamor that must have accompanied the building and operation of these industrial sites during the eighteenth and nineteenth centuries came to an end not long after the Civil War. On a national scale, of course, this postwar period saw the largest demographic shifts in the history of the nation. Between 1860 and 1920, for example, the country's urban population increased by 669 percent (Barron 32). More specifically, as Ann Douglas writes, the war itself partially decimated rural New England's male population. Then, in the war's immediate aftermath, many Yankees left upland communities like the Sawmill Valley, drawn away by "the attractions of western expansion and an increasingly industrialized economy" (18). One after another, the watermills closed up shop, so that, by the turn of the century, only a few continued to produce.

Even well before this time, even the remotest pockets of rural New England were beginning to be affected, both directly and indirectly, by the reorientation of the economy toward factory production, which in turn attracted record numbers of non-Anglo immigrants. The uplands had been settled in the service of a mixed economy based on natural resources. By 1900, however, that economy had been fully replaced by other forms of production. Several of the rich agricultural towns of the Connecticut River floodplain evolved into cities. In the period between 1870 and 1915, Hampden County—the site of such cities as Springfield, Holyoke, and Chicopee—experienced a 235-percent increase in population—the highest in Massachusetts (*Historic and Archaeological Resources* 119). Still closer to home, industrial sites in the Franklin County cities of Turners Falls and Greenfield (approximately ten miles distant from the Sawmill Valley) were producing, among other things, machine parts, cutlery, paper, and hydroelectric power. As hard as they worked, residents of the Sawmill Valley, like their counterparts in other rural sections of New England, could barely compete in such a booming, post-agricultural economy. Nor could they remain unaffected by the arrival, both on their periphery and in their midst, of French Canadian and Eastern European immigrants.

Large-scale non-Anglo immigration to the New England states began in the mid-1800s, with the arrival of Irish immigrants. This was especially true in eastern Massachusetts and its outlying districts, where factories, railroads, farms, and other economic sectors attracted refugees from the potato famine of the 1840s. But western sections of the state were touched by the Irish influx as well. Following the Civil War, as factory production in the Connecticut Valley replaced an economy based on natural resources, other immigrant groups began to arrive as well. French Canadians arrived by rail as early as the 1860s, most of them having been attracted by the prospect of work in the mills of Holyoke, Springfield, and Turners Falls. By the turn of the century, almost half of Holyoke's residents were foreign-born (*Historic and Archaeological Resources* 121). Polish and other Eastern European immigrants began their influx at the turn of the century as well. They were drawn not only by the Connecticut Valley's industrial sites, but also in order to cultivate the precious floodplain fields that an increasing number of Anglo families were selling off as younger generations were lured away from agriculture by the urban and industrial boom.

While the Sawmill Valley itself experienced relatively slight growth in its foreign-born population during the years between 1880 and 1920, even in comparison with the surrounding communities of Sunderland and Montague, the region certainly was affected by the presence of immigrants both within and beyond its immediate boundaries. Leverett's census figures for 1880, 1900, and 1920 indicate a relatively moderate increase in total population—700, 744, and 795, respectively. But in those years, its percentage of first- or second-generation immigrants increased from 1.4 percent to 10 percent. In 1880, 7 people of Irish origin and 3 people of French Canadian origin lived within its boundaries. By 1920, 22 residents of the town were either born in, or had one or more parents who had been born in, Quebec. Nine more were of Irish extraction, and 81 were of Eastern European (Polish, Lithuanian, Russian, or Bohemian) ancestry. The preponderance of the latter lived in the low-lying Long Plain district to the south and east of Brushy Mountain and the Sawmill Valley. To most residents of the Sawmill Valley, even as late as 1920, the settlement at Long Plain was outside and beyond daily geographical reach, but it *did* form part of the same politically constituted town and was subject to the purview of the same board of selectmen. In a community where most people could not help knowing one another by face if not by name, the impact of such an influx had to have been significant. The high concentration of so many recent immigrants and their families within the town bounds of Leverett itself could only have increased the valley's sense of its own exceptionality, and it helped valley residents fashion a self-consciously "upland" identity.

The agricultural district of Montague Center, where the Sawmill River empties into the Connecticut, was also relatively slow to change. But even here, the foreign-born and second-generation immigrant population grew from a mere scattering of French Canadian and Irish families in 1880 to, as of the 1900 census, a solid 10 percent of the total population of 1,500: 54 people of Franco extraction, 105 of Irish, and 18 of Eastern European. These numbers increased moderately during the next two decades, so that by 1920, 14 percent of Montague Center's population was of Franco, Irish, or Eastern European extraction. Indeed, even in the tiny upland town of Shutesbury, where the Sawmill River originates, residents of foreign (and particularly Eastern European) origin numbered 77 in 1920—*out of a total population of 240.*

Changes within the Sawmill Valley, then, seem even less significant than those occurring in neighboring communities. Throughout western Massachusetts, and especially in the industrial and agricultural communities along the Connecticut River itself, the period between 1880 and 1920 saw a complete transformation, due in large part to the arrival and widespread settlement of both French Canadian and Eastern European immigrants.

Around the turn of the century, men and women who either came from Quebec or were descended from French Canadian immigrants comprised New England's second largest non-Anglo ethnic group, following behind the Irish. Today they appear to be one of the nation's largely "invisible" immigrant groups; they did not have to cross an ocean to get to New England,

and perhaps half of them returned to Quebec (Brault 1). According to statistics gathered by immigrant historian Roger Daniels, however, between 1890 and 1920 their numbers in the United States as a whole grew from over 500,000 to 850,000 (259). New England was and remains their largest area of concentration. Americans of French ancestry (including people of Quebecois origin, descendants of Huguenots, and descendants of Acadian migrations) constitute the fifth largest ethnic group in the United States, behind African Americans and ahead of Italians (Brault 2). But the peak period of Franco immigration from Quebec to New England was in the decades following the Civil War, as the demand for cheap labor increased in the textile mills of industrialized portions of central and northern New England (Brault 54). Because they had relatively uncomplicated access to New England by rail, large numbers of French Canadian workers were drawn away from their Saint Lawrence Valley farms into the region (and, quite often, back out of it). French Canadians, like most other economically motivated immigrant groups, were responding in large part to worsening conditions at home. As both Daniels and Brault point out, the post–Civil War period coincided with a decline in farming *throughout* northeastern North America; rural New Englanders themselves were leaving *their* homes during this period and traveling either westward or into large urban centers. The Franco influx into New England, in other words, took place at, and also shaped, a critical juncture in the economic and cultural history of the region.

By the end of the twentieth century, even in places where their descendants constitute a large proportion of the population, Americans of French descent, like so many other white ethnic groups, have arrived at a state of nearly complete assimilation. Exceptions to this rule can still be found in sections of Maine, where bilingualism is still practiced in several border-straddling families. For the most part, the only large-scale hallmark of French Canadian ancestry in New England, aside from retained surnames, is membership in the Catholic church. Around the turn of the century, however, when the French constituted a relatively new immigrant group, assimilation was an impossibility. Distinguished by their continued use of the mother tongue at home, in church, and in the many church-run French schools that the first and second generation Francos attended, the French became known and discriminated against in some nativist Yankee circles as "the Chinese of the Eastern States" (Daniels 258). A common perception was that they *desired* to remain different—French-speaking, Catholic, and, in several industrial cities of New England, geographically restricted to so-called "Little Canadas." Because their mother tongue was such an integral part not only of their ethnic identity but also of their religious practice (one second-generation Franco-American whom I interviewed several years ago told me that priests in her parents' church continually warned their rural Maine parishioners that "if they lost their French, they would lose their God"), the French remained on the margins of Yankee culture well into and even past World War II. The anti-assimilation attitude also seems to account in part for this group's large-scale failure to participate in the various labor protests of the early twentieth century, including the famous Lawrence, Massachusetts, lockout of 1912, in which Francos "were instructed by their pastors not to participate" (Brault 63). This particular trend was not reversed, apparently, until after World War I.

From early in the migration period, the Connecticut Valley of Massachusetts was a major receiving point for men and women leaving Quebec. Both Holyoke and Springfield/Chicopee were built around large mills; as early as 1900, Franco-American families constituted over 20 percent of their respective populations. The town of Montague, whose major population center was situated within walking distance of the factories of Turners Falls Village (six miles distant from the Sawmill River's confluence with the Connecticut), also had a significant Franco population. In 1900, 1,190 of the town's total 6,100 residents (16 percent) either had been born in, or had one or more parents born in, Quebec. Although they were scattered throughout Montague's five separately incorporated villages, most French Canadians lived in Turners Falls, where the Yankee mill owners could look down upon them and their fellow ethnic outsiders (the town had large numbers of Irish, Eastern European, and German immigrants as well) from their sizable houses up on "The Hill."

Virtually no statistical evidence for itinerant laborers of Franco origin is available, but—according to oral historical accounts of the post–Civil War period—their comings and goings had a major effect on the Connecticut Valley (see chapter 3). French Canadian men participated in large numbers in the log drives that took place on the Connecticut River toward the close of the nineteenth century. Local legend has it that the town of Turners Falls (which happened to be the terminus point for the drive) owes its still high concentration of alcohol-serving establishments to the influx of loggers who periodically "invaded" the town to blow off steam.

Needless to say, the Anglo-Yankee culture that witnessed this French influx also was transformed by it. French-speaking Catholic immigrants represented a visible, undeniably "foreign" presence in western Massachusetts around the turn of the century. Their arrival—following relatively closely upon the arrival of another predominantly Catholic group, the Irish—signaled an end to the homogeneous Puritan heritage of New England. It reminded rural

New Englanders that their precious legacy was in danger of eclipse, and this in turn caused many of them—at all economic levels—to begin thinking of themselves as the last vestiges of a Yankee tradition nearly three centuries old. When Franco immigrants actually left the mill towns and settled the uplands (at least two families settled in the Sawmill Valley), they served as catalysts in an inevitable expansion of regional (on both the local and New England–wide levels) identity. Although most of these intrepid French men and women very well may have checked their ethnic baggage at the point of entry, their assumption of Yankee traits—a series of compromises that could be viewed simply as acts of assimilation—necessitated a profound revision of what an upland Yankee could be. First and foremost, their presence offered incontrovertible evidence that the terms of regional belonging were—had to be—subject to modernistic expansion. Whether they lived as Yankees in the Sawmill Valley or as foreigners outside it, French Canadians forced native-born Anglos to reconsider their own embattled ethnicity. The fact was that change—industrial growth and cultural expansion—was inevitable.

French and other millworking newcomers in the Connecticut Valley (along with their agricultural counterparts, the Poles) could not avoid effecting the transformation of New England during the early part of the twentieth century. Mere moments away from the Sawmill Valley, for instance, lay the polyglot village of Turners Falls, which had been built in the service of large-scale industry. As at least one of my informants has described it to me, Turners Falls was a veritable ethnic battleground, a town whose street life was dominated by ethnically affiliated gangs of Franco, German, Irish, and Anglo backgrounds.

The Poles who settled in rural New England represented a small but quite visible portion of the one to three million Poles who immigrated to the United States between 1870 and 1914 (Gladsky 429; Blejwas, "Inherited" 49). New England as a whole was home to approximately 10 percent of these Polish immigrants by 1930, and even sparsely populated rural New England—primarily the Connecticut Valley—was home to nearly 70,000 of these (Blejwas, "Inherited" 50). From central Connecticut north into southern Vermont and New Hampshire, the rich alluvial soil along the river banks—soil which had been cultivated by colonial-era English settlers and by Native American farmers before them—increasingly was tended to, and then bought up by, Polish families. Stanley Blejwas offers some startling statistics in connection with the transformation of Northampton (less than twenty miles away from the Sawmill Valley): between 1905 and 1930, though the population growth of Polish-American families increased modestly (from 4.9 percent to 7.1 percent), the proportion of land that they owned in Northampton increased from 5.2 to *89.2* percent

(Blejwas, "Inherited" 50). In other words, while their actual numbers assigned them minority status, the Poles and other Eastern European immigrants had an enormously transformative effect on the land itself in the towns bordering the Connecticut River.

The arrival of these groups also had a significant effect upon people's perceptions of regional transformation in *adjacent* areas, such as the Sawmill Valley. Between 1880 and 1900, Leverett's neighboring town of Sunderland—whose western boundary is the Connecticut River—experienced an increase from 0 to 65 in its Eastern European population. As a small farming community, Sunderland's total population in 1880 was 700. By 1900, that total had risen only to 771, so the coming of Eastern European immigrants could be seen as accounting for fully 90 percent of the town's growth. By 1916, at which time the town's population had risen to 1,040, 154 of its adult residents had Eastern European surnames. In 1920, 10 percent of Montague Center's adult male population was Eastern European in origin as well. In 1900, this number had stood at 1 percent. This is to say nothing of Montague's industrial and commercial districts, within which 10 percent were of Eastern European origin in 1900 and 12 percent in 1920.

No less significant than the huge increase in Polish landholdings in the turn-of–the-century period was the corresponding winnowing of Anglo farmers that helped to bring it about. Again, the psychosocial ramifications of this demographic change played an enormous role in shaping the upland Yankee consciousness and discourse. As more and more Anglos sold off their farms, Blejwas points out, native-born Yankeedom underwent an identity crisis of sorts. The landscape had been the Puritan birthright, but now, as Poles not only outbred but also outfarmed their Anglo predecessors, "the old stock was facing biological defeat in a Darwinian struggle for survival" (Blejwas, "Inherited" 55). Local Yankee reactions to this influx were not so much resentful as profoundly ambivalent. As soon as Anglos began to feel that the Polish were displacing them, they took a realistic look inward and considered their own failings, their own state of (perceived) cultural and economic degeneration. In his study of turn-of-the-century New England novelists and their treatment of the Polish immigration, Thomas Gladsky refers to Yankee fears of an imminent "Anglo-Saxon racial suicide" (431). It was the Anglos themselves, in other words, who were all too susceptible to the temptation to sell off their birthright. Polish newcomers were not necessarily guilty of anything other than showing up at the exact moment when the Puritan stock was giving up the ghost.

Indeed, in both literary portraits and in their oral traditions, Yankees occasionally portrayed the Poles who settled in the Connecticut Valley in a complimentary light. Who, after all, could blame them for working so hard to claim the birthright that their predecessors on the land so thoughtlessly had discarded? And even demeaning, racialist attitudes toward Polish farmers in New England, posited as they are upon an assumption of Anglo-Saxon superiority, betray a typically modernistic despair on the part of nativistic Yankees regarding the prospect of their own demise—a phenomenon Thomas Gladsky refers to as "the agricultural crisis facing America, particularly New England, at the beginning of the twentieth century" (438). The influx of Polish farmers into the Connecticut Valley occasioned, or at least coincided with, just the sort of ideologically infused nostalgia and cultural self-consciousness that accompanied New England's elegiac entry into the new era. It was a nostalgia fueled by a state of insecurity and conditioned by the invention of a past (the myth of a self-sufficient, homogeneous, and prosperous rural New England) which truly never had existed. It could have arisen only in a modern context, in a period when the life of the countryside was increasingly circumscribed by the encompassing influence of a market economy and attendant social changes.

To upland Yankees, Francos and Poles alike, both as they passed through or eventually stayed in the Sawmill Valley and as they lived in their own ethnic neighborhoods in nearby industrial towns, represented the inevitability of large-scale change. As long as they remained "different," they were guilty of heralding a new, less-than-welcome change: the end of old New England. If, on the other hand, they could be assimilated to upland Yankee values, as a (self-selecting) few were, in relatively short order, these newcomers, as Gladsky notes, invented a "new type, a new man [*sic*] who foreshadows an American of the future" (437). Lest we fail to account for the compromises entailed in such a reinvention, however, it is important to note, as Blejwas does, that this new Polish (or French Canadian) Yankee has been thoroughly de-ethnicized, fully adapted to the "existing Yankee social and cultural heritage" ("Puritans" 88). The "American of the future," in other words, is an American who willingly discards his or her ethnic past in order to assume a "Yankee" past instead.

Ironically, this sort of psychological reliance—by Anglos and immigrants alike—upon a continuum of invented pasts is exactly what gives the context in which all this identity shifting was taking place its decidedly *modern* character. For their part, both culturally resistant *and* assimilationist immigrants lived—and *knew* that they lived—in an increasingly uncontrollable world. Their methods for coping with the enormity which threatened to engulf them implicated them in an eminently pragmatic adherence to certain elements of the past and a careful, cautious engagement with the conditions of the present. As historian John Bodnar suggests, immigrant culture "drew from both a past and a present and continually confronted the limits of what was possible" (209). In this respect, the lives of turn-of-the-century immigrants were quite similar to those of the upland Yankees who received them, the men and women who are the subject of this book. To extend Bodnar's formulation, these Yankees, too, "accepted the world for what it was and what it was becoming and yet ceaselessly resisted the inevitable at numerous points of contact" (210). Yankee and aspiring Yankee alike, "since they could not control the direction of either elites or capital . . . placed most of their attention on the immediate, the attainable, the portion of the world in which they could exert some influence" (210). The invention of a specifically regional identity in the Sawmill Valley, one which united both native-born Anglos and a handful of recently arrived immigrants, was just one of these spheres of influence. For all its devotion to the ideals of the past, it was occasioned by the tumult of modernity. Its adherents—like its very geography, which straddled the worlds of mainstream and tributary—were "tied simultaneously to the lower levels of tradition, household and community as well as the higher levels of capitalism, industrialization and urbanization" (Bodnar 212).

Mentifacts of Region and Place: A Folkloric/Oral Historical Perspective

The rise of factory-based industry, as well as an immigrant presence not only next door to, but also (albeit to a lesser extent) in the Sawmill Valley itself, had profound effects on the cultural life of this upland region. As I researched the early twentieth century in the Sawmill Valley, however, I found myself returning repeatedly to the same questions: Why did so many of the old settlers' families *remain* in the valley so far into its period of industrial decline?[1] And how did the arrival of immigrants contribute to the reshaping of regional identity? On these questions, old mill remains and history books alike were mute. Only the old-time residents themselves, those men and women who had been born before 1920, might be able to supply me with answers. As I sat in their kitchens and living rooms and listened to their stories, I learned that their parents and grandparents had stayed in part because their collective identity was tied inextricably to their sense of *place*. Within their oral traditions and folklife, Sawmill Valley residents portrayed themselves as beleaguered and impecunious Yankee holdovers whose values of hard work, thrift, and simplicity were part and parcel of their devotion to an isolated stretch of upland geography. Contemporary historians might call their allegiance to this landscape a form of cultural resistance. To borrow a metaphor from Hal Barron, turn-of-the-century inhabitants of the Sawmill Valley were "island communities against the stream" (136). This condition of isolation was essentially an act of invention, the result of reactions to the forces of history bearing down on them. Far from being a survival from a prelapsarian rural America, Sawmill Valley cultural life during this period had been spurred into existence by modernity itself.

Several scholars have examined both "high" and "middlebrow" cultural forms that arose in New England during the latter decades of the nineteenth century in response to such modern upheavals. In her 1993 study of the tourist industry in New England, Dona Brown portrays the profound contrast that existed in the late 1800s between the "mythic region called Old New England" and the region's actual appearance. "By the last quarter of the [nineteenth] century," Brown writes, New England "was in fact highly urbanized, industrial and ethnically diverse." She continues: "Its city landscapes were dominated by huge brick factories where immigrants from every part of Europe sought work. But tourists sought out the isolated or remote parts of New England, looking for an imagined world of pastoral beauty, rural independence, virtuous simplicity, and religious and ethnic homogeneity" (19). Another New England historian, Stephen Nissenbaum, points to the ironies attendant upon this stark contrast between appearances and realities. Most likely, there is no coincidence in the fact that, as Nissenbaum puts it, "by 1860, when the New England small town was first being sentimentalized as a seat of pastoral Yankee stability, New England as a whole had become the single most urban part of the nation—the most industrial, the most Catholic, the most heavily immigrant in population" (39–40).

The residents of the Sawmill Valley, who lived within a few miles of factories and heavily (Catholic) immigrant neighborhoods, were not particularly *sentimental* in their attachments to the "Old" New England; they were too busy living in it, coping with its dissolution, and paying attention to the events taking place on its margins to be living in a world of illusion. But Brown's and Nissenbaum's formulations of conditions in late-nineteenth-century New England have as much relevance to the lives of upland Yankees as they do to the projections of mythicizing wealthy tourists. Residents of rural New England were experiencing a profound psychological transformation during the turn-of-the-century period. They were too fearful of change to discard their ties to the past and to the traditional land-based economies in which their ancestors had subsisted, yet too realistic and survival-minded to think that they really had any choice in the matter. Such ambivalence seems to have been characteristic of all levels of New England society at the turn of the century. Backcountry farmers, urban immigrants, and the fortunate members of the upper class, who had the luxury of shuttling between city homes and rural retreats, all had this double consciousness in common.

Sawmill Valley residents' self-imposed guise of rural isolation and difference closely parallels the vision of Appalachia that folklorist Cecil Sharp was publicizing in the new field of folklore during the same era. Marking the Southern Appalachian Mountains as the sole preserve of landlocked and culturally isolated Scotch-Irish peasants who sang Elizabethan ballads, Sharp failed to recognize the role that Germans and African Americans, among others, had played in the creation of regional culture there. The people of "these sequestered mountain valleys," the folklorist wrote, "have for a hundred years or more been completely isolated and cut off from all traffic with the rest of the world" (qtd. in Whisnant 119). His assertions exerted a long-lasting influence. Some sixty years after Sharp published his collections of Appalachian ballads, Richard Dorson still was referring to regional folklore as something which is "hidden away in nooks and byways" (*American Folklore* 75). Only recently have scholars come to recognize and treat the vernacular region as a complex and far from pristine phenomenon, one subject to some of the same upheavals that touch the largest cities.[2] Counsel on this subject, and admonition as well, come from many quarters. "We can no longer consider regions and regional variations to be isolated survivals in a standardizing world," argues critic Jim Wayne Miller (10).

Among other things, regional identity offers a given folk group a means of drawing protective boundaries around itself. Because, from our relatively fleeting vantage point, the land appears to be an unchanging fact, we sometimes make problematical associations between it and the homogeneity and stability we seek in our own lives. We want the land to be *ours*, and we forget that it precedes all of us. Of his beloved Gloucester, Charles Olson asks rhetorically: "Who can say who are/citizens?" One of the questions this book asks is: "*How* do they say it?" How do the culturally diverse inhabitants of a given region attempt to lay a singular claim to the land? Since a region must have boundaries in order to exist as such, residents and researchers alike often are tempted to *separate* it from other regions, to view it and its inhabitants in isolation. As Werner Sollors observes, "Explorations of region tend to be 'dualistic' in nature, built on a distinction between the region and unregion" ("Region" 449). Moreover, the sentimentalizing tendencies which so often have guided popular perceptions of folk subjects often cause us to regard people whose cultural existence involves a symbiotic relationship with the land as somehow stranded in both time and space. Hence the plethora of folklore studies pertaining not only to geographically isolated groups like the Southern Appalachians, Ozarkers, and Maine islanders, but also to essentially antimodern groups like the Pennsylvania Dutch. This book, on the other hand, treats regional identity as a dynamic, a text that invites multiple readings. The book treats place and region not as fixed or deterministic entities, but as matrices of cultural interchange, social tension, and economic upheaval. It reads the folk region as, to borrow Jim Wayne Miller's phrase, "evidence of natural diversity" (8).

Despite its centrifugal tendencies, regional identity is also a powerful impetus to cultural cohesion. Because place is never entirely malleable, it superimposes a form of continuity on human lives. I do not mean to propose a deterministic version of place along the lines of that posed by Sharp and Dorson, which reads topography as if it were an assemblage of walls somehow predestined to seal one group off from the next. Place plays a unifying role among cultural groups because it yokes them together on its own terms. Indeed, one of the assumptions of this book is that place often is an identity-forming *inheritance,* which *can* be powerful enough, as Alan Dundes observes, to resist being subsumed "under the concept of ethnic group," among other rubrics (*Folklore Matters* 13). Place anchors all humanity to a form of singularity, what geographer Etienne Juillard calls a "criterion of uniformity" (432). It does not create an indelible mark on cultural forms, but it does force people to share one another's company. The idealizations of the 1930s regionalists emphasize this point. "More socially intimate than the political nation," Simon Bronner suggests, in the New Deal era "the region [was] itself a model for *E Pluribus Unum*" (64–65). If Sharp and Dorson simplified place and understood it to function as a means of achieving cultural stasis, or racial and ethnic segregation, this book seeks to invert the equation. Rather than viewing place as an isolating factor, this project invokes the work of both 1930s and contemporary regionalists in order to understand place to function as a syncretic arena in which one cultural form is exposed to and challenged by others. Place imposes a unique form of dynamism on human life, or—as Allen Tate said—a "centralization of a different and better kind" (Dorman 12).

This book's focus on the dynamism inherent in the fashioning of regional identity mirrors recent work on the social construction of ethnicity and nationalism by such theorists as Werner Sollors, Benedict Anderson, and Eric Hobsbawm. As Sollors explores the "invention" of ethnicity, he points out acts of creation and adaptation that lie at the heart not only of ethnic identity but also, by extension, all other socially based versions of self and community. Like ethnicity, regional identity is a process rather than an established fact. Like ethnicity, it seems to emerge from a specifically modern milieu, a world in which doubt and flux are at the core of human experience. The concept of invention does not imply "a conspiratorial interpretation of a manipulative inventor . . . but . . . widely shared, though intensely debated, fictions that are continually reinvented" (*Invention of Ethnicity* xi). The members of a folk region such as the Sawmill Valley were not passive recipients of a stable, established set of traditions and norms, and they were not devious schemers either. Their sense of themselves was fashioned in the midst of modern tumult, and its function was to promote a feeling of wholeness in a fragmented world. As people in the turn-of-the-century period increasingly diverged, regional belonging—especially inasmuch as it offered a sort of rootedness in the landscape—offered its adherents what Ayers and Onuf refer to as "a form of identity that promise[d] to transcend ethnic boundaries, to unite people across generations" (3).

Like Sollors' discussion of ethnicity, Anderson's description of the origin of the nation-state is predicated upon the idea that countries are essentially *fictional* in their composition, based on ideas rather than facts. Nations, in Anderson's words, are "cultural artefacts [*sic*]" which have been created in response to "a complex 'crossing' of discrete historical forces" (4). In other words, nations, like ethnic groups and like regional cultures, not only are *made-up* things, but also are outgrowths of certain specifically *modern* conditions, such as the land- and power-grabs of post-Enlightenment Europe. A nation is forged because a group of people who inhabit one territory wishes to declare its independence from all others. But that same nation owes its existence to a series of engagements and encounters with the world beyond its frontier. Shaped by dynamic conditions, nations are in and of themselves ever-changing and reformulated entities. On a smaller scale, it seems to me, regions are defined by the same sorts of patterns. The growth of regionalism, as Robert Dorman suggests, comes at "a critical juncture in the . . . transformation of this country from a rural, frontier, centralized, producerist farm and village society . . . into the modern, commercialized, consumerist and mechanized mass society" (xi–xii).

Hobsbawm's analysis of tradition is useful here as well. The form that turn-of-the-century Sawmill Valley folklore assumed often was that of an "invented tradition," a set of oral narratives and pastimes based on a sense of stability whose roots were located in the valley's collective (and imagined) past, its shared historical landscape. That tradition, too, is a reaction to the fluctuating conditions of modernity and came into being because "a rapid transformation of society weaken[ed] or destroy[ed] the social patterns for which 'old' traditions had been designed" (4–5). Invented tradition, like ethnicity and nationhood, fills a void. As contemporary folklorists have applied insights like Hobsbawm's to the study of vernacular culture, they have offered a revelatory demystification of even the most pedigreed pastimes. In the interest of "anchoring their desire for a sense of place in the face of the mobilizing tendencies of increasingly commercialized culture," Roger Abrahams writes, "social elites" have contributed to the invention of simple-minded, untainted, premodern folk (391). The folk themselves, at least in a modern age, participate in these acts of invention.

Inasmuch as Sawmill Valley residents rooted their sense of region in a *reaction* to "outside" threats and influences, it was a fiction, a construct. Their reliance on an opposing Other resembled the appearance within mid- and late-nineteenth-century New England folklore and literature of a previous generation of morally upstanding, industrious, and self-sufficient Yankees. These antebellum Yankees owed at least part of their inspiration to the sectional conflict which had made New England and the South into mortal enemies. The plain-spoken New Englanders of mid- and late-nineteenth-century American literature had been *invented* by Abolitionists such as Harriet Beecher Stowe, as well as by a host of other storytellers and journalists, in order to stake a claim for New England as the seat of reason and straightforward morality in America.[3] The stakes undoubtedly are higher when a nation-state or a section (i.e., New England) declares its independence and wholeness in the face of surrounding moral or political dissolution. But the *process* by which a small region's inhabitants develop a sense of themselves as distinct is not vastly different from the process which guides the development of national or sectional identities. At its roots, the fashioning of folk regions, like the fashioning of ethnicities or nation-states or sections, occurs as people collaborate in order to set themselves apart from their neighbors. Such acts of collaboration are by no means the result of an easily won consensus; they implicate even "insiders" in a continuing series of compromises, reinventions, and power-exchanges. Most importantly, the individual members of such a group never are wholly in control of the forces which determine the terms of cultural belonging.

As Sollors, Anderson, and Hobsbawm's analyses suggest, acts of cultural invention take place in an abstract world, in which people's ideas about their communities begin to assume a life of their own. Regional identity is no exception to this pattern. According to Barbara Allen, "the idea of regional *consciousness* and regional *identity*—a regional sense of self—crops up in nearly every serious discussion of regions and regionalism" (my italics; "Regional Folklore" 2). Dorson himself, Allen observes, says that "the folk region lies in the mind and spirit as much as in physical boundaries" ("Regional Folklore" 3). And this point is refined further by Suzi Jones in her 1976 essay on "Regionalization." The "isolation" that folklorists such as Dorson (or Sharp) attribute to regional folk groups "is not for the most part a physical fact; it is more of a mentifact—a state of mind, a cultural-psychological attitude" (108).

Even people who occupy the same geographical region diverge in the ways that they articulate this regional *consciousness,* as Mary Hufford's study of the New Jersey "Pineys" reveals. The Pinelands, we learn, are home not only to Italians, Puerto Ricans, and Anglo-Americans, but to farmers, laborers, and trappers. Each group articulates its connection and claim to the land differently. Italians plant grape arbors behind their houses. Trappers fashion distinctive snares that are adapted specifically to the landscape and its indigenous fauna. No one group has a monopoly on the terms of regional belonging. In this respect, a regional culture can be a perfect example of what scholar Jay Mechling refers to as the "conflict" model of folkloristics—a group whose collective folklore is not the result of consensus-based sharing but of frequently opposing perspectives held together, in this case, by the facts of geography ("Sharing").

To date, the most workable definition of the folk region emerges from Jones's piece, with its assertion that the phrase "regional folk group" should be used only in "instances where people share a body of folklore because they live in a certain geographical area" (107). Jones poses as a fitting example of the regional folk group "the people in Oregon who live west of the Cascades and who share such folk expressions as 'going to the coast' (rather than 'to the ocean' or 'to the beach'), who refer to Oregonians living east of the Cascades as 'bunchgrassers,' who refer to themselves as 'webfoots,' and tell jokes about the rain, who know how to pronounce *Willamette,* and know who bigfoot is" (107). What strikes me about Jones's application of the term *regional* here is that it avoids the sorts of exclusions and boundaries that are only incidentally related to the physical fact of region. By concentrating on the geographical resonances of webfoot folk culture, Jones enunciates a version of regionalism that is a response to the immediacy of place and not to the countless other aspects of folklore that happen to exist within the state of Oregon. The "regional folk group" is one of many overlapping aspects of a given culture's identity. As Jones points out, "Many of the people in western Oregon may also (and certainly do) belong to other folk groups such as loggers, salmon fishermen, children, Norwegians, [and] Catholics, to name a few" (107). Their participation within these other groups certainly is an indispensable aspect of their sense of themselves; but, inasmuch as we seek to identify them as members of a specifically *regional* folk group, geography has to be a major criterion for analysis.

But landscape conditions are only one aspect of regional folk geography. As folklorist W. F. H. Nicolaisen explains, "Folk narrative material, speech habits, names, or superstitions and other non-material traits can [also] be used legitimately and successfully as indices in the determination of folk-cultural regions and landscapes" ("Folk and Region" 147). Geographical circumstance is the key to my understanding of region, inasmuch as it is the one factor which all members of a regional group share. But because the *mentifacts* of geography are informed by any number of disparate cultural forces—such as ethnicity, vocation, religion, economics, and so on—the folk forms which converge in order to create a particular regional style never are solely place-oriented. Regions absorb and adopt as their own all manner of vernacular traditions—from place legends to work habits to dance styles. In her article about ramp suppers in the Southern Appalachian Mountains, Mary Hufford refers to the diversity of verbal folk forms that inhere in the life of a vernacular region as a means by which local "women enunciate their place in the hills" ("Tending" 5). In other words, the terms of regional belonging and pride can be articulated in myriad forms, whether the subject is ramp-eating, local characters, or sawmilling accidents.

Hundreds of collections of folklore marked as "regional" do in fact exist. But, as William Lightfoot argues in his essay "Regional Folkloristics" (1983), all the collection activity that occurs "within regions of the United States" does not excuse the fact that "not very much attention has been paid to regional theory, methodology, or analysis" (in Dorson, *Handbook* 185). Folklorists almost always are faithful to the practice of carefully recording the particular provenance of each piece they collect; until recently, however, their use of provenance as a means of actively defining the term *region* has been limited. The recording of provenance begins, as W. F. H. Nicolaisen points out, by asking the questions "When?" and "Where?" But, in order for *region* to be clearly understood and articulated, the folklorist must follow these two relatively simple questions with two others: "Why there?" ("Folklore and Geography" 5) and, as Kent Ryden puts it, "What does it mean?" (57). Archie Green suggests that "it has been easy for us to collect within territorial bounds, but difficult to use place as a cluster point for theory" (qtd. in Allen, "Regional Studies," 7). I have attempted to do just that in the chapters that follow.

Conducting the Field Study

This book is based upon a series of audiotaped interviews that I conducted with eighteen elderly residents (or former residents) of the Sawmill Valley. Most of the sessions took place between February and June 1992, some as recently as

February 1999. The Leverett Historical Society's audiotape archive provided me with more material—a series of interviews dating from 1967 to 1984, with six additional informants, four of whom had died well before I even thought of the project. Within a few weeks of my first interviews, I already had collected several hours' worth of local and personal legends and anecdotes, occupational recollections, and descriptions of region-specific folkways. In many cases, I was recording the accounts of people whose knowledge and experience, if it had not been entirely overlooked, certainly was not widely accessible to the public. Almost exactly a year after I met and interviewed him for the first time, Robert Ripley—a ninety-three-year-old farmer, Sunday School teacher, storyteller, and maker of Montague's choicest maple syrup—died while conducting his church choir. Like many of his neighbors, Ripley had been too busy running a farm all his life to afford himself the luxury of writing any sort of a memoir. The same was true of nearly all my informants. Sadly, four other informants—Clifford LaClaire, Mary Keniston, Gertrude Carey, and Dave Mercier—passed away during the book's gestation period. Although I did "repay" some of my interviewees with jars of homemade jam, I could only hope that these people who were so helpful to me in creating a basis for the project were gaining a more lasting form of "return" by being offered the opportunity to recount their memories and experiences to a relative stranger who was enthusiastic about listening to them and eager for others to have access to their traditions.

In the course of the fieldwork, I often was struck by how *easy* it was to find new informants. I had not taken into account what I suppose most seasoned folklorists assume—that one informant inevitably leads to the next. I would come to the end of what to me had been a productive interview, only to hear the person who had just regaled me with stories and anecdotes for an hour and a half say, "But I don't remember anything." In March 1992, Clifford LaClaire and Clarissa Truesdell LaClaire told me, "If you want to talk to someone who *really* remembers the old days, get in touch with Vernon Aiken." As soon as I got home, I called Aiken and scheduled an interview with him. At the end of that talk, I came away with more names.

Although the tape recorder was absolutely indispensable to me as a means of gathering oral materials, I always spent at least fifteen to thirty minutes before each initial interview talking with my interviewees on an informal basis. Since these women and men were gracious enough to donate their time and energy to telling me—among other things—their life stories, I always took care to tell them who I was, what I was doing sitting in their kitchens or living rooms with a tape recorder, where I lived and worked, and so on. Everyone in the Sawmill Valley knows the "goat place" (a couple of my informants have memories of playing dress-up and going to dances in the farmhouse there), so I had little trouble finding common ground upon which to stand with local people. Arriving at someone's house in the middle of winter on a bicycle was another way of starting a conversation. Clifford LaClaire jokingly remarked that he had expected to see a Cadillac pull into his driveway when "the folklorist" arrived. In a sense, cycling put me on something like a par with old-timers who once had traversed the same landscape on either foot or horseback; the experience of topography always proved useful in the field as an equalizing reference point.

Before the first few interviews, I spent hours trying to invent particularly creative modes of inquiry, questions that would produce the highest possible yield of responses. Those lists usually started on their trip to oblivion by descending into my pants pocket. For better or worse, I decided relatively early on to conduct open-ended interviews. I etched a few fundamental questions in my mind, began the taped portion of the interview with them, and allowed circumstance, instinct, and opportunity to guide me the rest of the way. Written lists were of use to me in only one sort of situation: during follow-up interviews, when I had come to hear more about particular things. More often than not, the more informal the setting was, the more material it yielded.

A case in point was my interview with Willy Stone and Mary Williams Stone of Montague on 16 March 1992. When we first sat down at their living room table, I told them that I was interested in stories and traditions that people told and practiced in the Sawmill Valley. I explained that I was not so much interested in written history as I was in the ways in which people *remember* things. This explanation was sufficient to get both the Stones talking about their memories of life in the valley seventy or so years ago and about things their parents and grandparents had told them. Half an hour later, an unexpected guest arrived at the door and joined us at the table. At first I shut the tape recorder off, figuring that we had reached a logical pause in our session. But after the Stones introduced me to their guest, I asked him if he would be willing to participate in the interview also. As it happened, Dave Mercier was someone I'd been looking for. Without any incisive questions from me, he and Mr. Stone began to volunteer a series of woodcutting stories and anecdotes that, before Mercier's arrival, I had not heard. Working together, Mercier and Mary Stone provided me with a detailed genealogy of the Mercier, Howard, and Williams families, which included in it more detailed anecdotes and stories. I was so excited by the conversation that, when it was over, I raced home in order to listen to the tape—just to make sure they had really said all those things.

For all the meeting's informality, however, knowing that I was waiting for them to conjure up sometimes distant memories also occasionally had the effect of making the Stones feel as if they had been put on the spot. Indeed, a number of times during various interviews, an informant would respond to a very specific question that I had asked (i.e., "Do you remember so-and-so?") in this way: "If you hadn't asked me, I'd probably remember." At times like these, one realizes how much of an artificial imposition a folklore collection or an oral history interview can be. Most tradition-bearers are not accustomed to reciting or placing their memories of events or stories in the context of an outsider's interview. The materials that the scholar designates as "folklore" or "oral history" or "legends" or "personal experience stories" usually take shape all of a piece within the recollections of a given speaker. Only when the researcher sits down with her or his transcript can she or he draw the lines of demarcation.

One question which dogged me as I presented myself and my project to potential informants had theoretical as well as practical implications. Was this project folkloric or oral historical in its focus? Was I—in Richard Dorson's words—a *collector* of folklore or an *interviewer* of local historical personages (Dunaway and Baum 293)? Despite the fact that oral history and folklore research often converge, the differences between the two are anything but trivial. Simply put, we expect the folklorist to look for traditional structures within the oral materials that he or she collects, and to pay as much or more attention to form—or, as the case may be, *performance*—as to content. We assume that a folklorist cares less about a given account's historical accuracy than its adherence to (or deviation from) other, parallel accounts. The folklorist—at least one like me who has been trained in theories that have their origins in the humanities—is interested in oral materials because they provide insights into the interpretive frameworks by which a particular folk group *describes* the world around it. To the extent that this book is a study of regional *consciousness*, or mindset, it seems to me to be a study in folklore. My folkloric orientation also is borne out by the book's thematic—rather than chronological—organization. Accordingly, the story I tell here does not follow a single sequence of events or progression through time; it does not even proffer a cause-and-effect relationship of any sort. Rather, I have sorted the various textual materials upon which the study is based according to what I might call "clusters of meaning." I am offering what I consider to be a humanities-based perspective on one particular historical moment.

On the other hand, given the fact that this study addresses itself to a specific historical period, as well as to the overall implications of certain historical trends, such as immigration and cultural admixture, its oral historical component cannot be overlooked. For one thing, as I interviewed elderly residents of the Sawmill Valley about the early years of the twentieth century, I quite obviously was relying upon them as witnesses to history. But their historical authority was important in another, perhaps more important, regard; I could access the primary object of my study—turn-of-the-century folklore—only by calling upon their memories of things their parents and grandparents had told them. A purely folkloric study would have been simpler, but it would have restricted me to talking about the oral tradition's late-twentieth-century implications. Indeed, another book easily could be written about Sawmill Valley folk traditions in the 1990s. Readers familiar with contemporary definitions of folklore do not have to be reminded that oral traditions are not inherently "about" the old days, any more than popular culture is inherently "about" the present. In associating folk traditions with a period of history, I do not mean to imply that folklore itself is a backward-looking entity or to deny the currency or late-twentieth-century relevance of my informants' narratives. I have stressed these narratives' historical implications because I am interested in history and because an examination of oral traditions seemed to be the most practical approach to serving that interest.

As it happens, each of the excerpted accounts presented in these chapters very well might merit either a "folklore" or "oral history" label. Narratives which adhere to relatively strict structural and formal patterns and whose roots are quite clearly communal might be labeled "folkloric." Such accounts often differ in their presentation of details from corroborating versions of the same stories, and they lead the scholar away from historical accuracy and into the realm of interpretive breadth.[4] Stories and descriptions referring to particular events or practices in the valley's past could, under such a strict set of definitions, qualify as oral history.[5] The categorization of such materials occasionally may have its benefits; but, in the context of a study which explores the multifaceted composition of a regional perspective within spoken materials, labels such as "folklore" or "oral history" intrude rather disruptively upon the task at hand. As I began to collate the materials that I had gathered as a collector (or interviewer), I found that the terms "folklore" and "oral history" interfered with my analysis and obscured the oral traditions' applicability to regional identity.

Nearly every piece of "folklore" presented in a given study, once placed in a historical context, becomes a piece of oral history. In the process of "justifying" folk research as historically valid, William Lynwood Montell points to George Laurence Gomme's 1908 observation "that every folk custom and belief has roots in a historical event " (Montell, *Saga of Coe Ridge* xvi). Whether or not we are willing to accept such a blanket statement, Gomme's point *has* been echoed—perhaps less stridently—by any number of more recent folklorists. For all their properties as traditional and highly subjective forms, folk materials have a direct bearing upon the historical circumstances and cultural forces which surround and create them. American folklore, especially, bears out such an assertion. For example, despite the almost ageless motifs often embedded in them, as well as their largely West African origins, the stories that postbellum southern blacks told about such trickster figures as Brer Rabbit and John the Conqueror spoke as much to the historically specific conditions of slavery and racism as they did to their transoceanic origins. As cultural historian Constance Rourke puts it in *American Humor,* the hunting exploits of Anglo-American frontier heroes such as Davy Crockett and Mike Fink have an ancient ancestry, "going back to fairy tales of Europe in which a hunter or poor man wanders all day without finding game, and then encounters magical events in the forest" (61). But these same stories offer much more than echoes or modernizations of European motifs. The appearance of frontier demigods in such great numbers during the mid-nineteenth century was an outgrowth, among other things, of historical developments, such as American expansion into the West.

Verbal forms that appear to be primarily historical in orientation are just as likely to be influenced by folk belief and custom as they are by economic or social circumstance. When valley residents tell stories about people, events, and phenomena particular to their woodlots and to the region's turn-of-the-century lumbering industries, they are careful to ground their accounts in a historical context; accuracy is important to the narrator who wants to educate her or his listener in the methods and practices of past workers. But traditional folk motifs have a way of creeping into even the most detailed and historical-sounding contexts. Legends, which are—by definition—"told for true," often embroider old motifs within time- and place-specific accounts. Walter Carey—the most prominent of Sawmill Valley woodsmen in the early 1900s—was a real person who participated in a critical phase of the region's lumbering industry. But Carey also was a noted strong-man, a character whose superhuman abilities allied him with other centuries-old powerful heroes whose exploits spoke to folk beliefs in magic and giantism. Rather than agonizing over distinctions that served only to obfuscate this study's actual purposes, I decided to go into the field guided by the ideas and approaches I had gleaned from both folkloric and oral historical models. Whether I was a collector or an interviewer I leave to the reader to decide. The main question I asked myself as I began the transition from research to writing was not "Is this a folklore or an oral history project?" Rather, I asked, "How am I going to sort all these materials out?"

Organization of Materials

In each of the chapters to follow, I explore the various forms that acts of regionalization have assumed in the folklore of the Sawmill Valley. The chapter on local hills, for instance, looks at the most obvious form of place-oriented lore—local legends—and at personal narratives pertaining to specific tracts of land. The distinguishing features of the local landscape—its hills—have taken sufficient hold on the regional imagination as to inspire a proprietary form of story telling and narrative. In this form, valley residents stake a claim to the land by imbuing it with a sense of *meaning* based upon, among other things, a nationally derived frontier mythology. The next chapter, in which I examine the folk history of agriculture in the area, explores another form of regionalization: valley residents' descriptions of landscape and farming practices. The accounts that I have included in this section of the book distinguish the local geography from its surroundings and highlight an age of relative agricultural prosperity by contrasting the valley's once-productive hillside farmsteads with the forested slopes that have replaced them. Whereas I have framed the hill chapter as an exploration of folkloric materials, the farm chapter is built around a more or less oral historical focus on ethnicity. This factor is especially salient in the excerpted accounts in which local residents distinguish their upland existence from that of their (Polish) neighbors along the Connecticut River floodplain. On the whole, regionalization seems to be the outgrowth of just this sort of outwardly oriented contrast.

My third chapter highlights the acts of regionalization which pertain to the valley's woodlots and lumbering industries. The chapter includes an exploration of personal narratives and third-person accounts of what I have termed "near misses," as well as strong-man stories. I have interpreted these materials as evidence of the valley's relentless ethic of hard work and self-sufficiency, by which insiders and outsiders alike were judged. The chapter also includes a discussion of the effects of immigration on the region's lumbering history. That discussion, again, is built around an essentially oral historical set of accounts.

Chapter 4's focus on village traditions engages both folklore and oral history in its exploration of the regionalizing effects of town character anecdotes, as well as local social pastimes. As they tell stories about one another, and especially about the eccentric men and women who lived on the margins of local society, local residents reveal a fascination with the Other which calls our attention, once again, to the state of *permeability* inherent in regional culture. Residents' accounts of pastimes function somewhat differently; like the near-miss and strong-man accounts treated in the lumbering chapter, they help to define the parameters of membership in the regional group and, in turn, the ways in which those parameters took shape as a direct result of local people's responses to modern pressures.

The concluding chapter is a reassessment of the book's overall implications, especially in light of current trends in scholarship in American studies. True to my commitment to anchoring the book in the circumstances of local life, I also devote the concluding chapter to updating the reader on the current cultural life of the Sawmill Valley. This seems to me especially important in light of the fact that, for all their *historical* relevance, the oral materials I have collected in the Sawmill Valley comprise a *living* tradition. Indeed, my experiences as a visitor to the Senior Citizen Lunches that are held every Friday at the Leverett Town Hall convinced me quite some time ago that, however useful a folklorist might be as a *prompt,* his or her presence is not indispensable when it comes to storytelling about the old days in the Sawmill Valley. For an hour and a half once a week, the lunch tables in the Town Hall feature a continuous buzz of recollections, stories, and jogged memories, all of which probably would emerge in some form with or without outside listeners such as myself. As a guest at a few of these lunches, I always found myself wandering from table to table, trying to teach my ears to listen to three or more conversations simultaneously.

As I progressed in my interviews, I encountered yet another indication of the local lore's traditional character and its continuing applicability in the lives of valley men and women. I learned that a universally understood shorthand exists among many locals, allowing them to refer—in a few short words—to a particular story or phenomenon which occupies space within the communal tradition. As I made my rounds, referred from one household to the next, phone calls from one informant to the next would precede me: "Tell him about Baker Whipple," one person would tell the other; "Tell him about the hunter in Rattlesnake Gutter." This shorthand, as well as the communal network of local residents who utilized it, convinces me that—for all their apparent remoteness in time—the oral traditions of the Sawmill Valley *would* exist in a world without folklorists.

This is not to say, however, that the local people I interviewed for this book were not performing for me as I held my microphone to receive their memories. As an interviewer, I undoubtedly played a role in shaping the outcome of a given storytelling session. I reminded people of things that they had forgotten. More important, I was an outsider—someone who was approaching these people in relative ignorance, asking them to teach me about *their* place. The stories they tell each other, as well as the stories that they might tell their grandchildren, probably resemble the ones I collected but are by no means identical to them.

Before turning my attention to the oral legacy of the Sawmill Valley, I would like to offer some final observations about the texts that the reader will encounter throughout the remainder of this book. To begin with, in calling them *texts*, I quite obviously am abstracting them from their original conversational or performance contexts—whether these contexts are properly understood as in front of one's neighbors on the general store porch in 1914 or in front of a folklorist's microphone in 1992. Given the attention that folklorists, at least as far back as the 1960s, have paid to treating folklore as an act rather than as a set of bounded utterances, my text-centered approach very well may appear to be a sort of throwback to the pre–Young Turk days of folklore scholarship. It is my hope, however, that discerning readers will see adequate justification for the emphasis on text in my attention to the variations among, modulations within, and composite effect of those admittedly abstracted texts, which—I would argue—are not bounded at all but are related to one another integrally, much as a piece of patchwork forms a part of a quilt. A performance-based reading certainly would reveal much that this reading misses. Among other things, it would offer a much more deliberate sense of context—when these stories are told, where, and in what sorts of situations. Perhaps such a focus also would have highlighted the various roles that each informant plays in the community—the storyteller, the voice-changer, the local historian. Ultimately, however, such an approach would have limited the book's usefulness as a work of history; the emphasis would have been on the contemporary context and the local lore's current dynamic. What I *do* regret about the text-centered approach is that readers of this book miss out entirely on hearing my informants' distinct voices—their accents and pronunciations, their moments of hesitation and high enthusiasm, their laughter and sense of timing. In this regard, these texts fail to convey a certain text-ure that the interview sessions had. I have done my best, whenever possible, to offer verbatim, if occasionally clarified, pieces of transcribed text. Readers from outside western New England who search for "ayuh's" and other reputed regionalisms will be sorely disappointed, however. In the first place, western Massachusetts has never been a place where people say "ayuh" in their conversations. My informants do display other salient Yankeeisms in their speech,[6] but those would have to be subjects for another book.

As I have indicated, the most formidable challenge I have faced in writing this book has been how I might best balance my desire to allow informants to speak for themselves with my responsibility as a scholar to provide a framework for cultural interpretation. I cannot say that the final product has resolved the eternal discrepancy between the lives of the folk and the analytical impositions of academic folklorists. Like Silas Lamson and countless other resident outsiders in the history of the valley, I can be rooted in the landscape without transcending my (perhaps self-imposed) foreign-ness. Regardless of how much local mud accumulates on my boots or how many hours of interviewing my tape recorder has logged, I reach the end of this project in an ironic convergence with my informants, knowing that I have only begun to understand this place.

Yankee Moderns

Chapter 1

Back Up on Brushy

Rocky outcroppings at the crest of Rattlesnake Gutter, February 1999. Photograph by Janice Sorensen.

Place-related Legends and Anecdotes of Sawmill Valley Hills

Stories about Hills

Anyone traveling the length of the Sawmill Valley's main thoroughfare, North Leverett Road, cannot help noticing how firmly cultural endeavor is woven into the very fabric of the region's natural environment. The valley's earliest European settlers situated their farmsteads, mills, and villages at prominent waterfalls. They built their roads or added to existing ones along paths of least topographical resistance. But the steep hillsides of the Sawmill Valley were not entirely amenable to the civilizing ax. Wilderness exerts its own powerful influence upon people who live in close contact with it. In the local mindset, higher places exerted an enchantment that often inspired residents to mythologize their heroic past. In so doing, they explained their cultural life as an outgrowth of their geographical circumstances. The Sawmill Valley's hills, then, were integral to local residents' acts of *regionalization,* their efforts to take possession, in an imaginative and ideological realm, of the land they inhabited.

Oral traditions served a dual purpose here. On the one hand, stories about hills provided locals with an area-specific repertoire, a body of common topographical knowledge that was derived from a tangible reference point—the hills surrounding their homes. On the other hand, these same stories offer the most obvious evidence of external influence on local lore, of national and even transhistorical themes and motifs superimposed upon a local landscape. And the extraregional derivation is only one aspect of that landscape's permeability. As Suzi Jones and others have demonstrated, regionalization serves an ideological as well as a rhetorical purpose. When my informants first heard these stories from their parents and grandparents, their culture was in the midst of a major modernizing transition. Local legends and anecdotes about area hills recalled the heroic and survivalistic deeds of the valley's first settlers; the stories' invocation of a pioneer era allowed locals psychologically to resist the social and economic changes that threatened to eclipse their sense of cultural wholeness.

Within the folk history of the Sawmill Valley, hills and mountains have taken on a higher degree of symbolic significance than any other aspect of local topography. Brushy Mountain, a continuous ridge of timbered and sparsely settled land, separates the Sawmill Valley off from Leverett Center to the south. Even the advent of automobile transportation did not stimulate much travel between the Sawmill Valley villages and Leverett Center in the early part of the twentieth century. As Evelyn Skerry puts it, "The north end and the south end of town . . . didn't have that much contact because [of] the hill between." Clarissa Truesdell LaClaire echoes this view: "Leverett used to be a very separated town," she says; "North Leverett and . . . the Center didn't know anything about each other." For residents of the Sawmill Valley, passage northward was even rarer. Chestnut Hill, which, along with Diamond Ridge, forms the northern edge of the valley, has been settled for over two hundred years. But as Chestnut Hill levels out to a plateau along the town line that separates Montague and Leverett on the west and south from Wendell to the north and east, settlement becomes sparse. When local residents left their home valley, which they did with increasing frequency in the early 1900s, they usually followed the most obvious geographical trajectory and traveled westward toward the mouth of Sawmill River in Montague Center, from which point they easily could continue on the north-south axis defined by the Connecticut River itself.

In addition to regulating travel in and out of the Sawmill Valley before the advent of the automobile and contributing to its residents' collective sense of their topographical parameters, the valley's hills and the oral traditions inspired by them have done much to shape local notions of history and cultural identity. According to folk memory, the valley's hills were settled long before its lower elevations were. To many residents, these hilly stretches of wilderness represent the region's preindustrial past. Cellar holes and stone walls remind locals of the region's earliest European settlers—men and women who were only as "civilized" as difficult topographical conditions allowed them to be. Locals associate Brushy Mountain and Rattlesnake Gutter (the ravine that forms Brushy Mountain's western edge) with Indians, pioneers, ghosts, buried treasure, crime, and murder. In the oral tradition, men and women who inhabited parcels of land on Chestnut Hill and Brushy Mountain are inextricably linked with the enchanted past.

A consistent thematic focus on *place* sets hill-related folklore off from the valley's other oral traditions. Valley residents at the turn of the century grafted onto the landscape a regional folk heritage and sense of the past, imbuing the defining hills and wildernesses with primary historical significance. Most long-time valley residents in their lifetimes acquired at least a small repertoire of these place-related legends. Some of my informants abbreviated the details; others drew stories out to full length. These stories offered members of the regional group a common local past and, in a modern era, a way of setting themselves apart from their neighbors outside the region. Inasmuch as the hills marked an actual *border* with an outside world for the residents of the Sawmill Valley, stories about the hills give voice to the region's participation in a cultural fabric that extended beyond even the most imposing of topographical impediments. Stories about hills speak not only to the divergent cultural *origins* of Sawmill River Valley folklore, but also to its margin-making function, its service as a dual signpost of internal resistance to, and external influence upon, the valley's cultural life in the turn-of-the-century period.

It is easy to see how cultural landmarks, such as houses and public buildings, generate folklore. From the house where George Washington slept to the office tower that showers the streets below it with plummeting panes of glass, buildings invite stories, anecdotes, and traditions. Certain leaps of imagination and faith *are* integral to such formulations. More often than not, the people who tell stories about the early history of a given house did not build it themselves; their knowledge is based upon hearsay. But buildings exist because human beings have put them where they are; they are more accessible to human formulations than, say, hillsides are. We know the name of the family who built the house down the street from where we live; if we do not, a short trip to the Registry of Deeds will tell us. The story of a given boulder or pine grove is bound to be more of a mystery, however. In rural areas, where topography exerts a dominant influence on people's lives, the scenarios tend to multiply.

As Richard Dorson puts it, "Certain tale types have natural roots in geography" (*Jonathan* 138). Unusual topographical features, Dorson suggests, cause people to invent or adopt unusual stories: "Over mountain peaks leap distraught lovers . . . ; under trees and rocks lie buried treasure caches" (138). Stories and anecdotes which are inspired by natural landscape features constitute one of the most common forms of regional folklore. They allow people to see their history inscribed in the landscapes they inhabit. And they provide the folklorist with some of the evidence necessary to explore a local group's often strained attempts to define regional norms and parameters.

As most folklore scholarship suggests, legends are at once highly mobile and quick to root themselves in particular places. Indeed, the regionalization of particular legends is a key aspect of their classification as legends. A given legend may wander over vast reaches of time and space, but rarely will it be rendered by its teller in the language of timeless myth. Rather, a legend becomes part of a particular region's oral tradition by lodging itself as *securely* as possible within local geography. Suzi Jones cites as an example of a place-related legend a story about a convent whose basement turns out to be a catacomb wherein resident nuns bury their secretly birthed babies. She provides excerpts from three separate versions of this legend, each of which was collected in a different area of North America. Here I quote only the geographically significant lines of each: "On the south side of Milwaukee, at the corners of 27th and Greenfield Streets"; "Well, I once knew a guy who was from the Isle of Pines, off Cuba"; "Three doors down the street from a convent in his hometown of Akron, Ohio" (112–13). In each case, believability is enhanced by the regionalization of the story. The same is true of legends that I collected in the Sawmill River Valley. Stories recounted for me about buried treasure on Brushy Mountain, for example, differ little in content from thousands of similar legends about buried treasure that exist all over the world. But nobody who told me about buried treasure said, "I have a story for you about buried treasure." Indeed, when I asked informants obliquely for "old stories," usually I came away with little or nothing. The key to collecting these legends, I soon learned, was to ask people questions like "Can you tell me any old stories about *Brushy Mountain?*"

Life and Legend on the Frontier: The Brushy Mountain Tradition

As the old-timers tell it, the earliest European settlers of the Sawmill River Valley made their homes on Brushy Mountain. Local residents portray Brushy Mountain as the ancient realm of pioneers. Indeed, when responding to my questions about how long her family had lived in the Sawmill Valley, Loyce Glazier Dunbar, speaking of Brushy Mountain in the same way that one of my relatives might in referring to the Old Country, told me that her ancestors were "Brushy Mountain people, if you went back far enough." Dave Mercier echoed Dunbar's reference to the mountain settlement's "past-ness."

As he understood it, the area had not been inhabited since the middle part of the last century. As Willy Stone explained, the valley's earliest (European) residents made their homes on Brushy Mountain "before they settled North Leverett." Even informants whose families arrived in the Sawmill River Valley after Brushy Mountain's settlement period ended (people lived on the mountain in the years between the mid-eighteenth and mid-nineteenth centuries) were quite familiar with the mountain's history and traditions.

As Clifford Blinn sums up communal knowledge of Brushy Mountain, his description is ambiguous enough to echo any number of frontier legends from all over North America. "It seems as if everybody moved up onto the top of the mountains when they came," he observes. "Years and years and years ago. . . . That's where they first settled when they came into this area, was Brushy Mountain. And then years and years later they moved down into the valleys from there. . . . That's where they came when they first came into the area. That's where they built their houses and had their farms." As its name suggests, Brushy Mountain was relatively inaccessible even in the days before second- and third-growth forests took it over completely. Although the early settlers on the mountain cleared enough space to maintain small farms, the oral tradition tells us that, even when a settlement existed there, trees and brush were a predominant feature.

The settlers of Brushy Mountain had a definite purpose in situating themselves in the middle of an inaccessible tangle of growth. They were pioneers in the American tradition, and they were necessarily cautious about exposing themselves too broadly to the dangers of living in a valley. "As I remember it," said Vernon Aiken, "they settled up there so they'd be away from Indians." His recollection was corroborated by several other informants. Mary Keniston and Gertrude Carey offered similarly vague accounts of the mountain's history as a haven from Indians, based on what they remembered having been told by their parents. Forrest Briggs, whose pamphlet on Brushy Mountain history introduces a combination of personal reminiscence, oral tradition, and genealogical research, suggests that "an upland location would mean signaling and protection" when "dreaded Indians" threatened from below.

Only one family retained an actual story on this theme, however. Bill Fleming, who came to the Sawmill River Valley from New Jersey when he married into the Watson family in the 1940s, recalled that his mother-in-law (Verdie Watson) told him how the Watson house came to be situated where it is, just off the Dudleyville Road on the northeastern slope of Brushy Mountain. Amos Watson was the first member of this family to settle in the Sawmill Valley:

> I don't know if this was fiction or what, but anyway, she said when the original Watsons bought their land here in 1795 . . . he put his cane here and he said, "This is where we're going to build the house. . . . This is where the front door will be." . . . And that's where the house was built. And the reason, she said, why did you build it up on the hill, it's so hard to get to and everything, he [*sic*] says, the reason in those days, that Indians were still around and they would come up the river and hunt and whatnot. And although they weren't hostile, they still had to keep an eye out for them. So they were up on the hill and they could watch the Sawmill River. . . . This is the way I heard it anyway. So what Indians they were I don't know.

Indeed, none of the informants who mentioned the mountain settlement's origin as a refuge from Indians had any specific knowledge as to the tribe or tribes in question, not to mention the historical period during which settlers might have been on the lookout. Naturally, the focus in these references to Indians was on the men and women who were watching them from above. Whether or not Amos Watson actually used his cane as a cornerstone, the existence of a family tradition that he did so proffers an image of the quintessential American pioneer—a man with the self-assurance of a prophet.

The part of Bill Fleming's story that mentions Indians is sufficiently vague as to suggest that the Brushy Mountain legacy fits squarely in the tradition of stories of beleaguered and vigilant pioneers that we have come to associate with towns and villages in all regions of the United States. In the Schoharie Hills of Upstate New York, for example, the pioneer and Revolutionary War hero Timothy Murphy is said to have "taken his family along and left his home in the valley for a winter residence on the mountain from which he could more easily command the movements of his Indian enemies" (Gardner 27). Although Amos Watson's experiences pale beside Murphy's death-defying exploits (Murphy's time on the mountaintop came to an end when, in flight from the Indians, he survived a leap from a hundred-foot precipice), the two stories of leading a party of kinfolk to safety and strategic advantage atop a mountain belong in the same category of frontier place-legends.

Aside from reminding us of other pioneer legends, what does the story of Amos Watson on Brushy Mountain tell us? In particular, what does it tell us about the specifically *regional* identity of people who have passed such a legend along from one generation to the next? To begin with, it indicates that the people of the Sawmill River Valley, for whatever reasons, have retained a cultural memory of the days when the wilderness was a refuge as much as it was an impediment to civilization. In keeping with a frontier tradition that endures in many regions, Brushy Mountain is remembered as a waypoint in the civilizing process, a point where cultural and natural landscapes converged. What its settlers were on the lookout for or in hiding from may not even matter. Dave Mercier, whose French Canadian grandfather arrived in the Sawmill Valley and settled on Chestnut Hill decades after the Brushy Mountain settlement already had been vacated, recalls having been to one of the early building sites on the mountain during his many hunting trips there. Because of the mountain's reputation as a frontier settlement, Mercier's assumption was that the building once had been a garrison of sorts, set up for defensive purposes. As he acknowledged his lack of substantive information concerning the building's origins and purpose, Dave Mercier participated in the collective act of mystification that surrounds the oral tradition's treatment of Brushy Mountain's history. Any regionalized resident who ascends through its thickets is engaging in time-travel.

Brushy Mountain's original settlers left several types of evidence of their presence on the hill, including vegetative ones. "You know, I hadn't been up there I bet for ten years," says Harriet Bourne LaClaire in a 1967 interview with Audrey Duckert, who asked her about the mountain's homesites. "And I went up and couldn't believe my eyes. . . . There were trees, I'll bet, as high as this house. And all the lilac blossoms with little tufts, was up at the top of the trees. . . . I couldn't get over it."

Both Dave Mercier's and Harriet LaClaire's experiences of the Brushy Mountain legacy usefully illustrate how accounts of personal experiences can attain a communal or even a traditional purpose. As local men and women talk about their own visits to Brushy Mountain, they attest to the legend's continuing role as an arbiter of regional culture. Following quite literally in the footsteps of Forrest Briggs, several members of the regional group have made pilgrimages to the site of the Brushy Mountain settlement and its cellar holes. Briggs himself was famous locally for having labeled each of the house sites and drawn maps of the original settlement. In a 1984 interview with members of the Leverett Historical Society, he provided a brief overview. Personal observation—direct experience of the landscape—figured prominently in his description. "It's quite a little history altogether," he says, "about the life on Brushy Mountain."

> House number one was Noah Torrey. That's why they call it the old—the first place you come to up the mountain—the Torrey place. There used to be Torrey Brook, that come down into—. And then Aaron Pike, and Simon Pike, lived up there up the road a ways. That's where he was born—on Brushy Mountain. . . . House number three was Mason Pike. That was my

> grandmother's father. . . . House number four was Jonathan Glazier. That's where my mother came from, was from Jonathan Glazier. He came to Brushy Mountain in 1790. He married Azubah—an Indian girl. There's Indian blood in me. They had ten children. . . . Nathaniel Maynard lived up there, at house number five. And he had a big family. . . . House number six was Josiah Hemenway. That's where the Hemenway family—part of it anyway—settled. And I think their place must have been the nicest place. I know the cellar hole—the stone work, the way they laid it out and everything—seemed like it must have been a very nice place.

The original settlers made an impression on more than the actual landscape. In the minds of their descendants, their example merited a ritualized remembrance. Forrest Briggs refers to the practice in the same interview. The Brushy Mountain settlement happened so long ago in the minds of local residents that its very *memorialization* begins to sound like an ancient practice. "Years and years ago," Briggs recollects for his interviewers, "the people walked on Brushy Mountain—used to go up there every year and have a picnic at the old Glazier place." Clearly, on the basis of Forrest Briggs's and other corroborating accounts of an annual picnic at the site of the original Glazier place, the memory of the Brushy Mountain settlement played an active role in the way the valley fashioned a regional identity at the close of the nineteenth century.

Valley residents were hardly alone in their commemoration of New England's pioneer days. As writers like Dona Brown have demonstrated, the turn-of-the-century period saw a burgeoning interest in the development of historical pageantry and the canonization of heroes, much of which was intended to elevate the old (homogenous) New England at the expense of the new (heterogeneous) one. When local residents made their annual trek up the steep, wooded slopes of Brushy Mountain and paid homage to their unencumbered predecessors, they also were commenting—albeit inadvertently—on their own lamentably modern lives in a valley that long since had relinquished its garrison status in favor of engagement with the outside world.

Like the inhabitants of other long-settled regions in the United States, the residents of the Sawmill Valley cultivate the memory of a time when time-worn farmsteads, villages, and fields did not exist, when daily life was full of hardship and danger, in contrast to the apparent luxuries of modern existence. The stories that perpetuate these memories are necessarily vague; they tap into broad, essentially ideological concerns that exceed immediate regional boundaries. Compare the language of this (written) memorialization from Forrest Briggs's Brushy Mountain pamphlet to any number of other ideologically infused accounts of pioneer adventures: "Most of the early settlers were probably poor in worldly goods, but because all shared both hardships and success, life was a great adventure. They were a brave, hardy[,] but uncultivated race of men. They knew little of the etiquette of refined society, were blessed with few of the advantages of education[,] and were destitute of the elegancies, and in most cases, the common conveniences of life." Brushy Mountain indeed was settled in the years before either Moores Corner or North Leverett existed; for all we know, it even may have been settled in order to provide its inhabitants with a means of protecting themselves from whatever threats existed in the valley below. But the lack of detail in these stories about Indians and pioneers is telling. The stories of Brushy Mountain's early settlement speak to the contrasting forces at work in the creation of place legends, to the similarities—real and imagined—between local experiences and national myths.

As these stories invoke such things as personal memories of particular cellar holes, they point to a collective impulse on the part of locals to root themselves in the visible and experienced landscape, to attach themselves and their progenitors to *this* place. As they echo accounts from other regions of North America about intrepid pioneers facing the unknown, on the other hand, they suggest that the inhabitants of this landscape are participants in a cycle of storytelling that is at least national in its overall scope. The residents of the Sawmill Valley may have carried this mythology with them from other places, or they may have integrated it into their sense of local history as they encountered an influx of people from other regions. They very well may have absorbed the frontier myth in their schoolhouses and then begun the process of adopting it as their own, of superimposing it on the local landscape. In any case, the existence within the Sawmill Valley of a pioneer legend associated with Brushy Mountain suggests that the folklore of this region is not a byproduct of cultural insularity or physical isolation. On the contrary, the Brushy Mountain frontier legend could have resulted only from a series of exchanges with people and traditions from the "outside" world. At the turn of the twentieth century, by which time life in the uncivilized wilderness was a far-distant memory, the legend was a valuable last remnant of departed bravery and virtue. In all its vagueness and imprecision, it still offers considerably more insight into its tellers' reluctant descent into modernity than it does into the actual eighteenth-century settlers who once cleared local forests.

Buried Treasure on Brushy Mountain

No Brushy Mountain tradition is as prevalent (or as varied in its forms) as the series of stories and anecdotes that treat the mountain's reputed cache of buried treasure. Here it is worth recalling Richard Dorson's observation that geographical features inspire folkloric traditions; for a few of its tellers, the buried-treasure story is related directly to the presence of an enormous boulder on the mountainside. For other tellers, the buried treasure has proven elusive for so long that no visible landmark ever could hold out the promise of its recovery. Landmark or no landmark, this group of tales has all the earmarks of the buried-treasure legends that folklorists have recorded across North America. It also shows how locals have imbued one of their region's harshest landscapes with potential and the capacity for redemption. The buried-treasure legend offered turn-of-the-century residents—even those who did not take it terribly seriously—at least the *image* of a wealth-bearing past, a hidden or even mystical store of economic or psychic power that their premodern progenitors providentially set aside for future discovery. Buried treasure, in other words, offers symbolic evidence of the enriching presence of the past amid present-day economic despair. It accumulates value over time.

Dave Mercier was the first person who told me about the burial. Sometime during the first half of the nineteenth century, he explained, two unnamed brothers who made their home in Brushy Mountain's tangled woodland stole money from a Greenfield bank. Upon returning to their mountain hideout, they got drunk on hard cider. When one of the two proceeded to bury the money, the other set upon and killed him. The secret of the treasure's whereabouts has yet to be revealed. The fact that the money's burial hinges upon an incident of *fraternal* strife at once alerts us that this legend bears upon the internal struggles inherent in any regional context. Indeed, fraternal strife and dissent among otherwise successful thieves is a common component of many buried-treasure legends. Of the 102 buried-treasure legends from across the United States that Gerard T. Hurley includes in his 1951 survey of the genre, 11 make reference to murders that accompany either the burial itself or (attempted) recovery of the treasure. Dave Mercier's version of the Brushy Mountain legend incorporates a narrative tradition that can be found in other regions of New England, as well as in Arizona, California, Florida, Louisiana, Missouri, New York, North and South Carolina, and Oregon (205–14). The fratricide that precedes the act of placing the treasure in the ground suggests that psychological proprietorship of the landscape has a potentially disruptive effect on even the most natural alliances. Instead of being a place where kinfolk can meet on equal terms and for mutual benefit, Mercier's Brushy Mountain is a site of internal fragmentation, of contention. In symbolic terms, it contains the seeds of regional dissolution.

Dave Mercier's telling of the Brushy Mountain legend is not the only rendition that takes us beyond the immediate boundaries of the Sawmill Valley. The buried-treasure legend also evokes the outlaw tradition that has pervaded American folklore for at least two centuries. In Joe W. LaClaire's version, the men responsible for stealing the money (the Pike brothers, who were residents of the Brushy Mountain settlement in the mid-nineteenth century) had quite a time dodging the law even after they reached their homes on the wooded mountaintop. Joe W. LaClaire and his wife Harriet Bourne LaClaire were interviewed in May 1967 by Audrey Duckert:

> HBL: But Simon Pike lived up there [Brushy Mountain] and—. And was it Simon that, somebody stole some money and then they—was that Simon's father, or who was that?
>
> JL: Seems as though it was his brother.
>
> HBL: A couple of them. They stole some money and then they—
>
> JL: Well, the cops come to get them, and they jumped out the window and they buried the money in the road. There's a big stone there—all of us thought it was under that stone. . . .
>
> HBL: According to the other fellow, before he ever told anybody, he died. So there's buried treasure up there.

This version of the legend is echoed by at least one other local resident. "I've heard about it," Willy Stone says in reference to the buried-money story. "That was just a rumor that went around that there was money buried up there. . . . Some bandits . . . robbed somebody and went up, back up there, and they got caught. And they figured the money was buried up there, but they never could find it. I've heard that story." Whether the robbers are the Pike brothers or more generic "bandits," their (fleeting) wealth amid the Spartan conditions of the Brushy Mountain settlement marks them as having achieved at least a small measure of folk hero status. As a result of their transgression, the undeveloped acreage of Brushy Mountain is distinguished by an intriguing story and by the possibility that it conceals wealth.

Tellers of this story are dividing their narrative loyalties. The legend's references to a local landscape and to local characters are aspects of its specifically regional scope. On the other hand, the fact that it echoes other legends about bank robbery, murder, and hidden treasure tells us that its derivation cannot by entirely local. Like the tales of intrepid pioneers making their homes on top of a mountain, the buried-treasure tales suggest that a nationally derived ideology is at work within local tradition. Ultimately, the challenge posed by the hidden money is the primary means by which the legend resonates with others of the same genre.

In a 1978 article on buried-treasure legends, folklorist Patrick B. Mullen writes that such tales, especially in their references to a search that may continue into the present, have a "bearing on the folk idea of unlimited good" (209–10), the belief that hidden stores of wealth can be recovered through some combination of hard work and luck. A particular landscape is the recipient of a tradition that spans an entire continent. Inasmuch as "unlimited good" is an aspect of buried-treasure tales like this one, the legend has a populist ring to it. The legend posits a landscape whose fate is not yet sealed, a landscape still open to the possibility that local residents (or enterprising outsiders) might discover its hidden store of wealth. Dave Mercier's perspective seems to bear this out. He told me that he himself always had a hankering to find the secret trove. "You don't have to go up [Brushy Mountain] too far to find this big boulder," Harriet Bourne LaClaire tells her interviewer; "that's buried treasure."

As unrecoverable as the buried money seems to be, the fact that its story is continually retold within the Sawmill Valley suggests that one purpose of the legend may be to render an otherwise bewildering, heavily forested mountain accessible to native and outsider alike. It gives an all but deserted landscape a human dimension. Unlike currently inhabited cultural landscapes, hills like Brushy Mountain constitute a sort of no-person's-land, regardless of their actual proprietorship. This may explain why, for example, Sawmill Valley residents who have no genealogical or ethnic link to the Pike brothers—or to the Brushy Mountain settlement, for that matter—have adopted the buried-treasure story as their own. Joe W. LaClaire, whose father was a French Canadian immigrant and whose mother was of Ulster Irish descent, was not born into one of the "Yankee" families who made Brushy Mountain their home, as the Pikes apparently did. Having spent all his adult years as a woodsman, however, he must have come upon the buried money tale early in his career, because it was standard *regional* fare.

Geographical circumstances play a greater role in Brushy Mountain stories than any other factor. For Harriet LaClaire and Joe W. LaClaire, the boulder under which the money is said to have been buried is the primary touchstone for memory. The boulder fits the tale into a personal as well as a communal context. "That boulder ain't half as big as it was forty years ago," Harriet LaClaire said. "It used to be immense, you know. Now it isn't much higher than I am. . . . It's settled into the ground." For the LaClaires' daughter, Marion LaClaire Norwood, geography is also a prominent factor. Thus, for her, the details of the buried-money legend become intertwined with the stories that valley residents tell about Indians and ghosts. Unlike her parents, Marian Norwood supplies a version of the Brushy Mountain story which makes no mention whatsoever of robbers. In its transmission from one generation to the next, her parents' story about the buried money somehow became linked with the mountain's "Indian" heritage: "The only ones I remember about Brushy Mountain— . . . A girl was buried up there. A young girl. I suppose she might have been seventeen or eighteen when she died. And . . . they've often seen her ghost up there, by her, where she used to live. And there's . . . [a] story about someone that buried treasures up there at one of the Brushy Mountain areas, you know. . . . Those are all kind of things that I heard as was growing up. . . . Something about the Indians coming and he buried his money, and it's up, still up there somewhere, you know." Because Brushy Mountain is the focal point for both the pioneer and the buried-treasure legends, it is easy so see how Norwood might have entangled the scenarios. Of course, it is possible that she simply came upon an errant version of the tale that her parents missed. Gerard Hurley's survey of buried-treasure legends records a Linceum, Louisiana, provenance for the following plot: "Men escaping from Indians in the early days buried their gold here. Later, the men quarreled among themselves and all were killed" (210).

Loyce Dunbar's version of the legend resonates with other local legends and anecdotes that feature stinginess as a common attribute of the Sawmill Valley's most colorful "local characters" (see chapter 4 for a full discussion): "All I know, a man, I guess he buried it [the money] because he didn't want anybody to know how much money he had. And then he died and he never told anybody where it was." Divergent versions of the Brushy Mountain buried-treasure legend should not surprise us; this is folklore, after all. Only one thing links all these renditions: the fact that the events are said to have taken place on Brushy Mountain. As a place imbued with a considerable amount of folk history, Brushy Mountain is simultaneously a point of communal convergence and a point where differences among individual experiences give rise to at least a few narrative departures from group experience.

Compare all the above versions of the Brushy Mountain legends with the one provided by Vernon Aiken. Aiken says that, in all his years living in the Sawmill Valley, he never has heard anything about *buried treasure* up on Brushy Mountain. He does, however, have a story to tell about the Pike brothers, and it takes place on Brushy Mountain:

> The Pikes lived up there. Mrs. Pike, and she had two sons, Steven and Simon. And this fellow had got in some bad trouble, and the law was after him and he came up and he got in the house and he told them, he says, "If you don't make any trouble for me," he says, "I won't hurt anybody." Well, he didn't know that Steven was . . . sleeping up in the loft. [And so]—They [the Pikes] were part Indian— . . . Steven bailed out the window, and he run from Brushy Mountain to Montague, and then stopped. And he got the sheriff and come back, and the fellow was still there, and the sheriff took him. But they said he run non-stop. The sheriff lived in Montague, and he hitched up his horse, and I don't know whether he got a deputy to go with him, or what, but anyway, Steven got a ride home.

Even though buried treasure is not an aspect of Vernon Aiken's Brushy Mountain story, his narrative has other elements in common with the stories his neighbors tell about the mountain. Although in this story the Pikes figure as law-abiding citizens, the tale does have an outlaw; if Brushy Mountain was not *home* to those in flight from the law, it still served as a refuge for one such fugitive, at least temporarily. In this story, too, the roles assigned to Indians are reversed. Instead of hiding from Indians, the story's protagonist turns out to be "part Indian" himself—a circumstance which apparently accounts for his stealth and speed.

If the Pike brothers were the central focus of the tales told about Brushy Mountain, it would be difficult to find any correlation between Vernon Aiken's story and those provided by the other informants. But Aiken refers to his narration as "the only *Brushy Mountain* [my italics] story I ever heard." Aiken has many stories to tell about particular *people*, but this is not one of them. Like his neighbors' buried-treasure stories, Aiken's account tells us that Brushy Mountain has a history of somewhat wild and unpredictable occurrences. It is a place where the staid life of the villages below it gives way to lawlessness and danger. Many communities in the United States revere as precious the memory of a frontier, a borderland where confrontation between wilderness and civilization never was fully resolved. For residents of the Sawmill River Valley, Brushy Mountain is that frontier.

As the quintessential borderland, the American frontier stands in the folk memory for more than unusual occurrences. Rather, it is a metaphor for the conflicts—internal and external—that occur even in seemingly homogeneous vernacular regions. Indeed, such conflicts create those regions in the first place. In Dave Mercier's version of the treasure legend, fratricide is the key metaphor for cultural tension. For Vernon Aiken, that same collapse is embodied in an outside threat, a man in "bad trouble" with the law. Within the

Sawmill Valley, moreover, only Brushy Mountain is represented as having any Indian history. It should come as no surprise to us, therefore, that the "part Indian" Pikes made their home there, even as some informants call attention to the mountain's history as a *refuge from* threatening Indians. Presumably, people of racially mixed heritage would not feel at home elsewhere, would be unable to conform to the ordered patterns of village life. But the wilderness, never completely settled even after it was dotted with homesteads, apparently accepts those who exist at society's margins, whether frontier folk or Indians or some mixture of the two. Like Coe Ridge in Kentucky and Tennessee, which after the Civil War sheltered former slaves and errant whites (see William Lynwood Montell's *The Saga of Coe Ridge*), Brushy Mountain tolerated more deviance than the valley below it could or would. Whereas the more prosperous early residents of Brushy Mountain had made it "off the mountain" by the middle of the nineteenth century, apparently the Pikes were neither prosperous enough nor sufficiently assimilated to make the final descent into village life.

Despite its temporal and spatial removal from the life of the valley, Brushy Mountain's folk history collapses the simple distinction between purely "natural" and purely "cultural" landscapes. Even the most settled denizens of Moores Corner and North Leverett seem to have come from the original settlement on the mountain. Loyce Dunbar, whose Glazier and Hemenway ancestors both came from the mountain, told me about her family's association with the settlement. As distant as they were from their counterparts in the villages below, the Brushy Mountain people had ways of keeping lines of communication open:

> My great-grandfather, Ebenezer Nigh Glazier, lived on Brushy Mountain, and his brother Benjamin came from Oakham [a town in Worcester County, Massachusetts], you know, he moved with a pair of oxen. And . . . my aunt [Ruby Hemenway] wrote down a lot of things, and one of things was, of course, there weren't as many trees on Brushy Mountain then as there is now. Probably was brush. But they said on a clear day, they could look, you know, and see the steeple down in Leverett. Of course the trees weren't growing then. And they if anyone [in town] was sick, they'd [Brushy Mountain people] go out and listen at morning and night. And . . . the bell would toll for the number of years they were. And they would ring the bell to tell in how many days the funeral was. They knew what they were listening for. . . . She [Ruby Hemenway] said that great-grandma's daughter walked all the way from the top of Brushy Mountain to the North Leverett Church. . . . I guess they didn't see their neighbors or friends very often, especially if you lived on top of Brushy Mountain.

On its surface, Dunbar's description suggests that the Brushy Mountain settlement was located at an enormous remove from North Leverett. Because of the mountain's perceived remoteness, the two miles separating the communities imposed a sense of isolation on the "Brushy Mountain people." Ironically, this same feeling of isolation contributed to the mountain's role as a centralizing feature of the Sawmill Valley's folk history.

Were we to dismiss Brushy Mountain as an anomalous exception to the regional norm, we would be misreading the oral tradition. In fact, Brushy Mountain is located at the very center of the valley, both geographically and psychologically. Its folk heritage has been adopted by many Sawmill Valley residents, regardless of actual lineage, as a universal regional past. Brushy Mountain is the Sawmill Valley's internalized cultural Other, its microcosmic version of the "outside" world.

The mountain's oral legacy shows us that a regional folklore never is a self-contained or sealed entity. The stories and anecdotes that feature Brushy Mountain are devoted to a particular piece of geography and, at the same time, to the wide-ranging and extraregional fare of American folk themes. That these narratives privilege an enchanting and wealth-bearing past suggests a direct correlation between local legend and the regional group's response to the daily compromises imposed by modern life. The Brushy Mountain legend, in other words, flourished among people whose own lives made them feel as if they themselves were poised on the edge of another sort of frontier.

Death Among the Rocks: Legends and Anecdotes of Rattlesnake Gutter

Brushy Mountain's legacy of Indians, bandits, hidden treasure, and apparent lawlessness bespeaks its reputation among locals as a frontier outpost. For all its history as an occasionally dangerous place, however, Brushy Mountain's promise of buried wealth, as well as its status within the community's collective memory as the original Sawmill Valley settlement, suggests that locals also viewed it as a potentially redeemable landscape. Moreover, it was a source of cultural pride, even vegetative renewal. Loyce Dunbar's own memories of the mountain, which date from after the end of human occupancy, are of a landscape rich (by rural New England standards, at any rate) in natural resources. "When I was a child," Dunbar says, "I used to go blueberrying up there with my grandmother. And the road was good enough at that time so you could drive a horse. There are quite a few roads on that Brushy Mountain. And you could drive your horse up there, pick your blueberries. And then in the fall we used to go ferning. She'd bunch all of her ferns, and Mr. Bannaker [a manufacturer of palm-leaf hats] would come from Boston, would pick them up. 'Course it's grown up now. . . . And I remember one year we had a horse that went lame, and so we took him up there, it was a pasture, it was all fenced in at that time."

If Brushy Mountain legends and anecdotes represent the generative and regenerative forces of the frontier in modern circumstances, those associated with Rattlesnake Gutter represent the frontier's potentially lethal and damning consequences. The deepest recesses of Rattlesnake Gutter, unlike those of Brushy Mountain, never have been settled. Brushy Mountain is somewhat steep and heavily wooded along its slopes but more or less level at its summit. It is bisected by one old woods road which, though full of dips and slight jogs, is devoid of any thrilling jump or precipice. Rattlesnake Gutter, on the other hand, is a forbiddingly steep, boulder-strewn ravine. The road that cuts through it is a glorified ledge, one that offers travelers a tight squeeze from end to end—an impossible mountainside on one side, a chilling drop on the other. Local inhabitants are quick to point to the Gutter's spectacular geological features, its varied flora and fauna. But the Gutter's oral tradition is weighted heavily toward the various misfortunes and close calls that, over the years, those same natural features have caused. Generations of Sawmill Valley residents have associated the Gutter with accidents, deaths, and near misses. As wild as it has grown to be since it was abandoned in the mid-nineteenth century, Brushy Mountain for many valley residents represents the old homeplace, even those men and women whose families never lived there. Not even the families longest settled in the valley retain any sort of sentimental attachment to Rattlesnake Gutter, however.

Not surprisingly, the steep topography of the Gutter figures quite prominently in each of the narratives I collected in the field. Informants retain traditional stories about the Gutter that in some way bear on their own experiences. Indeed, all the communally based stories about Rattlesnake Gutter reminded narrators of their own adventures. Every resident of the Sawmill Valley has at least one anecdote to share about her or his experiences coping with the dangerous and occasionally lethal *passageway* between Moores Corner and Leverett Center. Over the years, Rattlesnake Gutter's geography has made it yet another internalized Other within the local mindset; the stories locals tell about it highlight its unpredictability and its proximity to the outside world. Never settled but continually in use, Rattlesnake Gutter always has been, for residents of the Sawmill Valley, the quickest entry and exit point to the south and west. Even today, there is no quicker passage from the

Sawmill Valley to Leverett Center than via the Gutter. Rattlesnake Gutter stories are stories of a margin, of sacrifices, of the sorts of risks inherent in any comings and goings.

One set of stories about Rattlesnake Gutter concerns misadventures surrounding the history of horse-drawn travel through the Gutter. Indeed, automobiles have proven hardly more adaptable to the Gutter's terrain than horses were. As a result of the many accidents which still occur there, the road no longer is plowed and therefore is closed during winter. In any case, the story of one particular accident in Rattlesnake Gutter's past which occurred back in "horse-and-buggy days" points to the dangers woodsmen faced as they transported lumber over the Gutter. As Clifford LaClaire tells it, "They used to haul lumber over there [Rattlesnake Gutter], with a pair of horses, you know. Then they'd put runner-chains on, underneath the runner, so they'd hold back the sled. But evidently the runner-chain broke, as far as the story goes, and two horses went over there. The men, that were driving the horses, jumped off the sled and the horses got killed, of course, because it's a long ways down to the foot of the Gutter at the end of the ledges there. I think that one horse got killed and the other was badly injured and they killed him, as the story goes." Sacrifices such as this latter one, it seems, were inherent in the use of Rattlesnake Gutter. Any local woodsmen who elected to participate in extraregional commerce using this quick but perilous exit point risked their own or their horses' lives. For all the temptations of such an efficient passage, accounts like LaClaire's served woodsmen and all valley residents as salutary reminders regarding the nature of the choices which modernity was foisting upon them.

As Loyce Dunbar recalls her own father's telling of the same anecdote, the trauma associated with the sacrifice is all the more pronounced: "I have a memory of my dad tell[ing] about it. You know, how the horses cried, because they were in pain. . . . It was right up in the steep part of the Gutter. I don't know what happened or anything. But they went off the edge. And one of them got hung up somewhere. . . . I guess they had to shoot them." Given the great economic value of such a horse to its owner, as well as whatever emotional attachment existed between the two, the price paid by the woodsman in question was sufficiently heavy to have ensured this brief anecdote a place in local lore.

Vernon Aiken provides another anecdote in which the Gutter's unforgiving precipice inflicts a wrenching loss on a woodsman. Here, the loss is compounded by a different sort of (financial) bloodletting. In this case, however, a touch of ironic humor gives the story an alternative form of narrative interest. Once again, a man is forced to make an impossible choice. "A fellow up in Wendell," Aiken says, "lost one of his horses over the edge, down into the Gutter. The horse was hanging there. And he had to do something, or he'd lose the other horse. So he took out his jackknife and cut the harness. And it dropped—there was nothing they could do. That was sad. . . . He used to tell it because he got a lawyer to go to the town for him, and he went to court. And . . . they awarded him a hundred dollars for his horse. And he got . . . the check, the bill from the lawyer. The lawyer wanted ninety dollars. So he only wound up with ten dollars. He endorsed his check and sent it back. Says, 'You've got most of it, you might as well have it all.'" Modern life, in other words, exacts a harsh price from men and women who (mistakenly) think that they might gain some economic benefit from its litigious innovations. This anecdote and its teller temper the implied sacrifice with a humorous twist, but any listener even slightly sensitive to the economic constraints placed by twentieth-century life upon the lives of valley residents cannot avoid the sobering message at the heart of this account: during this period, to attempt quick commercial passage out of the Sawmill Valley was to suffer loss and other unpleasant consequences in an unforgiving world.

Forrest Briggs's more detailed version of the same anecdote (he names the woodsman in question and mentions having seen the dead horse himself) is elicited by his interviewer's series of questions regarding North Leverett's "stepchild" status, compared with "the main part of town." In other words, the loss of the horse in Rattlesnake Gutter is linked directly to the Sawmill Valley's isolation and the perils faced by those who attempt to move beyond it to sell their goods and so better their economic and social positions. The teller himself is not exempt, of course. "I used to go down there with great loads of lumber and so forth," he explains. "I remember Donald Stewart with his team, uh, I don't know how it happened, but he was going there with a load of lumber and, uh, I guess found a slippery spot or something. And one horse went over the edge . . . see, and there he hung. . . . And, why he had to, just cut the harness and let him [the horse] drop." In both versions of the horse-harness story, the woodsman in question is humbled by the forbidding topography of the Gutter. The choice that is forced upon him bears the thematic weight of a natural consequence; having made the problematical choice to trade outside the valley, perhaps he should not be surprised that he faces a life-or-death choice en route. In these variants, the horse-sacrifice itself seems to bear a specific metaphorical significance, in other words.

In a slightly different Gutter-related anecdote provided by Vernon Aiken, the most heavily weighted symbolic act occurs in a separate sphere, although it, too, has implications for extraregional travel. An element of supernatural protectiveness not evident in the horse-sacrifice anecdotes sets this two-part story apart from the others. Aiken heard this account from his father: "Did anyone ever tell you about the fellow coming down Rattlesnake Gutter with his pair of horses and a load of lumber? And the neck yoke broke. And the fellow didn't jump off, he hung right to them horses. And of course with the neck-yoke broke, that brought the horse back so their rear ends was kind of against the load. But he rode it to the bottom." The primary difference between this story and the ones about horses hanging over the precipice seems to be one of logistics. Instead of a broken runner-chain, for example, Vernon Aiken attributes the accident to a broken neck-yoke. Moreover, rather than letting go of his horses, the driver in this version holds tightly to them. The neck-yoke story may be making a case for the driver's heroism. While the sacrifice stories properly are understood as versions of an anecdote ("a single episode story about a place or event" [Brunvand 173]), the neck-yoke narrative seems more like a full-fledged legend. It is a more carefully crafted and performed narrative, one which bears signs of incorporating an overall theme (i.e., the driver's heroism) and perhaps aspects of certain migratory motifs. In asking me if "anyone had ever told me about" the event in question, Aiken frames his story, calling attention to its construction as a deliberate and bounded narrative contained within a communal tradition.

The impression that the story is constructed becomes even stronger as Aiken develops its second half, whose outcome distances his version still farther from the horse-sacrifice anecdotes: "The school superintendent, Miss Stearnes, had been to Leverett Center, visiting the schools. And she was coming up to Moores Corner, and back to North Leverett, so she was coming up the Gutter. But somebody had a beef about the school, and they see[n] her and they stopped her and was talking to her. Well, if they hadn't stopped her and talked to her she would have, she would have met them, she would have met that pair of horses and that load of lumber head on, 'cause there's no place to turn out." The coincidence that preserves Stearnes's life indicates that this legend is a sort of "remarkable Providence" story, quite possibly formed by joining an event from local history with a story from elsewhere. The fact that this story takes place in and around Rattlesnake Gutter is no accident, however; as the shortest passageway between the Sawmill Valley and the rest of Leverett, Rattlesnake Gutter is in fact the *only* logical place where such an event could have occurred. With its precipitous drops, strewn boulders, surfeit of shade, and foreboding name,[1] Rattlesnake Gutter invited near misses and catastrophes. Whatever temptations the ravine may have offered in the way of direct access to Leverett Center, its narrowness and unpredictability—at least in Aiken's story—precluded its simultaneous use by woodsmen and schoolteachers. The providential interference of people like the local "who had a beef about the school" could not always be counted on to prevent disaster. For the most part, Rattlesnake Gutter's legacy within local legend was a deadly one.

Easily the most chilling account I collected in the Sawmill Valley is the story of Leon Pratt and Antoine LaFogg. This tale imputes a malevolent quality to the dark landscape of Rattlesnake Gutter itself. Significantly, though neither of the participants lived in the Sawmill Valley (both were residents of Leverett Center, according to Loyce Dunbar), one likely setting for the actual events is Rattlesnake Gutter, the quintessential regional borderland. Dunbar was the first person to tell me about it: "Well, this Leon Pratt was a widower. He had four boys. And there was a LaFogg family, they lived down Leverett Center. . . . This LaFogg's son went with Leon. They used to go blueberrying, and they'd take the blueberries and sell them. They had a horse. Well, they [the Pratts] came home one night and, I don't know what happened, but they found Leon up in the Gutter, down in the ravine, dead. And come to find out, LaFogg had hit him over the head with a rock and killed him, to get what little blueberry money he had." What sort of desperation, we might ask, would lead a man to kill his friend for blueberry money? A story like this one does not appear to hold out many possibilities for place-based interpretation; it records a seemingly random act of violence, a murder which may or may not even have taken place in Rattlesnake Gutter (see Vernon Aiken's version, below). Whether or not the murder took place in the Gutter, the fact that one informant is convinced that it did is an indication that valley residents have attributed ghastly qualities to Rattlesnake Gutter's jagged topography.

Vernon Aiken, my other informant concerning the LaFogg-Pratt murder, is sure that the events took place at quite a distance from Rattlesnake Gutter, within the town limits of Woronoco.

> But . . . Leon Pratt had lived around here. And they went blueberrying together, and Leon didn't want to give Antoine [LaFogg] . . . his share of the money. So there was a piece of two-by-four in the back of the car, so he took it and hit him on the head, and didn't intend to kill him. But he see[n] he killed him, so he threw him down over the bank. And he took off and, it was along later in the fall, some boys were down in this ravine picking grapes, and

> they found the body. But they never found Antoine 'til he come back. He, you know if he'd stayed away they'd never caught him. But he came back and somebody recognized him, going into the theater down in Amherst. So they pulled him out of the theater and took him to court. He had to serve time for that. . . .It was Woronoco, where he murdered him. But I guess they were living up this way somewhere. . . . I went to school with Leon Pratt's kids. And I remember their telling about it, at school. 'Course we'd never heard anything like that before and we thought that was pretty hideous. . . . 'Course they'd probably both been drinking. Drink don't help any.

Aiken's version of the story proposes more than a different location for the murder. Among other things, it tells us that—due in part to his state of intoxication—LaFogg killed his friend by accident, panicked, fled the scene, and eventually was caught. What it does have in common with Dunbar's version is its mention of a motive and a scenario for the murder, as well as its clarity on the matter of where the body was found—at the bottom of a ravine. A murder like this one, both versions suggest, could only result in a body's being dumped into a dark and inaccessible recess in the surface of the earth. "That would be the logical thing to do," says Loyce Dunbar.

It seems to me that the lack of consistency between the two informants' accounts of which town was the site of the murder does not detract from this story's implications, not only for Rattlesnake Gutter and its legendary reputation, but also for the entire region and its impending dissolution. The study of folklore, after all, never has been a matter of discerning the *accuracy* of a given account; the folklorist's job is to work toward that account's meaning and implications within a community. Even if Dunbar were the first person to interpret this story as having taken place in Rattlesnake Gutter, her having done so would not constitute a spontaneously generated reinvention of the story's geographical setting. Somewhere along the line, Loyce Dunbar came to associate Rattlesnake Gutter's proximity to the outside world with disastrous events like this one. Like the other Rattlesnake Gutter legends and anecdotes, "true" or "untrue," her version of the LaFogg-Pratt incident emerges from a communally based association of the Gutter's dangerous, forbidding, and borderland topography with death and disaster. If disagreement exists within that community as to the geographical setting of a particular event within the folk memory, it is because wild places like the Gutter exude a form of enchantment that invites continual regionalization.

Let us suppose, for instance, that the murder did actually take place in Woronoco, as Vernon Aiken suggests, or in any town other than Leverett, for that matter. Like the characters, circumstances, and motives featured in both narratives, a specific *topography* is a core element of the murder tale. If Aiken's version were the more accurate of the two in its geographical references, Dunbar's moving it to Rattlesnake Gutter only would underscore the facility with which one geographical location can be substituted for another without substantially changing a story's thematic or narrative core. Unsettled mountain tracts, whether in Rattlesnake Gutter or any other place, represent unpredictability and social strife within the regional group. Perhaps we ought not to pay too much attention to the fact that, in an age when a substantial influx of immigrants was occurring, Leon Pratt was an Anglo Protestant and Antoine LaFogg was a Franco Catholic. But even if ethnicity were not an issue, the story poses extreme economic desperation, such as would drive one man to kill another over blueberry money. This potentially modern theme is impossible to ignore. Whatever the actual motives or circumstances of the murder, the fact that members of the regional folk group have consigned a struggle of this sort to the deep recesses of a ravine suggests that Rattlesnake Gutter has taken on symbolic value within the regional imagination. This value, at least in part, is derived from the Gutter's borderland qualities.

A related interpretation may be relevant to yet another feature of the Gutter's folk history—the presence at its southern end of a place referred to by locals as "the tomb lot." The origins of the story of this tomb appear to be in the mid-nineteenth century. Of the three informants who tell it, only one (Loyce Dunbar) is still alive; thus the tale must have gone out of fashion relatively early in the present century, with the result that—except for Dunbar—informants born since 1900 were not old enough to have been exposed to it. Ruby Hemenway, who was born in 1884, told the story to Audrey Duckert in a 1967 interview, as Harriet Bourne LaClaire and her husband Joseph W. LaClaire listened and provided context. "That's where they used to keep the people when the ground was froze," offers Joseph W. LaClaire, introducing a purely practical Yankee perspective on the mystery of the tomb's origin. As Ruby Hemenway calls upon her memory of the place, however, a tale follows:

> Well, there's some story told, about two-three graves, and that tomb down there by Maurice [Glazier]'s. And I wish that I had written it down. I had Lucy Fiske write it down. She knew it and her mother knew about it. And her mother was a Marvell . . . and as I remember what she said, I think that it was somebody lived, I don't know whether it was in that place where Maurice did live, down at the foot of the Gutter. And she was terribly afraid of being buried alive. It was an obsession with her. And so she left it in her will, or got somebody to promise her that she would be put in the tomb, and left there a certain

> length of time before they buried her, so she'd be sure that they wouldn't bury her alive. And she's one of those, and Lucy told me the name that's on one of the stones—there's only two-three-four stones—and hers is one of the names. I don't know whether I got it exactly right or not.

How can the prospect of premature burial fail to bring listeners to the brink of their own fears? In keeping with the other Gutter-related legends, the story of the tomb lot specifically reintroduces a chilling fear of borderlands—in this case, the uncharted middle ground between life and death implicated in any premature burial. In this respect, the tomb (like the Gutter itself) is a transition point between this world and another, a literal threshold. Its existence "at the foot of the Gutter" lends an even greater symbolic weight to the ravine's essential "in-between" character, its positioning at the farthest edge of both regional topography and the human psyche.

Internalizing the Landscape

Both Forrest Briggs and Loyce Dunbar offer similar—though slightly less detailed—versions of the same anecdote. In both cases, the telling comes to an almost verbatim convergence with that of Ruby Hemenway on this particular point: the girl in question insisted on being placed in the tomb "for a certain length of time" (the Dunbar anecdote). She wanted "her folks to look in on her every little while" (the Briggs anecdote). In other words, the tellers emphasize not only the transitional and transitory character of the tomb lot (i.e., halfway between life and death), but also its function as an extended present that serves as a psychological bridge between past and future.

The tomb lot anecdote is hardly a "ghost story," however. Indeed, belief in such things was quite rare among the practical Yankees with whom I spoke in the Sawmill Valley. "My folks didn't believe in ghosts," said Loyce Dunbar, "so I never heard of them." Rather, this story offers a relatively "factual" perspective on one particular girl's relatively rational fear—not even of death *per se* but of the less tangible space between it and what precedes it. The tomb lot story reinforces the Gutter's symbolic function within the regional group as an edge of sorts, as the reification of an inherently transitional realm.

Like the barely penetrable thickets in Nathaniel Hawthorne's fictional accounts of early New England, the wild places of the Sawmill Valley have acquired a form of moral and transitional ambiguity that suggests an association of unsettled landscapes with flux and unpredictability. Stories about both near misses and the LaFogg-Pratt murder suggest that the uneven topography of the area's hills and recesses invites sinister, or at least shadowy, events. Implicit in both Loyce Dunbar's and Vernon Aiken's versions of the murder story is the idea that dangerous terrain is a "logical" site for desperate and tragic occurrences. Fond as many of old-time residents of the Sawmill Valley are of the Gutter's unique topography, they have not retained any *communally based* stories about the Gutter that do not feature a brush with death or death itself. Valley oral traditions fail to ascribe any redeeming qualities to a wild landscape that has claimed so many lives and haunts so many imaginations. But this does not mean that valley residents have consigned *all* mountainous wildernesses to the forces of doom.

As the example of Brushy Mountain suggests, when a place retains at least a few visible signs of past human presence, it often inspires stories which actually *privilege* its wild qualities. Inasmuch as the Brushy Mountain settlers lived atop a mountain, they enjoyed a reputation as intrepid pioneers. The landscape that they occupied was all the more remarkable for having been so resistant to cultural intrusion. The Brushy Mountain settlers inhabited a landscape of possibility, a landscape whose wild and uneven topography was destined to enchant future generations of *valley*-dwellers. In this sense, the wilderness of a place like Brushy Mountain evokes the triumphs of earlier generations, whose ability to subsist at a (relatively) distant remove from the Connecticut Valley's settled portions set them apart from their more comfortable descendants in the modern age.

Wilderness constitutes the core of any cultural landscape. Without an unruly terrain against which to measure themselves, women and men who settle and dwell within a given area have no means of defining themselves. This is why Brushy Mountain and Rattlesnake Gutter inspire more place-related legends than any other sections of the Sawmill Valley. They call attention to the trials and accomplishments of previous generations, who were inherently braver than their living descendants. When the present-day residents of the valley recall their ancestors, their narratives suggest that previous generations coped with, and in fact prospered as a result of their familiarity with, the local wilderness. Apparently, the features that still endanger those who travel through the wilder portions of the local landscape did not impede current residents' determined predecessors. The earlier generations carried infallible maps of the local landscape in their minds. Their facility with the terrain was the key to their survival.

The blizzard of 1888 was the occasion for a story provided by Vernon Aiken. It concerns the Chestnut Hill settlement and recounts how one man's familiarity with the landscape saved his life. Like Brushy Mountain, Chestnut Hill exists at the margins—geographical and psychological—of the Sawmill Valley. The Hill comprises the northern edge of North Leverett village:

> My grandmother had a sister in Orange. And she and grandpa wanted to go out there and visit while they could still go with the sleigh. . . . So my father's older brother . . . came home to stay with the kids while they were gone over the weekend. And it started snowing. There was another fellow . . . [there, and] he had a cow somebody had to milk. So my uncle went and milked that cow. And he got the cow milked and the woman told him: "Don't you try to come in the morning, Willy," she says. She says, "I milked a cow when I was a young girl," she says, "we'll take care of her." . . . [When it came time to go home] he had to go cross-lots, from one house to the other. And he got out there a ways and it was snowing so bad that he was lost.

In the face of a bewildering snowstorm, even returning home from a neighbor's barn is an impossible task. The 1888 blizzard rendered a familiar landscape nearly illegible.

Using the map he carried in his head, however, the traveler was able to find his way home: "He stood there and strained his eyes. And it was all open land. But he remembered there'd been a clump of bushes right by a ditch. He strained his eyes 'til he could see that clump of bushes. And he got to the clump of bushes and my grandmother—of course it got dark—always lit a lamp and put it in the window. And so the girls just automatically, one of the girls lit the lamp and put it in the window. Well when he got to the clump of bushes he could see that light and he made it. If it hadn't been for the bushes and for the light, he'd never made it. He'd have perished in that storm." Willy Aiken's narrow escape from death is the result of a telling confluence of "natural" and "cultural" beacons—a clump of bushes and a lighted lamp. In actuality, this apparent combination of opposing circumstances amounts to a virtual merger of natural and cultural landscapes. It also points to the local tradition's tendency to locate wildness at the center of cultural endeavor, and vice versa.

The traveler's internalized map presages actual topography. Willy Aiken finds the brushy landmark by conjuring up his memory of it. Having located the clump of bushes within his mental template of the landscape, the traveler cannot fail to find it in front of him. He "strains" his eyes, laboring to make them see what his previous experiences of the landscape have taught him to see. Having adopted the landscape's most minute features as components of his consciousness, the traveler locates wilderness at the center of his own awareness. A seemingly random clump of bushes, far from having been consigned to the realm of unknowable Other, proves indispensable to the survival of the self. By lodging itself firmly within the traveler's internalized map, the clump of bushes has become an aspect of the *cultural* landscape. Similarly, the girl's lighting of the window lamp collapses the ordinary distinction between "natural" and "cultural" landscapes. Having been lit "automatically," the light in the window becomes a part of the insentient, apparently random landscape that precedes and contains human consciousness.

This family anecdote's juxtaposition of seemingly disparate reference points, its removal of a distinction between landscape and consciousness, indicates the centrality—even well into the twentieth century—of wilderness and difficult terrain within the regional group's oral traditions. The collective memory of unsettled land speaks to the dynamism and permeability inherent in the local consciousness—a generalized state of being unsettled that lies at the core of the group's sense of itself and its history. Within the Brushy Mountain traditions, local history and legend regionalize a pioneer ideology that is at least national in scope. Moreover, through the wilderness legacy left them by their ancestors, valley residents distinguish themselves from their lowland counterparts. As they tell stories about death and near disaster in Rattlesnake Gutter, local residents point to the mortal dangers that await those who think too lightly about entering or *leaving* the valley. In stories about the Gutter, the wilderness wreaks a form of revenge upon residents who attempt to make an easy peace with a surrounding market economy. Success in this (largely psychological) wilderness seems to have been predicated upon a delicate balancing act. As valley residents—willingly or not—entered the modern age, they had to make some sort of peace with the facts of life in an outside world that increasingly impinged upon their lives. Their survival and integrity were no less dependent, however, upon their measured embrace of the wilderness legacy and the unpredictability at its core. As we see from Vernon Aiken's anecdote concerning the 1888 blizzard, even the most bewildering climatic and topographical conditions yield some beacons and ensure the prospect of human perseverance. Over the years in which they have inhabited the variegated landscape of the Sawmill Valley, members of the regional group have made their homes at the center of these apparent contradictions.

Chapter 2

"In Those Days You Never Made Any Money"

One of the Sawmill Valley's few remaining open prospects—the view southward toward the Sawmill River from the Ripley family's sugarhouse on Chestnut Hill, March 1999. Photograph by Janice Sorensen.

Subsistence Farming and Regional Identity

The Small Farm

Valley hillsides played an active and determining role in the economic, as well as the imaginative, lives of local residents. Having chosen to settle an upland topography, the men and women who made their homes in the Sawmill Valley from the mid-eighteenth century onward knew that they were contending with less than ideal farming conditions. In fact, for all the open and cultivated land that surrounded them, few residents of the Sawmill Valley ever thought of themselves as anything but part-time farmers. As Robert Ripley explains, farming was only one aspect of the valley's yearly work cycle: "In the winter it was a busy time. Everybody drew, cut logs around and drove them into mills. And that's the wintertime of farming, was cutting wood and cutting logs. Then when it got to spring, you had to tend to sugaring and then you had to get out to manure and plant your corn and cultivate it and hoe it. And that was the summer's work. Then you started all over again the next fall."

Like the inhabitants of most other Connecticut Valley hill towns, people in the Sawmill Valley farmed on a small-scale subsistence level. The cultivation of the soil, like woodcutting and mill production, was but one aspect of the valley's mixed, resource-based economy. If nothing else, the valley's stony hillsides were not conducive to any sort of specialized, single-crop cultivation. In the early days of settlement, diversity in production had been a means of guaranteeing regional self-sufficiency and rural independence. By the late nineteenth century, however, no level of crop variety could protect local residents from the economic and social changes that were causing the decline of rural New England.

If locals felt a measure of pride in their adherence to the sort of mixed production that their preindustrial forebears had engaged in, they could not share their ancestors' conviction that they actually could subsist on the fruits of their labors. Valley residents farmed according to eighteenth- and nineteenth-century patterns, but their livelihoods depended upon their adaptability to twentieth-century economic and social conditions. Social historian Hal Barron finds a similar pattern in his study of Chelsea, Vermont, at the turn of the century, based on a review of statistical evidence and other written records. "Rural Chelsea," he observes, "represented an enigmatic combination of attributes: kinship ties and social interactions reminiscent of a preindustrial village coupled with the economic lines and organizational structure of modern society" (134–35). Correspondingly, the oral traditions that pertain to farming practices in the Sawmill Valley at the turn of the century reflect both a pious devotion to the farming techniques of previous generations and a more modern despair concerning their potential economic viability.

Nearly every land-owning family in the Sawmill Valley engaged in some type of farm production during the years preceding World War II. These families' collective identity as upland-dwelling, subsistence-level cultivators set valley farmers apart from their neighbors along the Connecticut Valley floodplain, who mostly grew single crops in relatively vast fields. Clifford LaClaire's depiction of his family's acreage in Dudleyville suggests that it conformed in every way to a regionwide pattern. I asked him if the LaClaires were farmers.

> Not to any extent. We had a little farm, raised our own vegetables, had a pig and a cow and a few chickens. . . . Of course in those days you never made any money—[if you] made three hundred dollars in a year that was tops. But you lived off the farm, you know, such as it [was]—if you want to call it a farm. Today it wouldn't be a farm, but in those days you had a farm. Where I lived with my grandfather I think there was something like five acres up there. That's all we needed—seems so anyway. Enough to feed the cows, cut hay. . . . [People] raised a family, . . . lived on a farm, which was, as I say, about five to six acres of land, maybe. Had a cow and a pig and a horse or two.

"Everybody had a little farm," says Robert Ripley. "They had a few cows and they had a horse or two, had a pair of cattle—oxen—and they'd raise . . . everything but . . . sugar and things."

Generations of New England farmers have aspired to the modest ideal that Clifford LaClaire and Ripley outline in their descriptions. Before the

American Revolution, even the most prosperous residents of eastern Massachusetts recognized that the small, mixed-cropped farm, with its relentless demands on the family who tilled its acreage, was the key to instilling a Puritan work ethic and insuring a successful errand in the wilderness. Compare Clifford LaClaire's and Robert Ripley's descriptions of Sawmill Valley farms in the early twentieth century with Edward Johnson's discussion of a typical mid-seventeenth-century Massachusetts Bay colony farmstead: "'There are not many towns in this country, but the poorest person in them hath a house and land of his own, and bread of his growing if not some cattel'" (Russell 51). In terms of their production goals, upland farms in the Sawmill Valley and second-generation Puritan farms differ little.

Even at the outset of New England's colonization, however, small farming was but one facet of a vigorous mixed economy. Early New England farmers filled their storage sheds and pantries with the foodstuffs they produced on their modest, hard-won acres, and they were active participants in an economic exchange spanning oceans and continents. The famous "triangular trade," by which the products of the New England hinterlands were implicated in the slave trade, is merely the most economically spectacular example of rural New England's involvement in transoceanic commerce. But by the early decades of the nineteenth century, the period of New England's agricultural preeminence, the sort of small farming which LaClaire and Ripley describe already was more or less limited to upland communities like the Sawmill Valley. And at the beginning of the twentieth century, small, mixed-production farms were an ideal held by fewer and fewer people.

Residents of the Sawmill Valley who cultivated small plots undoubtedly were aware of their status as a nearly extinct class of farmers. Distinguished by their adherence to a hillside existence, Sawmill Valley residents developed an acute sense of their geographical singularity. Like their counterparts in Chelsea, Vermont, they may have thought of themselves as bulwarks of Americanism holding out against a shifting urban (immigrant) tide (Barron 35). Author Rollin Lynde Hartt, himself a resident of Leverett (Center), encapsulated the plight of the uplands during the era at the turn of the century: "'The people of New England are running down hill[;] Massachusetts has built the factory and mortgaged the farm'" (qtd. in Russell 257). Regional identity in the Sawmill Valley was shaped largely by local resistance to the "down hill" trend. The small farmstead provided locals with an idealistic, if unstable, footing in the hills.

In keeping with the Puritan ideal of hard work for small but sufficient recompense, the residents of the Sawmill Valley honor their hardscrabble, upland existence. Understandably, however, relative poverty and economic insecurity lend a measure of defensiveness to the celebration of simplicity. "Everything was hard work, you know," said Clifford LaClaire, as he described the conditions under which he grew up. "We used to cut hay by hand, wheel it in a wheelbarrow. . . . Did it with a scythe. Today nobody knows how to swing a scythe snathe. That was the main industry here in Moores Corner, North [Leverett]. . . . They either lived on a farm or worked on the highway department. Some people was lucky to get into the [Leverett Center] box shop." LaClaire's portrayal voices both pride and some bitterness. In his actual description of hay cutting, LaClaire allows the facts to speak for themselves. He honors hard work and simplicity along with the scythe. But he does not stop with a straightforward reference to advances in farming technology, as scythes have been replaced by mechanized harvesters. He remarks instead that "today nobody knows how to swing a scythe snathe," indicating that recent generations have lost a vital connection to the demanding standards of the past and consequently no longer are capable of appreciating their ancestors' sacrifices.

The orally transmitted record of Sawmill Valley farming at the turn of the century is marked by three sorts of simultaneous pronouncements: paeans to simplicity, laments concerning near impoverishment, and observations of present-day degeneration. By no means is such ambivalence purely the product of a late-twentieth-century idealization of rural New England. The very fact that my informants' parents and grandparents remained in the Sawmill Valley in the face of their contemporaries' downhill and westward scramble suggests that an anxious version of regional pride was a force in *their* lives, too, and that the valley's difficult landscape and economy inspired its inhabitants' allegiance and concomitant bitterness even in the days when people *did* know how to swing scythe snathes. The oral traditions recounting the history of Sawmill Valley farming are marked at every turn by simultaneous pride and envy, insularity and awareness of the outside world.

For all their allusions to the virtue and simplicity of the old farm life, my informants' accounts of local farming traditions show that they recognized the hardships and disappointments inherent in the life of the upland farmer at the turn of the century. While the valley's current lack of arable land and enterprising farmers may make past eras seem preferable to the present, the period when each of the valley's families farmed its own little plot of land was a trying phase of history. "Everybody had to struggle in those days," says Willy Stone. Even if they were able to raise enough in the way of foodstuffs, valley farmers still had to grapple on a daily basis with the hard truth that the small farm faced imminent eclipse by a cash-based, industrial economy. Regional identity was the product of just this struggle, as local people's desire for self-sufficiency confronted their recognition that, in order to maintain even the slightest semblance of independence, they would have to enter into a commercial exchange which, by its very nature, was destined to overrule self-sufficiency. Farmers in this period were profoundly ambivalent—eager to keep up with certain modernizing trends, reluctant to give up their small-scale and occasionally antiquated methods. As Hal Barron points out, their spokesmen—the people who wrote advice columns in agricultural journals—gave voice to this ambivalence. These writers "advocated responding to market pressures and adopting rational scientific techniques. On the other hand," Barron points out, "they advised contentment with a complete or a modest independence and berated those who went after greater and quicker returns" (Barron 36). Occasionally impassioned but more often even-handed, valley residents' own depictions of farm life are suffused with a sense of impending obsolescence. Folk descriptions of farming practices and patterns no longer extant serve as telling indices of the region's attitudes toward the changes that befell it in the first two decades of the twentieth century, as self-sufficiency gave way to permeability and decline.

Farming in the Hills: Upland (Self-)Consciousness

By most accounts, the Sawmill Valley's largest farms at the turn of the century were those owned and operated by the Aiken, Howard, and Ripley families. The Ripleys, who lived just north of the Leverett town line on Chestnut Hill in Montague, kept more stock than any of their neighbors. In addition to the sheep that Washburn Ripley raised in the years leading up to World War I, the family also owned a considerable herd of cattle—some fifty head. When he moved to North Leverett from Chestnut Hill in 1910, John Aiken was raising some ten to fifteen head of cattle and selling the milk that they produced. Wayne Howard remembers helping his father to raise about fifteen cows, also in North Leverett.

Considerably smaller operations represented the norm in the Sawmill Valley, with subsistence the main goal of valley farmers. The guiding principle behind small farming, at least as my informants remember it, was to be able to feed one's own family and have enough surplus to trade with one's neighbors and town establishments. "We used to raise all our own vegetables and all our own meat," explains Clifford Blinn:

> I think at that time most of the, most of the ones had at least vegetable gardens and gardens and animals of some kind. At least chickens and so forth. And there used to be two or three, you know, two or three dairy farms in Leverett,

> where they had several cows and sold milk and so forth. Now it's all gone. . . . You had vegetable gardens and, like I say, the cattle and chickens and so forth, but that's not a, not a big time-consuming thing. Unless you have twenty-five or thirty cows—then you didn't do anything but that. . . . Milk the cows in the morning and at night afterwards. But they worked longer hours than they do nowadays. We had chickens and we had eggs and butter and meat and everything that we raised, all our own.

"I think in those days they had more barter than there is now," recalls Loyce Glazier Dunbar; "you know, trading, swopping." Wood products, as the valley's primary "exported" commodity, were a source of income in nearly every family. But valley residents earned money by other means as well. Willy Stone's father "bought and sold land" often enough to generate some income. Gertrude Maynard Carey's father owned a grocery business, in addition to "a cow and a horse and . . . chickens." Robert Ripley remembers, "over to the other side of . . . [Chestnut] Hill," a man by the name of A. B. C. Coolidge, who "used to raise blueberries . . . and . . . peddle them over to Millers [Falls] and over to Turners [Falls] and Lake Pleasant. . . . He had a little sugarbush there and he'd do the same thing." In their devoted pursuit of supplemental forms of income, the farmers of the Sawmill Valley gave the lie to any notion that they could maintain total, cash-free self-sufficiency. In order to remain viable as small farmers, they had to look upon farming as one of many necessary economic endeavors.

Mary Williams Stone, whose family owned a few cows and chickens and raised a garden, explains that, because her father's primary occupation was lumbering, "we just had [the farm] on the side."

Willy Stone's family farm was more or less comparable: "[We] done quite a lot of family farming, that's about what it was," he says. "My father was at that time more or less in the wood and lumber business. So he worked in the woods, made maple syrup and raised potatoes and corn."

Shifting one's occupational orientation from time to time was a practice common—even inevitable—in the Sawmill Valley. Loyce Dunbar's father, Maurice Glazier, "used to be in lumbering. . . . And he owned a sawmill. And then he lost his hand in the sawmill so he kind of got out of that business and he used to have a chicken farm."

Most valley residents supported themselves by working at as many of these local pursuits as possible, making the most out of the yearly work cycle and hiring themselves out whenever possible to neighbors who could afford to recompense them for their labor. Vernon Aiken's father, John, moved to North Leverett in order to work a larger farm than the one he had owned on Chestnut Hill. But he also "work[ed] out," his son says, "to supplement his income."

Occasionally, valley residents took advantage of their proximity to large industrial towns like Turners Falls and hired "outside" (often immigrant) help on their farms. Sometimes these employees settled in the valley permanently. By the decade after 1910, the Sawmill Valley was reaching the earliest stages of its present status as a "satellite" region of the Connecticut Valley. To the more prosperous immigrant workers of industrial towns who preferred rural surroundings, the Sawmill Valley's relative quiet and undeveloped hillsides and pastures offered a respite from urban crowding. Vernon Aiken remembers two Polish families who lived up on Chestnut Hill. Willy Stone mentions a household of Italians: "They were people that moved in, lived there for a couple of years and moved away." Most of the immigrant families who lived near upland areas like the Sawmill Valley could ill afford to leave their communities and churches behind, much less their factory jobs; certainly those who came to places like Chestnut Hill were exceptions to the general rule. Lionel Girard, who grew up in a French Canadian neighborhood in Turners Falls, told me that, until well into his teens, he never "knew that Montague Center existed," much less Anglo-dominated upland villages of the Sawmill Valley, like North Leverett. Most members of his community had no such knowledge, either.

Nonetheless, by holding jobs in larger towns and at the same time owning small farms in the Sawmill Valley, a small group of immigrant families set a precedent for a practice that, at least by the 1930s, also became the norm for Old Yankee settlers in the Sawmill Valley. "The year-after-year settlers were just about all Yankees, I guess," remembers Willy Stone. In terms of actual residence and land-ownership patterns within the Sawmill Valley, Stone's memory is corroborated by town records. But, by the decade after 1910, the social and economic effects of the Sawmill Valley's proximity to immigrant and industrial centers were considerable.

As Robert Ripley describes the arrival of Polish farmers "down in the Meadow" (the Connecticut River floodplain), he captures the valley's feeling of being under siege. Upland farmers always had felt that their neighbors along the Connecticut were blessed with richer soil, but as Polish farmers "took over" the fertile fields of the floodplain, Sawmill Valley farmers appear to have been relieved that their ancestors chose to farm hillsides. The farm-related oral tradition conveys a sense that, increasingly, Sawmill Valley residents came to feel that their small subsistence farms represented the only viable means to perpetuate the Old Yankee tradition. Ripley says:

> I can remember when the Polish began to move in, well, probably in the early 1900s. 'Cause father used to hire a green Polish man for do chores, every winter

> sometimes. He didn't know how to do anything. And then they begin to come in. And the Polish, like now, they used to come in and they'd go to farming. They'd take over. Romansyk's farm down here, and they take over Sidofsky's and down through the Meadow they took over all of those Old Yankee farms from the old Yankee people. . . . I guess they [the Old Yankees] got very old or got so they didn't want to farm anymore and they just sold them, that's all. I don't know. 'Course some of them died. Some of them, I know one or two moved to town because they quit farming, they wasn't able to farm. And, that's how they got their start. And then they began to move in more and more and then they got into Sunderland.

Ethnic stereotyping may play a role in Ripley's assertion that the Polish hired man "didn't know how to do anything." But for all its repetition of the phrase "taking over," which seems to hint at a conspiracy of sorts on the part of the Polish, Ripley's comments actually indicate that the Old Yankees themselves were largely responsible for their own economic demise.

By the early 1900s, the cumulative effects of emigration to the cities and to the West, along with the lure of increasingly lucrative jobs in nearby factory towns, had led to the displacement of the Old Yankee population of the Connecticut Valley lowlands by an immigrant population eager to begin farming. In most rural areas of New England, Anglo farmers had no alternative but to recognize that their eclipse could not be blamed on the arrival of any particular ethnic or social group. Rather, their collective demise was the result of a volatile and expanding economy which had little use for subsistence farmers.

Robert Ripley remembers the succession of events which put one of his neighbors out of the dairy business. This particular farmer "had a big barn . . . and he used to keep, I don't know, probably twenty-five head or so. . . . He didn't keep so many young stock. But he used to milk and so forth. And, well, he got so he couldn't take care of the farm and it kind of went down. The boy didn't want to take care of the farm, he wanted to work down to Amherst. So the barn burnt, fell down and everything else."

Immigrants had little direct effect on the rural status quo; as farm historian Howard Russell suggests, most of them lived "in cities or manufacturing towns where they could get wage jobs" (290). The most noteworthy exception to this rule, Russell points out, was in the Connecticut Valley of Massachusetts, within a few miles of the Sawmill Valley itself.

The Poles' evolution from hired hands to owners of land and farms was gradual, the result of hard work: "Outfitted in straw hats and blue jeans, and in bare feet, boys and girls of Polish families did the kneeling jobs in the onion fields. Through hot summer days they planted the sets and later weeded the seeded rows, while their elders with horse-hoes took care of the tobacco and cut the hay. Little by little these families accumulated money, bought farms, and at length came to own much of the best land in the tobacco-onion towns of Hatfield, Hadley, Whately, (North) Amherst, Sunderland, and Deerfield" (Russell 308).

Most Polish farmers worked toward their eventual status as landowners in this fashion. As hired workers on Connecticut Valley farms, they assisted the Old Yankee farmers in their single- and double-cropping endeavors, but they had arrived at a time when their employers' own economic viability, due to aging, was coming to an end. Moreover, Polish farmers were not alone in their rise to prominence on the floodplain. By the 1920s, the Poles, Ukrainians, and other Eastern Europeans who had "taken over" the Meadow were joined by a cohort of farmers who had come directly from the region of the Pyrenees in France. Lionel Girard, who knew these farmers because they interacted with local French Canadians like himself at the "French Church" (St. Anne's) in Turners Falls, recalls a sizable Franco presence "in the Meadow." The Perinet, Socquet, and Paillet families formed part of this group. As far as I could tell, the Sawmill Valley's oral tradition did not register the fact that Polish farmers were sharing the Montague "Meadow" with French people. Perhaps the Yankee farmers in the uplands were too busy worrying about their own impending obsolescence to notice exactly who their lowland neighbors were.

One Anglo family whose members otherwise might have been interested in leaving the Sawmill Valley for better farmland amid the economic upheaval of the late nineteenth century hesitated to do so. The family's lore reflects the uplanders' loyalty to place. Robert Ripley remembers that his father (Washburn Ripley) told him many times about how the family at one time almost moved to the floodplain: "Father always told me, he says, they had a chance to buy a farm over on the Greenfield Road towards, just this side of Montague City a little ways. Nice, level flat land, no stones, he said, but his grandfather couldn't leave Chestnut Hill [laughs]. Every time he'd go that way he'd say, 'Oh, plowing up there amongst all those rocks, and look at this nice level land, no stones.' But he [Washburn Ripley] lived, he lived around Chestnut Hill all his life. . . . He inherited it [the farm on Chestnut Hill] from his father."

Unlike many of the people who left upland farms, the Ripleys appear to have been prosperous enough to make their own choices about where to go and what to do. Nonetheless, a type of regional fealty and devotion to their upland landscape were sufficiently powerful to keep the Ripleys on Chestnut Hill. For a family who had farmed hillsides for generations, the fields of

Montague—which were no more than three miles distant from Chestnut Hill—seemed culturally distant. The Ripleys' decision to remain on Chestnut Hill, after all, marked them as participants in a general demographic trend that had as much to do with ethnicity as with heartfelt allegiance to a hilly landscape. For many residents of the Sawmill Valley, farming the hills was a means of retaining one's Yankee identity in the face of the changes taking place along the Connecticut River.

The key to the "hillside consciousness" present in Robert Ripley's account of valley farming is not ethnicity *per se,* but rather regional identity and pride. Ethnicity is an undeniable factor in such allegiance, but it is only one of many facets of the upland identity. If a specifically Anglo-Saxon folklife and cultural identity once had existed in the Sawmill Valley, any traces of these had disappeared by the beginning of the twentieth century. Supplanting them was a regional style which took its primary cues from the local landscape and had all but forgotten its roots on the other side of the Atlantic. Reluctance on the part of upland families to move to the towns and villages of the floodplain may have had something to do with fear or resentment of "foreigners," but regional identity (that is to say, allegiance to Yankee settlement patterns and farming practices) was the primary means by which uplanders *expressed* whatever anti-immigrant sentiments they may have harbored.

While the oral tradition offers no evidence of overt ethnic tension, actual settlement patterns in the immediate vicinity of the Sawmill Valley speak to the cultural differences that separated hill dwellers from floodplain dwellers at the turn of the century. As Willy Stone puts it:

> It was . . . more or less Polish people in Turners Falls. . . . And this area would be more or less Republicans and over there they'd be about all Democrats. . . . But we never thought too much about that when we was kids. I had just as many Polish friends as I did Yankees. . . . Down . . . near the Connecticut River there were a lot of farmers, they were mostly Polish people that had the farms down there, whereas we were up on the Hill and we didn't have anywhere near as nice farms as they did down near the River. But at that time we were farming to eat. At that time . . . we didn't have any money, but we lived good as far as eating. . . . And my folks had to work pretty hard to do it, same as everybody else.

Whether Sawmill Valley farmers harbored any bitterness toward the Poles and other ethnic groups who bought and worked the rich farms along the Connecticut River is difficult to determine. Stone suggests that, for children at any rate, ethnic differences were insignificant. What we can note is that—in accounts like Willy Stone's—landscape and regional identity function as primary markers of ethnic difference. Observations like Stone's and Ripley's suggest that Sawmill Valley residents at the turn of the century considered their cultivation of unyielding hillsides to be an aspect of their *cultural,* as well as their geographical, identities. Willy Stone's remark that "we were up on the Hill and didn't have anywhere near as nice farms" as those of the Poles along the Connecticut River, on one level, merely states a geographical/agricultural fact. Indeed, farms along the Connecticut River had much higher yields than farms on the Sawmill River. Stone's suggestion that Sawmill Valley farmers "had no money" and were "farming to eat," however, relies upon an extraregional Other to provide contrast.

Ambivalence concerning the upland lifestyle inspired a noteworthy place-related oral legacy. In the spirit of New England's often humorously self-deprecating attitude toward its own landscapes, Sawmill Valley oral traditions pay wry homage to the stony character of the local soil. Pride in their ability to farm such difficult terrain occasioned a potent form of local wit which enabled valley residents simultaneously to celebrate their hillside fields and to vent frustration at having inherited such a difficult fate. Local accounts of farming rocky land gain added significance in light of the fact that an onion and tobacco boom occurred on nearby floodplain farms at the turn of the century. Robert Ripley's anecdote about one Chestnut Hill farmer shows the famous Yankee wit at work on the Sawmill Valley's agricultural decline: "I don't remember [Mr. Ware], . . . but I heard them talk about him. And he had a little farm, . . . and it was awful stony. But he never picked up one. Somebody asked him one time, says: 'Why don't you pick up these stones? [Don't] they bother you?' 'Well,' he says, 'I knowed those stones was made for something,' and he left them right there."

Ware's answer to the inquiring "somebody" suggests two things: first, that he is well aware of the problem; and, second, that he is determined to work around it. His response is a fine metaphor for the Sawmill Valley's attitude toward the prospect of "easier" farming. The farmer's lack of interest in removing the stones from his fields suggests his reluctance to alter nature's or God's preordained designs in the local landscape. Ware is a true conservative, a man content to abide by the difficult terms of his upland existence.

Ware's acceptance of the rocks on his farm is not merely a stereotypical example of New England stoicism, however. His reluctance to do anything about the stones occurs in a particular sociogeographical context. Like Ware, many Old Yankee farmers had to convince themselves that, difficult as it was, their upland existence was preordained and unchangeable. Removing the rocks would involve more than physically taxing labor, Ripley's anecdote implies; it also would entail admitting that the conditions of hillside farming are far from ideal. Accordingly, Ware had developed a dry wit delicately attuned to his situation. His response to the inquiry indicates the regionally sanctioned attitude toward the local landscape. Like the stones themselves, Ware seems to be saying, farmers like him have been "put there" on Chestnut Hill for some reason. For all the landscape's foibles, it is home. The men and women who cultivate it are well aware that they easily might live elsewhere, but their first allegiance is to place and its social concomitants. On the other hand, the farmer's answer, for all its condensed wit, might be construed as a defensive response to a perfectly reasonable question. Ripley's anecdote expresses both the region's dedication to "staying put" and its awareness of the limitations of self-sufficiency.

While Robert Ripley's anecdote about Ware serves as a metaphor for valley residents' *attitudes* toward their landscape, it does not represent the *practices* typical of local farmers. Willy Stone, who also grew up on a farm on Chestnut Hill, recalls the steps that most farmers took to remove the stones from their fields. "As far as I know," he told me, "there was a lot of stones on every farm up there. [It] was pretty stony country." Removing the rocks was one of the most tedious tasks undertaken on an upland farm: "Well, they'd cut the wood. Usually they'd . . . let the land lay for a few years, and then dig out the stumps. And then plow it. And then pick the rocks. A lot of rocks. I spent a good many days picking rocks. We used to hate it. On our farm—we weren't clearing land on our farm because it was cleared, but every time we plowed it, a lot of rocks. We had to pick the rocks and carry them over and dump them over in a pile out in the pasture somewhere. Hard work. Especially for a kid. Those are some things I remember. Hoeing corn and picking rocks was the jobs I didn't like."

Farmers took various approaches to removing the rocks from their fields, depending on the sizes of the rocks. Willy Stone explains: "We had lots of rocks that you couldn't pick. . . . The man before my father was quite good with dynamite, so he used to blast the big rocks that we wasn't able to move. And . . . anything we could get down small enough so the horses could move it we'd hitch a rock on and snake it away on a stone boat." A piece of simple but indispensable technology, a stone boat was a necessity on any upland farm. As Stone describes it, "A stone boat is a couple or three planks. It used to be, as I remember it, about two feet and a half wide, and it had a little lip on the front of it. The planks were level and it had a lip on the front of it, so it would slide over and you'd get your rock onto that and then the horses would drive it off. That way you wouldn't mark up all the land . . . leave tracks, you know, where the stone was digging in." The coordinated use of dynamite, muscle power, and stone boats in rocky fields suggests that farmers like those on Chestnut Hill were prepared to combine whatever tools they needed to remove stones. Crude as its construction may have been, a stone boat was the most adaptable means by which farmers could get the stones out of their way.

Gasoline-powered tractors, introduced in the 1920s, failed to solve the problems presented by stony soil. In 1925, Robert Ripley tells folklorist Michael Kline, "We got the Caterpillar tractor and drew off a lot of them [rocks]. But there's lots of ones underneath. It's pretty stony. It's good for team of horses or oxen plowing, but it ain't no good for a tractor. . . . [A] tractor's good if you didn't get any stones, but you . . . got stony and you hit a stone and you either break something or stop or something. But with horses, of course, if you hit a stone, stop. And tip your plow over top of it and go to the other side. But with a tractor you got to back up and lift it up and put it down the other side and drive around it." To be sure, tractors were welcome additions to the hill farmer's repertoire of cultivating tools. But, as Ripley's discussion of their limitations indicates, older farm implements were better adapted to certain tasks. In the New England tradition, Sawmill Valley farmers always were enthusiastic about technological innovations. At the same time, however, their devotion to the local landscape and their interest in cultivating it intelligently precluded unthinking dependence on the most modern tools.

For the single- and double-cropping farmers of the Connecticut River floodplain, the tractor arrived at the perfect moment, enabling them to cultivate even vaster acreage than they had been able to manage previously. But full-fledged dependence on the latest cultivating equipment would have meant abandoning hillside farms; Sawmill Valley farmers preferred to adapt their use of tools to the landscape at hand, even if it meant continuing to use livestock for certain tasks. Their willingness to do so implicated them in a form of cultural/geographical self-consciousness. They were well aware—indeed, were proud—of their adherence to the practice patterns of traditional, subsistence-oriented farming. What farmers along the floodplain did was their own business, in the upland estimation. "As you get nearer the Connecticut River," explains Willy Stone, "there aren't hardly any rocks. They say you can plow all day long and not hit a rock, I guess."

Sawmill Valley farmers like Willy Stone knew the advantages enjoyed by the farmers "down in the Meadow," but they liked to think that they were above envying them. "They raised a lot of potatoes down near the Connecticut River," says Willy Stone, "but we figured the potatoes were better up on

[Chestnut Hill]. My father always said, 'Potatoes up on these hillsides are much better than they are next to the river.' But I don't know, as that was what we were brought up to think, because he was doing it, I suppose." Stone's qualification of his father's preference for Chestnut Hill potatoes speaks to the sort of rationalization that was a necessary component of upland agriculture. Regardless of which potatoes actually *did* taste better, the Stones' assurance that theirs were not merely good, but better than those grown next to the Connecticut River, illustrates the self-consciousness associated with the practice of cultivating hillsides. Like her husband, Mary Williams Stone remembers her father raising a full field of potatoes on Chestnut Hill, as well as a good deal of sweet corn. Both crops apparently did well, as a result of growing in the Spartan soil of the Sawmill Valley. Having invested so much of themselves working the local landscape, valley farmers were bound to think—or at least speak—highly of their fruits of their labors.

Cows, Sheep, and Open Fields: Livestock-raising Traditions

Potatoes and corn are not the only farm products well suited, or at least reputed to be well suited, to the hillside farm. Throughout the nineteenth century, settlers of upland areas like the Sawmill Valley, eager to make full use of every available acre, viewed livestock as a reliable and well-adapted means to a food supply and, occasionally, some small income. Hillside pastures are rich in folkloric, as well as nutritional, possibilities. The steep grades of Vermont's Green Mountains, for example, which have fed many generations of dairy cows, have inspired an inventive form of region-specific tall tale. An article from the *Haverhill (Massachusetts) Gazette,* excerpted in B. A. Botkin's *Treasury of New England Folklore,* tells of the legendary *gyascutus,* whose legs were short on one side and long on the other, in order to help it negotiate Vermont's steep mountainsides. Vermont farmers interbred their cows with *gyascutici* in order to alleviate the problems inherent in hillside pasturage. The newspaper article explains: "Obviously, the ordinary cow cannot clamber over Vermont pastures. The early settlers, bringing cows from other states, quickly learned this, and for several years a problem worse than Indians . . . was that of getting cows to and from pasture. It took two men for each cow, and the task was comparable to teaching her to go up and down a ladder" (Botkin 281). Washburn Ripley's and Robert Ripley's cows were not expected to clamber up and down ladders, but the barn that housed them, because it was built into a hillside, featured another sort of vertical challenge. As Robert Ripley tells it, the family's cows "used to go up a stairway on the east side, and it was made out of flat stones. . . . And they'd walk up and down that stairway, and boy, it never wore out. But sometimes . . . you'd get a new, different cow and they didn't want to go up and down that. But after a while the rest of them pushed him and they had to go." Sawmill Valley cattle certainly were not as advanced as Vermont cows in their anatomical conformity to hillside pasturage, but farmers such as Robert Ripley tell stories that reflect in a more matter-of-fact manner upon their cows' adaptability. If the cows themselves were not built on an incline, the pastures that fed them and the buildings that sheltered them occasioned a good many pastimes and stories specific to their upland existence.

Although the barn still stands, Ripley explains, it has been out of use for many years:

> Today they'd never let you do that, 'cause . . . those stone steps for the cows to go on would be a no-no. 'Cause they might slip and break a leg or something. . . . It took them a long time to get used to go up and down. 'Cause the steps was that [steep]. But after they'd been up a few times, they didn't have any problem. Used to have to drive them down in the wintertime, downstairs to drink. And let out a few, and they'd go down and come back, and some more would go down. But . . . that's the only way they could get into the stable, was going that way. . . . They didn't use to think of anything like that then. You know, like building a barn on the ground floor and having cows go in there. But they made it. They made it.

Though it lacks the extravagance of the *gyascutus* tall tale, Robert Ripley's description of his father's barn pays similar homage to the hard facts of hillside existence. He presents the barn's staircase as a perfectly logical structural feature of the hillside farm, suggesting that, for hill farmers of his generation, "building a barn on the ground floor" was literally unthinkable. While different in form and genre from the Vermont farmers' stories about crossbreeding cows with *gyascuti*, his description of the cow-steps achieves the same ends; it distinguishes the hillside farm from its lowland neighbor and establishes the former as the locus of true ingenuity. In 1900 or so, when it was built, the Ripley's two-story cow barn was not a novelty. For farmers on Chestnut Hill, who encountered no level landscapes, buildings set on an incline were a natural choice.

Raising stock in the Sawmill Valley necessitated more than imaginative barn structures. In order to keep one's livestock well fed on silage and hay, valley farmers had to mow their sloping fields on a regular basis. Without constant attention, any given field could be reclaimed by trees and brush within a few summers. The few open fields visible today in the Sawmill

Valley are mere remnants of what once was an enormous expanse of meadow. Cleared hillsides were commonplace in the years before the 1930s, as they were in most areas of western New England. Men and women who describe the Sawmill Valley's pre-1930s appearance are unanimous in their descriptions of a largely open landscape. Valley residents took a good deal of pride and satisfaction in their dedicated maintenance of cleared land. To locals, open land was a sign of prosperity, evidence of local farmers' ability to put their difficult landscapes to proper use. The return of forest cover to once-productive pastures, on the other hand, was an incontrovertible visual indicator of the imminent decline of small farming. The presence of trees and brush in fields that once fed livestock suggested the existence of a crisis.

"Back where I lived in Moores Corner, at my grandfather's," says Clifford LaClaire,

> You could see the Hemenway Road, you could see people haying and farming. Of course . . . they hayed with their horse and wagon in those days, you could see the men pitching hay—before they put it in haybales, you know, they pitched it loose. Up [at] the Watson property I used to watch my grandfather and all the people in the summertime over there in the hayfields. There was a huge barn up there and they used to fill that full of hay, all by hand, pitch it on, pitch it off. But you can't see anymore, you can't see off anymore, because the trees are all grown up. . . . From where I lived over to the Hemenway Road must be three miles. You could look off in the distance, you know. But nobody cuts the trees down no more.

LaClaire's description of open pastures reminds me of a panoramic landscape painting. But the broad view of the Sawmill Valley that he provides in this picture allows for much more than a look at the actual landscape. From his perch up by the old Watson house, Clifford LaClaire could see *people* he knew, working fields that he'd been in. This panoramic view of the Sawmill Valley is of a thoroughly *humanized* landscape, one in which farmers at work are more distinct than the fields themselves. Owing to his own experiences with farm work, LaClaire is able to impart a great deal of detail to the human figures who—at a distance of three miles—actually would appear within the verdant fields as small dots, if they were visible at all. The picture evokes a sense of regional coherence, a feeling that one could see all one's neighbors and all the townspeople at the same time. With the arrival of brush and trees, however, regional fragmentation begins. No longer being able to see open fields means no longer being able to see farmers; not seeing farmers is tantamount, in LaClaire's account, to seeing nothing at all ("you can't see anymore"). Given a verbal picture like this one, it is easy to understand how crucial such open fields must have been to the region's sense of itself.

Other informants corroborate LaClaire's depiction of the valley as having once hosted wide-ranging pasturage, as well as his account of how the grassland gradually was replaced by brush and trees. Wayne Howard provides a view of the land which lies to the south and west of the area surveyed in LaClaire's vision: "From North Leverett Center going over Cave Hill, that was a lot of open fields, farmer's hayfields, cornfields. Now it's brush—I say brush; trees under six or eight inches . . . The fields are all grown up to brush. From North Leverett towards Montague you can see the same thing. The farmers kept the brush cut right to Sawmill River. You could drive along the road and you could see the river practically all the way." "Seeing the river" from any of the valley's hills today is not even a remote possibility; trees and brush grow all along the river banks. The fact that locals *would* have seen it back in the days when Wayne Howard was growing up only emphasizes the fact that the Sawmill Valley itself, as a derivative of an actual river, was a much more tangible, visible entity than it is today.

I asked Robert Ripley to tell me how the landscape of the Sawmill Valley has changed since his childhood in the decade after 1910. We were looking south, toward the Sawmill River, from his living room window on the side of Chestnut Hill:

> Well, it's grown up. . . . When I come here in 1930 I could look over there and it was all bare. . . . Woods. Woods. And they built houses, a lot of houses, everywhere along there. And everywhere they built houses—over here. Up on the hill here there wasn't only a few houses in 1936. . . . Just a few houses. But they built, I don't know how many now, I can't count them there're so many. Even way up on the top, they built some. . . . But over there was a big pasture, that was all open. Up in back here . . . all open. . . . All the way up, you could go to all open land. . . . There was a farm up here, right opposite. That's all grown up. We had twenty acres of good meadow land over there. That's all grown up, I guess—I ain't been there for years. Up on the hill is the same way. There used to be farms and they're all grown in, most of them. But you go all along up the river, it's the same thing.

According to Ripley, open land began to give way to forest cover as farmers "died out" or moved away. Myron Graves was one such farmer. The Graves' property bordered the Ripleys'. Graves "had a few cows, he had a lot over there [pointing], it was all open. He died, nobody carried on after, that all grew up. And the folks died and they never did anything to that land, . . . and that's growing up. And down on the hill, we used to pasture there, and it just grew up—nothing to keep it down. Of course we used to turn cows in there and . . . any little stuff they would eat." Livestock were the key to maintaining an open landscape. When the residents of the Sawmill Valley—for whatever reasons—stopped raising cows and sheep, their need for pasturage naturally came to an end.

"Before the [Second World] War," explains Wayne Howard, "they tended to . . . small farms. . . . A lot of people had a cow or a horse or something, so they . . . tried to keep the field big enough so they'd get hay enough to feed the cow for winter or whatever. And when they did away with . . . having the farm animals, they didn't take care of the fields. They just grew up, to brush." Because of its implications for the entire valley's landscape, keeping one's fields mowed and generally free of brush—or one's inability or failure to do so—was a crucial aspect of one's participation in the life of the region. Owning livestock and working to keep them fed and housed properly were important measures of a given family's *belonging* in the Sawmill Valley. Pasturage certainly was not communal property in any legal sense, but it did provide valley residents with a form of visual cultural cohesion. In the early years of the twentieth century, however, as one farm after the next began to yield to the sorts of economic and social forces which were to strip Sawmill Valley residents of their sense of enterprising self-sufficiency, the landscape's changing appearance served as a stark reminder of that cohesion's imminent end.

Most of the verbal accounts that informants provide of their own and their ancestors' work as livestock raisers evoke a distant, unrecoverable past. Like the woods-related traditions which assert the unequaled strength of long-departed heroes, such as Walter Carey (see chapter 3), stories and descriptions concerning animal chores seem to suggest that small farming enjoyed a Golden Age in the turn-of-the-century period. Nostalgia reverberates from one livestock-related account to the next. Even so, within their accounts, informants provide hints of how fickle the small-farm economy actually was in the years preceding its outright collapse in the 1930s. From our vantage point late in the twentieth century, it is easy to understand why Sawmill Valley old-timers might look back fondly, as they often do, on early mornings spent in the milking shed. What is less obvious but no less crucial is why these same informants intersperse their nostalgic accounts of animal care with references to the economic precariousness of the farming enterprise.

Robert Ripley's memory of his father's flock of sheep is anything but nostalgic. By the time he was born, the Ripleys, for better or worse, had implicated themselves in a market economy that took them beyond the confines of the Sawmill Valley. In order to earn the cash necessary to keep his family in the farming business, Washburn Ripley began to raise sheep. He hoped that selling their wool would yield a profit. What is particularly striking about his son's account is the fact that it focuses on the *last days* of his family's sheep farming, on the exact moment when valley farmers no longer found it economically feasible to raise sheep. Washburn Ripley "used to raise sheep at one time. And he had, oh as much as two hundred sheep at one time, but . . . right after the [First World] War there it got so you couldn't sell the wool. The last time he sheared a sheep he took them, took the wool down to Holyoke somewhere to a woolen mill and they'd knit blankets. Virgin wool blankets. And they would buy just enough wool to make, they'd make your blankets, enough that would pay them for making them. But they wouldn't buy the whole wool."

"We got rid of the sheep after that," says Ripley. With as many as two hundred sheep in their flock, the Ripleys obviously were farming for more than the clothes on their backs; under these circumstances, it is no wonder that, when Robert Ripley remembers his father's sheep, he remembers the moment of crisis, "the last time he sheared a sheep." The Ripleys' foray into the market economy proved no more lucrative than their subsistence farming had been.

It is worth comparing Ripley's memory, which is utterly devoid of nostalgia, with Loyce Glazier Dunbar's account of related events. Lacking Robert Ripley's connection as the son of the shepherd in question, Dunbar nevertheless recalls *seeing* the sheep go past her home and supplies much visual and circumstantial detail that Ripley's account lacks. Dunbar remembers seeing Washburn Ripley drive his flock right through the center of North Leverett in the years around 1915: "I can remember h[im] going up through in the spring time. Of course . . . it was all dirt roads, there was not much traffic. . . . He'd go up through town in the spring with this whole flock of sheep. And he always had a hired man. And that little dog would run around. I don't know for sure, but I think they said he was taking the sheep up on Brushy Mountain. Brushy Mountain used to have open meadows." Dunbar's account looks back at an apparently obsolete pastime—its novelty is the image it evokes of a shepherd driving his flock through a village which now has cars and trucks passing though it. It posits an unrecoverable landscape, "all dirt roads" and "open meadows." Nothing that Dunbar says is contradicted by Ripley's account; what makes her description different from Ripley's is how it (understandably) abstracts this particular farming pastime from its painful economic context.

The Problem of Gendered Spheres: Small-farm Domestic Production and Foodways

For residents of the Sawmill Valley before 1930, the farm was essentially synonymous with the home. Barns and fields had no monopoly on farm-related work. In addition to tending hay, corn, and potato crops and all the tasks associated with raising livestock, valley men and women who considered themselves small farmers kept vegetable and herb gardens. They maintained busy kitchens and work-related outbuildings for the purpose of storing their farms' fruits, vegetables, and meats. Sustenance-related work such as canning, curing, and baking formed a focal point of farm life, but many locals also participated in some other form of home manufacture in order to earn extra income. Moreover, events such as husking bees created a sense among locals that their farms were not merely individually held plots of land, but veritable social centers. The work and social activities associated with farming were sufficiently all-encompassing as to shape the entire cultural life of the Sawmill Valley.

A key factor structuring these farm-related activities was a widespread belief on the part of many farm patriarchs in a strict division of labor along gender lines. The line between female work and male work was not always drawn as sharply as some farmers would have liked, but its presence—even as an ideal incapable of realization—bolstered the region's sense of itself as a last bastion of Old Yankee tradition amid twentieth-century degradation.

Unlike their neighbors along the Connecticut River floodplain, hill farmers like those in the Sawmill Valley tended to divide almost all labor into separate gender-based spheres. Descendants of Polish and other Eastern European immigrants who settled in towns like Sunderland and Deerfield remember both boys and girls being sent out to participate on an equal basis in heavy farm labor; evidently, their parents had determined that economic efficiency was more important than gendered propriety. Indeed, according to Stanislaus Blejwas, the collective success of Polish families along the Connecticut River resulted directly from their belief in "old world tradition"—the notion that women and children belonged in the fields alongside their husbands and fathers ("Inherited" 50). Upland Yankees saw things differently. As they observed their Polish neighbors tending farms along the floodplain, often they were disturbed, as the protagonist of Edna Ferber's *American Beauty* (1931) is, by the sight of "women working in the fields of New England like cattle" (Blejwas, "Inherited" 55). I could not help noticing, on the other hand, that, among my eighteen Sawmill Valley informants, not one of the eight women recalled having worked on a regular basis either in her family's fields or among the livestock. Women *do* remember working as girls in their families' homes—in kitchens, among younger siblings, and—less frequently than I had expected—in gardens. By no means were women and girls spared the rigors of farm life, but their participation in the work of maintaining the small farm was regulated in a manner that at least appears to run counter to what we might expect in an economically marginalized region like the Sawmill Valley.

If valley residents were concerned about the continued viability of their small farm–based economy, why would they not allow some flexibility in the maintenance of gendered spheres? Many aging upland New Englanders were forced to abandon their farms because they were unable to convince their sons to continue farming when they had to leave off; Robert Ripley's memory of the Graves farm's decline comes to mind. Why, we might ask, would they not have been more disposed to putting daughters to work? Although the oral record of Sawmill Valley farming does not supply direct answers to such a question, it does provide indirect clues. The gendered division of labor, as economically impractical and socially restrictive as it may have been, offered the (male) proprietors of land in the Sawmill Valley a type of continuity with New England's peak period of economic influence in the early and mid-nineteenth century. Strictly separate gender spheres formed a key feature of the social structure at that time. Accounts by women whose work on a family farm was restricted to domestic chores evince both resignation to and frustration with the strict division of labor. Those women whose work took them beyond traditional gendered roles figure prominently within the valley's oral record, but their examples more often than not are cited as notable, if not rare, exceptions to the rule. Most important, the dual tone of acceptance and regret marking local accounts of domestic production and the gendered division of labor is linked to the fact that, by the early 1900s, small farming in the Sawmill Valley was in crisis. Like accounts of how pastures gradually were transformed into second- and third-growth forests, the recollections that men and women supply of their participation in, and departure from, traditional domestic pursuits and pastimes suggest that regional mores were in a state of flux during the turn-of-the-century period. Strict adherence to genteel nineteenth-century gender roles, like valley residents' loyalty to unyielding, stony fields, was essentially a defensive gesture, an effort to maintain the old-fashioned belief in regional self-sufficiency and Yankee conservatism, in a world which no longer could sustain these.

Mary Williams Stone, whose father's primary occupation was wood cutting, remembers having been asked to do small tasks in the outdoor portions of her parents' small farm: "I used to take care of the cow. . . . Back then, he [Mr. Williams] didn't have any fencing, so we had to tether her out. And I would do that and carry water to her and bring her back to the barn. I never milked in my life. And I didn't like chickens. . . . I remember one job that I did— . . . my job was to pick the potato bugs off the potato plants. And I guess I did a little weeding and so forth." Mary Stone never was called upon to milk the family cow, because she had brothers whose duties included milking. Her work in the garden was limited, because her father's evident enjoyment of gardening as a recreational pursuit: "Dad enjoyed it so much he didn't require much of our help." Instead of working outdoors, Mary Stone would "help [her] mother with household chores. And," she says, "I also did a lot of baby-sitting for my younger brother and sisters." Even as the local economy faltered, girls like Mary Stone had to be content with helping their mothers indoors. Their participation in outdoor tasks might have signaled their fathers' collective failure to realize the ideal of Yankee self-sufficiency. Moreover, the constant demands of the homeplace itself—all the childrearing, cleaning, and cooking tasks—required the attention of as many hands as could be mustered in one family.

Most female children, according to Loyce Glazier Dunbar, were put to work immediately upon returning home from school in the afternoon. A mother like hers could not participate in such tasks as livestock raising and gardening; she was too busy raising children and maintaining a home. Her daughters were taught not to expect anything different:

> Of course they [the Glaziers] were married nine months and had the first child. And—no modern conveniences. No indoor plumbing whatsoever. I'd come home from school, the lamps would all be lined up on the table. I'd have to fill them all with kerosene, wash the globes, wash the chimneys. . . . We always had running water—and that was it.. . . . A big barrel of water . . . came down from the hills and of course your water was heated in a reservoir on the stove. I can remember going out [to] that outhouse—was my mother fussy. We used to have to go out every day with a pail of water and a scrub brush. Scrub those seats, scrub that floor. She had to keep everything so clean. . . . I don't know how she did it.

From her standpoint as the occupant of a home equipped with many of the amenities common in American homes in the late twentieth century, Dunbar seems perfectly justified in wondering at her mother's ability to raise eight children in a rural home before the advent of electricity. Lack of "modern conveniences" aside, the ability of a woman to succeed at such a task is noteworthy primarily because it marks her as equal to the region's difficult standard of self-sufficiency. Like the valley's old-timers who still know how to swing scythe snathes, Loyce Dunbar's mother—at least in her daughter's eyes—exemplifies now-departed rigor.

In her own day, Mrs. Glazier (Loyce Dunbar's mother) herself must have been somewhat awed by her own mother and mother-in-law. As if the traditionally sanctioned domestic work were not enough to keep them fully occupied, Dunbar's two grandmothers performed tasks ultimately inconsistent with the ideal of a complete division of labor along gender lines. Although neither kept a full-fledged farm, Dunbar remembers both her grandmothers as exceptionally well versed in traditionally male pursuits, as well as in the tasks usually expected of women. By necessity, women like Dunbar's grandmothers participated in regional and extraregional commerce as actively as their male counterparts. "My grandmother Glazier," Dunbar says, ". . . was very energetic; she used to go ferning. She used to . . . go blueberrying. That's one way she had of earning money. She used to make Panama hats—beautiful. And of course they had a good driving horse; she would go to Greenfield and, apparently, they had rummage sales the way they do now. She'd go and . . . buy shoes, you know, if she thought that they would fit somebody that she knew. Buy hats. Anything that she thought she could sell, bring home, make a little money." The scale of Grandmother Glazier's industriousness makes it clear that she was engaged simultaneously in market-oriented exchange and efforts to maintain farm-based self-sufficiency. Inasmuch as "earning money" and not mere maintenance of domestic order was her primary goal in these market activities, Grandmother Glazier was disregarding the valley's traditional separation of spheres. If husbands, fathers, and brothers ever had been able to restrict women from participating in farm work that took them beyond the walls of their homes, the replacement of a subsistence economy with a cash-based economy rendered such restriction obsolete.

In a world where so many men were subject to sudden economic ruin, women were just as likely as men to become models of self-sufficiency within their families and the community. Vernon Aiken describes his how his grandmother, after her house burned down, came to buy the property of a man whose fortunes had failed:

> I remember her [Grandma Latham] telling about, she was making maple syrup in, she called it a back kitchen. Up on Chestnut Hill. And she got a little too much fire going and the house caught afire. And she was there all by herself. Of course the neighbors, some of the neighbors see[n] the smoke and they came

but it was too late then. But the sewing machine was right near the door so she snaked that out, so she had her sewing machine. She bought a house down the road a little ways and the[re] must have been, oh, I would say there must have been fifteen acres of land, and the house and it was all furnished. The fellow, the fellow couldn't live by himself any longer and he'd gone up to the Town Farm to live. And she bought the house, all furnished and, I think there were about fifteen acres of land. Four hundred dollars.

As the gap between economic viability and poverty narrowed, valley residents fashioned a version of self-sufficiency which at least occasionally allowed women as well as men to play the central roles. Loyce Dunbar's Grandmother Hemenway was widowed at the age of sixty. As Dunbar describes her, Mrs. Hemenway, like other valley women, was as successful as any of her male counterparts in meeting the demands of self-sufficiency:

My Grandmother Hemenway . . . was a widow—well, I'd say young. . . . She lived up on the Hemenway Road. Lived there all winter long—alone. After grandpa died, [she] shoveled a path to the barn, kept a horse. And the same with her as the rest of us—no modern conveniences. . . . After Grandpa died I can remember Grandma used to putty in all the windows every fall. If, after she moved to Montague, and if anything happened like a flatiron or a lamp, she knew how to rewire it. I don't know how she knew, but she did. And of course another thing about women—if they had a spare moment they sewed. Everything they had. My clothes were all made by my grandmother or my aunt. And they used to make the boys' shirts. . . . They didn't have any spare moments.

Given the circumstances under which she performed tasks that otherwise her husband might have done, Grandmother Hemenway was not living in direct violation of the regional code. Dunbar's account does not suggest, however, that Mrs. Hemenway *learned* to rewire flatirons and lamps only after her husband's passing. Evidently, work on the Hemenway farm was not gendered as carefully as we might think; Mrs. Hemenway knew how to execute tasks that, given a strict adherence to the gendered division of labor, she would not have been expected to perform. In truth, no family could meet the economic and social demands made upon it without allowing some flexibility in gender roles.

Nonetheless, most valley women usually were so busy meeting their obligations in childrearing and food preparation that they could give little thought to other aspects of farming. "If you have eight children," says Loyce Dunbar as she describes her mother's experience, "you don't have much time for farm work." Women were expected to do a great deal of work in the farm kitchen. In many cases, the kitchen fed more than family members. On the Howard farm, a number of hired hands could be expected to partake at all meals. The same was true at the Ripley farm on Chestnut Hill. Luella Streeter Ripley was responsible for all her family's meals; her involvement in gardening was an inevitable aspect of her work as a cook. The family "always had one or two hired men. To do farming and help around haying. And in the winter time we always had one man would help do chores. . . . There was always something going on, like . . . threshing, or haying or something. You hire a couple of extra hands, they all expected to go to dinner. . . . And she'd cook for them."

Food preservation was no less time-consuming than cooking. Like most of her neighbors, Luella Ripley "used to can beans and everything." Mary Stone remembers watching her mother can all the usual vegetables, but she also recalls—"way back"—seeing her canning meat. "They used to can [meat] with a . . . regular canning or they would put it in a brine," remembers Robert Ripley. "And then when they wanted meat they'd fish it out and freshen it up a little."

Even as late as the 1920s, most farming families in the Sawmill Valley aspired to self-sufficiency when it came to kitchen production. Women were expected to prepare meals which did not violate the code. Every single one of the foods that Robert Ripley mentions in his description of family meals was a product of the Ripley farm: "One thing she [Luella Ripley] used to have in the fall, we'd have . . . ham and potatoes and cabbage and all vegetables. . . . She'd cook . . . a lot of potatoes. Never thought we'd had breakfast unless you had potatoes. Fried potatoes. And eggs, for breakfast." Having grown up in a family where lumbering was the main source of income, Marion LaClaire Norwood remembers that both her mother and grandmother worked diligently to prepare the sorts of foods that woodsmen, at least in the Sawmill Valley, expected to find in their lunch boxes. Self-sufficiency was not the only principle guiding the work done in the LaClaire kitchen. Woodsmen had strong personal likes and dislikes which often determined what sorts of foods were to be cooked in valley homes.

Kitchen production was an indispensable aspect of the valley's work patterns, as well as a means by which women propagated regional preferences. Valley lumbermen often insisted on eating pies for breakfast; the LaClaire women worked hard to accommodate this preference, among others. When I asked Marion Norwood if her family ate any traditionally French Canadian foods, she explained that, to her knowledge, they had not. The LaClaires had been regionalized in every way; apparently they had a strictly Yankee diet:

> I know my father was very fond of johnny-cake or cornbread. And pea soup. . . . And then they used to make what we called doughboys. I don't know if they still call them doughboys. It was fried dough, or just take bread dough and deep-fry it. I know my Grandmother LaClaire, when she was still alive—she's supposed to have been an Indian, but I haven't been able to find that out—but anyway, she went into desserts a lot. So I don't know whether the French did or whether that was just because they had been rather poor. And she just thought pies were especially really good and she always had pies around. Although she was a rather sickly woman, you know, you wondered how she could even make pies, but she did. Every time my father or his brother—he had no sisters, just brothers—would go out, she'd have pies for them.

Mary Stone recalls an elderly relative who insisted on being fed a different sort of workman's meal. "Two or three times a day," Mary Stone remembers, her great-grandfather "used to eat milk gravy, salt pork, and potato." Stone's husband Willy reports that his grandfather had a strong preference for exactly the same meal and also insisted on eating it three times a day: "That wasn't all [he ate], but he wanted that every meal. He got pretty upset when my grandmother wanted to eat . . . cereal. Oatmeal he didn't kick so much on. But when she went to . . . shredded wheat . . . he thought that was terrible to eat that stuff." These men very well may have insisted on being fed the same meal three times a day because of taste and their perceived nutritional needs. But the rejection of shredded wheat may have had to do with the upland farmer's preference for foods that his own family farm could produce. Implicit in the grandfather's loathing of shredded wheat might be a dislike of any store-bought foods. Not only were milk gravy, salt pork, and potatoes traditional New England fare, but also they were foods that the Stone farm was capable of producing. Indeed, Willy Stone himself makes the point that, since his family lived a half-mile away from the nearest store, they relied as much as possible on foods they could produce. Like other valley families, they bought a few staples at the store; but, unlike people who lived in town, they did not buy any prepared goods.

The Valley's Last Husking Bee

The successful operation of a small family farm was contingent upon more than the full participation of family members. In the "old days," when small farming was the normal pattern, not only in the Sawmill Valley but throughout rural New England, cooperation among families was a vital aspect of agricultural life. Tasks like barn-raisings, hayings, and corn-husking occasioned large gatherings at which one's neighbors, family, and friends came together to work and to socialize. Of all Sawmill Valley's farming pastimes, corn-husking involved the greatest degree of community interaction. A successful corn-husking bee was an outward manifestation of a successful regional farm economy. It brought more than festivity to farm production; a husking bee signaled economic bounty. Moreover, the husking bee allowed men and women who occupied the same valley to assist one another to achieve regional self-sufficiency.

As is often the case with recollections of culturally charged "moments," local memories tend to differ as to details. As Loyce Glazier Dunbar remembers it, "[Washburn Ripley] was a deacon. And he had a pair of oxen. He used to have a husking bee every fall. Out in the big barn, and big big bushel baskets. If you could get a red ear you could take it and jump up and kiss any woman you wanted to. My father always took a red ear from home with him. And then after the husking bee, you'd go in your house, you had doughnuts, cider, coffee, cheese, and [then] you'd go out [to] the barn. They'd sweep away all the corn husks and you'd have a little square dance." Robert Ripley, the deacon's son, remembers differently: "We had one [husking bee] one year but we never raised corn, much corn to husk, . . . but a lot of people around the country used to have husking bees. They used to have one up to the Hemenways quite often. . . . They'd get the corn and pick it and dump it along the barn floor or else they'd bring in the fodder and let them pick it up themselves. It was a little community affair, that's all."

On the surface, the differences between Dunbar's and Ripley's recollections may seem to reflect simple confusion, but the fact that each locates the bee at *the other's* family farm (the Hemenways were Dunbar's maternal grandparents) suggests that the reversal is symbolically significant. As one family after another reduced its farming operations to a bare minimum of activity, it may have appeared as if only families *other than one's own* still were capable of adhering to the old ways. Corn-husking bees still "happened every year," but only the neighbors were in a position to hold them.

"I was a little too young to participate much," Willy Stone recalls about the few husking bees he went to in his childhood: "They had a good time. They had cider, both sweet and hard and . . . sandwiches, I guess. They had a little party anyway. Probably had . . . somebody playing the harmonica or something. It seems as though I remember music . . . seems as though they danced some." Willy Stone's description of husking bees, like Loyce Dunbar's, concentrates primarily on the social aspects of the pastime—the food and drink served, the music, dancing, and so forth. In such descriptions, the corn-husking itself is little more than a sidelight to everything else that occurs at the bee. To be sure, the event's festive air had at least as much to do with its social aspects as with the harvest. Men took advantage of the fact that red ears of corn allowed them a degree of licentiousness forbidden by the strict standards of daily life; Loyce Dunbar remembers, for example, that her father always went to husking bees with a red ear hidden on his person.

When corn-husking bees eventually disappeared from Sawmill Valley folklife, their passing probably did not seem as momentous as it does now. Well into the 1940s, valley residents engaged in a great many church- and community-based social activities that, like the husking bees, involved food, drink, music, and dancing. What once separated the husking bee from these other activities was its context—its origin and functions in the social and economic life of the small farm. By the time Dunbar and Willy Stone had come along, this connection was well on the way to being severed.

The last husking bee that Stone remembers attending very well may have been the region's very last husking bee. His account of the event is a requiem of sorts, a fitting description of a folk pastime which, at least by the mid-1920s, was merely a relic of a former era. The bee took place "up to the Hemenway place. . . . They had a big scaffold up over . . . where you drove in. . . . And I remember . . . they were drinking cider some and somebody fell off of the scaffold. They got fooling around. Somebody fell off and got hurt some. I guess nothing serious, but I remember that put an end to the husking that night." The disappearance of this rural pastime in the 1920s marked the passing of an era. When informants recall corn-husking bees of their childhoods, they are recalling the eclipse of the small-farm economy and its associated way of life.

Vernon Aiken, with Michael Hoberman, January 1999. Photograph by Janice Sorensen.

Loyce Glazier Dunbar and Charlotte Glazier Abbott, March 1999. Photograph by Janice Sorensen.

Robert Ripley, 1990. Photograph by Paul Frantz, *Greenfield Recorder.*

Willy Stone and Mary Williams Stone, February 1999. Photograph by Janice Sorensen.

Clarissa Truesdell LaClaire, March 1999. Photograph by Janice Sorensen.

Bill Fleming and Marion Watson Fleming, February 1999. Photograph by Janice Sorensen.

Wayne Howard at the ruins of the Howard coke kilns, with Michael Hoberman, March 1999. Photograph by Janice Sorensen.

Ruby Hemenway, 1984. Photograph from private collection of Audrey Duckert.

Clifford Blinn during sugaring season, February 1999. Photograph by Janice Sorensen.

Marion LaClaire Norwood, January 1999. Photograph by Janice Sorensen.

Lionel Girard, February 1999. Photograph by Janice Sorensen.

Chapter 3

Self-reliance and Ambivalence

Wintry view of the North Leverett Baptist Church and parsonage from beneath the old Glazier lumber mill, February 1999. Photograph by Janice Sorensen.

Life and Lore in the Lumbering Industries

Woods Lore

Small dairy operations and kitchen gardens notwithstanding, the farmers of the Sawmill Valley, at least by the close of the nineteenth century, produced very little in the way of surplus goods. But because the valley's steep hillsides offered settlers a bountiful supply of lumber, locals both harvested timber and processed it in their many sawmills. Thus the woods became a last bastion of regional self-sufficiency, and the men who worked in them gave local residents images of themselves as fittingly independent and strong-willed. During the turn-of-the-century period, rural New England experienced a general economic decline, documented by many historians; and the valley's own lumber operations underwent a gradual decline of their own during the same period. Consequently, adherence to an ideology of self-reliance seems to me best understood as a *reaction* to social, economic, and political tendencies that were making self-reliance, at least on a regional basis, impossible. In effect, the preeminence of self-reliance and hard work as character traits of regional heroes was a tacit admission on the part of locals that the days of viable self-reliance had passed. For all their strength and bravery, valley woodsmen and their families during the turn-of-the-century period no longer were in a position to control their region's economic and social destiny, and their oral traditions reflect this reality in a number of ways.

Valley woodlots and woods-related industrial sites were not the first places to be affected by the changes attendant upon rural New England's economic decline. Farming had experienced its most dramatic decline in the middle of the nineteenth century, as many New England farmers joined the vast exodus which was settling upstate New York, the Great Plains, and the Far West. Prosperity and regional self-reliance within the lumbering industries did not taper off appreciably until the 1890s, however. At that point, the uniformly Anglo-Saxon woodcutters and sawyers of the Sawmill Valley found themselves no longer able to compete economically without hired, immigrant help. By the turn of the century, the local woods were being worked—for the first time since the earliest days of European settlement—by men and women whose ethnic stock was different from that of the early settlers. Furthermore, within a short time, even the arrival of immigrant help was insufficient to keep the valley's once-lucrative woodlots and sawmills going. Local enterprises gradually ceased operation, until by the 1930s only three of the Sawmill River's original twenty-two mills was still functioning.

The narratives and anecdotes that pertain to this period in the valley's lumber history are marked by a peculiar blend of self-congratulatory wistfulness and tight-lipped stoicism, both products of modernity. Self-consciousness is the dominant tone, perhaps because, for valley residents, the woods were no less important psychically than as means of literal sustenance and commerce. For one thing, among local men the forest was a key proving ground for physical strength, endurance, and resourcefulness. Skilled woodsmanship was a crucial means by which recently arrived locals were able to gain acceptance as natives. Like the accounts which locals provide of farming practices and traditions, the stories told by valley men and women of life in the lumbering industries are fueled, in large part, by a sense of being besieged and directing attention toward the world outside the valley. The chapter which follows features two sorts of accounts—stories which highlight the character trait of self-reliance among valley woodsmen and narrative treatments of the immigrant, or "outsider," presence in the valley. Among other things, the immigrant presence called into question the belief in regional self-sufficiency.

Images of stereotypical Yankee hardheadedness and self-sufficiency abound, not only in New England folklore but throughout American storytelling and literary traditions. From the formative years of our national culture right down to the present day, New England character traits have been rendered by symbol-obsessed authors as the backbone of American independence and ingenuity. Benjamin Franklin can be said to have nationalized this trait; in moving from his birthplace in Boston to his adopted home of Pennsylvania (not to mention representing America in the capitals of Europe), he held up the New England tradition as a model for the world. New England resourcefulness and practicality are nowhere better represented than in Franklin's *Autobiography.* Despite his heterodox embrace of Deism, or more properly as a direct result of it, Franklin offered the world an example of moral strength and virtue based on self-assurance and humble reason, as opposed to fear of the unknown. His optimism was the outgrowth of his faith in himself and his abilities, and in this regard he can be said to be an early and highly visible exemplar of post-Puritan New England pragmatism and modernity. The folklore of nineteenth-century New England offers a similarly inventive emphasis on self-reliance and rationalism. Exhibiting an uncompromising faith in the self, Yankee traders and travelers got the better of their fellow Americans in tale after tale.

By mid-century, however, westward expansion and urbanization not only had depleted rural New England's population but also had made its legacy of modest self-reliance a trait that was rare—indeed, nearly obsolete. By the time my informants were born, their ancestors' strong-mindedness had been supplanted by a thoroughly *Americanized* ideology of brash—as opposed to understated—individualism. The rural New England character had become a subject eliciting nostalgia, and residents of the Sawmill Valley were no exception to this pattern. When they talked of their exploits in the woods, they did so portraying themselves as the last of a dying breed. New residents of the valley, including the offspring of French Canadian and other non-Anglo immigrants, were accorded conditional acceptance into the regional fold if and when they embraced the ideology of hard work and simplicity. Even so, their arrival constituted a clear challenge to the notion of regional impermeability.

Most of the immigrants to the United States at the turn of the century lived in cities, of course, and more often than not in clearly defined ethnic neighborhoods. But non-Anglos settled in rural areas as well; large-scale settlement of the Upper Midwest by Scandinavian immigrants is a well known, but by no means singular, case in point. The Great Plains topography, as well as the decentralizing tendencies which held sway west of the Mississippi, allowed for a relatively large measure of cultural difference among rural settlers. Rural New England, however, whose settlement history was considerably more centralized and village-oriented, had been thoroughly dominated by men and women of East Anglian stock for nearly three centuries and was not as readily disposed to accommodate open displays of ethnic difference. Consequently, the immigrant presence in places like the Sawmill Valley is difficult to track. On the whole, either immigrants *passed through* the valley without much more than a trace, or they became thoroughly assimilated Yankees, so driven by the local ethic of hard work that whatever recollections they may have had of a previous cultural life were rendered trivial. Places like the Sawmill Valley were not impervious to the syncretic patterns of turn-of-the-century American life, however; even the domination of Old Yankees could not insulate locals from the modernizing influence of immigration.

Self-reliance in Legend: Near Misses and Strong-man Stories

The Sawmill River Valley seems to have held fast to only one "traditional" character trait: belief in the power of the clever, level-headed, and witty individual. The woods in the Sawmill Valley were full of "originals"—"characters" within the storytelling tradition whose unusual resourcefulness and eccentricity transcended the need for any sort of supernatural faith. Within this tradition, pragmatism is regarded so highly that its practitioners, as well as those who fail to exhibit it, stand at the center of nearly every personal legend, anecdote, and first-person narrative that emerges from the woods. For all their religiosity (almost all my informants were brought up in church-going households), the Sawmill Valley's oral tradition hardly ever mentions faith in God as a prerequisite for preservation in the woods. Rather, it is the protagonist who maintains a calm fortitude in the face of imminent death or disaster, as well as a sense of confidence in self and in the lessons of experience, who emerges as a hero. If woods-related traditions were our only gauge of local cultural practice, we might assume that a secular belief in the ability of the individual to overcome obstacles and threats was the local religion. Following one's instincts in these woods was a matter of avoiding panic and placing one's faith in the power of intelligent and measured decision making.

Sawmill Valley informants sometimes tell stories about times when faith—both in oneself and, to a lesser extent, in one's equipment or livestock—offered the only chance they had to escape from death in the woods. Vernon Aiken tells about an incident that happened early in his career as a lumberman, in which a usually lazy horse proves his worth:

> I remember coming out of the woods with a big load of wood. And a stick caught the nose of the runner of the sled. And put it up in the air all of a sudden and I lost my balance. And I gave a jump and I kind of landed on the bank. And I got clear of the sled except for one foot, that was under the sled runner with a big load of wood on it. And I knew I could lay there, [until]

> dark, you know, before anybody would come after me. I knew I couldn't make anyone hear. So, I had a pair of horses. One of them, nobody ever drove him too much except me. And he was known for being kind of lazy and he usually let the other horse start the load, you know, unless I see[n] to it that he kept his end up. So, I don't know, I said, "I may smash that ankle if I let him pull it off of me," but I says, "I can't lay here." So I said "Brent," I said, "Gee!" And just like that he'd always done it, you know, he pulled right over to the right. That kind of pulled the thing off my foot instead of dragging it the whole length.

Aiken, who is also the source of the "remarkable Providence" tale about Rattlesnake Gutter, considers this story a record of a common occurrence in the woods. "I had a lot of close calls in the woods," he says; "seems as everybody else did that worked there." For him, as for other men and women in the regional group, the woods were places where remarkable things occurred on a relatively regular basis.

Aiken's account of his horse's reliability speaks to his own and his fellow locals' belief in self-reliance. "I knew I could lay there, [until] dark," he says. "I knew I couldn't make anyone hear." In refraining from making a futile call for help, Aiken is not merely stoical. When a lumberman was off by himself in the woods, the oral tradition tells us, he knew that his success and survival were predicated not only upon learned skills, but also upon character traits such as calm and forethought. The lumbermen featured in woods-related oral traditions survive and prosper as a result of their adherence to the regional group's standard of self-reliance. Indeed, the individual cases of self-reliance can be seen as metaphors for the entire region's sense of itself and its capabilities.

A LaClaire family story provided by Marion LaClaire Norwood corroborates Aiken's near-miss story. As if to underscore the absence of the trait of self-reliance among members of more recent generations, Norwood recalls her father's telling her about an instance in which self-reliance on his part was the key to survival. She might as well be making the case for a form of religious belief. Norwood's father, Joe W. LaClaire, owned a horse who was not as dependable as Aiken's Brent turned out to be: "He was [cutting wood] way off in New York State. . . . Somebody had to stay up there with the animals when the rest would come home for weekends. . . . And he stayed this one time and somehow or other he was taking care of the horse and the horse broke . . . my father's leg. You know, he says, 'It wasn't the horse's fault. I did the wrong thing at the wrong time.' But anyway, he was up there all by himself way out in the woods. And he fixed that leg the best he could, I don't know how, and he stayed there for, oh, this particular time I guess it was at least a week before anybody came to help him. He set the leg himself." The anecdote makes clear the high regard in which the regional group held those who had passed the test of self-reliance and had acquired the knowledge and skills needed to survive in the face of life-threatening adversity. Moreover, LaClaire's refusal to blame his horse for the mishap suggests that the true woodsman must hold himself accountable for whatever happens to him on the job.

Calm and self-reliance figure prominently, too, in an account of a sawmill mishap narrated by Joe W. LaClaire and Ruby Hemenway. As he describes the operations of Bourne's mill (described in more detail below) to Audrey Duckert and Ruby Hemenway, LaClaire recalls the day in March 1915 when Maurice Glazier lost his arm there: "You know, when Maurice Glazier got his arm cut off I was working with him. . . . We sawed a hundred and three thousand that morning, we was going to get a hundred and twenty before night, see. Then at nine o'clock he cut his arm off, see. But he walked right up to the camp . . . and never fainted or nothing."

"I heard him say that, or somebody say that, the rest of them were petrified," interjects Ruby Hemenway. The ensuing dialogue between LaClaire and Hemenway completes the picture: "And he had to tell them to go and unlace the lacing that held the belt together where it was pieced, or where it came together," Hemenway recalls. "Unlace that and take it and make a tourniquet out of it. He had to tell them what to do."

"I remember; I was there," adds LaClaire. "I was sticking lumber down the pit there, the day he got it cut off." Having been on the scene, LaClaire recounts details that do not appear to have any direct bearing on the accident. How, we might ask, is it in any way relevant to Maurice Glazier's losing his arm that the men had cut 103,000 board feet in the morning and were planning to finish the day with 120,000? Marginal as this detail may seem, it speaks directly to the facts of life in the lumbering industry. Notwithstanding the lost limb, the sawyers in Bourne's mill were working hard on the day Maurice Glazier lost his arm. For years to come, they would look at Maurice Glazier as an example of fearlessness and resourcefulness. They would look at themselves as examples of dedication to the exacting standards of the work ethic.

Sawmill Valley tradition-bearers also were in the habit of privileging locals who displayed extraordinary determination to resist the inevitable changes being wrought within the increasingly demanding regional milieu. When the accident described by Norwood took place, LaClaire was cutting wood in a faraway section of the Adirondack Mountains. He and his sons traveled there regularly in order to supplement whatever income they were able to derive from the local woods. The residents of the Sawmill Valley liked to tell stories about their neighbors who had mastered the art of coping unflinchingly with oppressive economic conditions.

Families and individuals who were having trouble meeting the financial demands of an early-twentieth-century market economy had three options. The least palatable of these was to submit wholeheartedly to the decline and move to the Town Farm. As if to underscore the scorn with which most valley residents greeted the Town Farm option, Vernon Aiken supplies the following anecdote, which also describes the second option available in coping with economic decline. This second option is hard labor in which the worker risks physical harm.

> I remember Old Mr. Miller used to live up Chestnut Hill a ways. And my dad and I were going up to get a load of wood one time and he, we got opposite his wood-lot. And he hollered to us, he says: "What time is it?"
>
> My dad says, well, he says, "About a quarter of twelve."
>
> . . . He [Mr. Miller] says: "Can I ride up to the house with you?"
>
> Dad said, "Sure." And that man come out of the woods on a pair of crutches. He'd come from his house down on crutches and he was cutting wood so to get two, three cord of wood out that he could, you know, sell to somebody. But I never forgot how courageous [an] old fellow he was, to get down there on his crutches and get a little wood so he could sell it, you know, and buy his food, clothes, or whatever. Wasn't much welfare back in those days—Town Farm, when they got to where they couldn't take care of themselves.

Vernon Aiken's attention to the looming prospect of the Town Farm is a testament to the economic and social instability that pervaded the Sawmill Valley in the period between 1890 and 1920. Being sent to live on the Town Farm was tantamount to being subjected to internal exile.[1] Implicit in such a fate was a perceived admission that one was irreversibly incompetent and needed to be looked after. Since no federal mandate existed for the support of unemployable people, the community itself was the only source of whatever monies might be available to keep poor people fed, clothed, and housed. Rather than subject themselves to the sense of indebtedness and helplessness they would feel if they relied upon local taxpayers, the men and women who are admired within the Sawmill Valley's oral tradition attained hero status by working hard and refusing to complain in the face of poverty.

Near-miss stories, as well as recollections like Vernon Aiken's story about Old Mr. Miller, point to the centrality of self-reliance within the regional consciousness. But they also reveal the tenuous nature of this inordinate faith in the individual. The region's devotion to the principle of self-reliance placed enormous demands upon individuals, even to the point of requiring a cripple like Old Mr. Miller to cut cordwood to support himself.[2]

The third option open to those facing economic hardship was the one that Henry Mercier evidently took. Vernon Aiken is the source of this anecdote, too: "He [Henry Mercier] was kind of crazy. You never knew what he was going to say or do. A good little guy. But . . . you never could tell what was going to happen with [him]. He was one of the guys who went to the welfare board, said he didn't have anything to eat. And . . . Mr. Marvell [the head of the welfare board] . . . asked him if he had a ax.

"'Oh yeah,' Henry said, he got a ax. Well, he [Mr. Marvell] said, 'Go right up there in the woods and cut some wood.' Says, 'Soon as you get a cord,' says, 'I'll pay you for it.' Henry moved to Montague and got a job down there. He wasn't about to cut wood."

Aiken's anecdotes about Old Mr. Miller and Henry Mercier both capture their protagonists' determination to stave off imminent economic—as well as psychological—collapse. Old Mr. Miller and Henry Mercier are men who have been backed into a corner. The folk tradition that has shaped them doesn't allow for easy resolution of their despair. Miller opts to risk life and (withered) limb in order to remain within the regional fold; Mercier, the more modernist of the two, chooses to attach himself to a neighboring economy, leaving home to take a job in town. Perhaps faith in God would have redeemed both these men in New England before the Civil War, when a pious optimism provided the ideological solution to even the most desperate situation. But this modern oral tradition does not shield itself from the hard realities of poverty.

As a region whose residents prided themselves on their prosperity and self-sufficiency, the Sawmill Valley was confronted, at least by 1890, with the fact of its economic and social permeability. Only occasionally did the women and men of this valley look back longingly to a time when (at least according to their reckoning) life had been uncomplicated by the looming prospect of the Town Farm. Economic prosperity, which valley residents experienced in the period of New England's industrial preeminence, might have given some of them the illusion that their region was in fact self-sufficient, capable of operating independently of extraregional markets. By the time when my informants were born, in the 1910s and 1920s, however, most families accepted the fact that neither their economic conditions nor their cultural institutions were immune to trends in surrounding and distant regions of the nation. As a consequence of this realization, local men and women crafted an oral tradition which celebrated the only means of subsistence still available to them: hard work.

The generation of valley residents who passed anecdotes like the one about Henry Mercier on to my informants had a penchant for yet another folkloric form featuring a problematic attachment to the self-reliant code of a departed past. This is the "strong-man story." In the face of general economic decline and the end of any illusion of self-sufficiency, local storytellers came to celebrate men like Joe W. LaClaire, Old Mr. Miller, and Henry Mercier. As human strength was replaced by machine power, those same storytellers coped by recounting the deeds of men whose physical power exceeded the norm. Propelled by some of the same social forces that gave rise to the John Henry tradition, the tradition-bearers of the Sawmill Valley inflated the reputations of their own superhuman heroes. Like the tall-tale heroes of the mid-nineteenth-century American frontier, the heroic woodsmen of the Sawmill Valley display enormous strength as a means of coping with underlying fears.[3] Beneath the strength and simplicity that these narratives appear to celebrate, however, we can discern a form of insecurity.

As we have seen, two characteristics vital to the heroic status of local woodsmen were genius and proper use of instinct. The presence of these qualities within the local tradition signals a somewhat modernistic fealty to acquired knowledge and the immutable laws of nature. If you cut down the tree the right way, it will not kill you. If you trust the horse to do what you have taught it to do, it will save your life in a pinch. Folklore celebrating unusual human strength, on the other hand, seems to be the result of a troubling lack of self-assurance. Physical strength, after all, usually is more of a last resort than a renewable cultural resource. Those who display extraordinary ability to lift heavy things in a world which is in the process of inventing and implementing machines to do the same tasks are, by their very nature, a dying breed.

Bragging sessions were common among Sawmill Valley woodsmen. According to Dave Mercier, the lumbermen would visit the local store and boast to one another about how many board feet they could cut. As Willy Stone remembers it, "They used to tell yarns about the different prowess of . . . people that were particularly strong." Certain woodsmen had remarkable reputations for productivity and strength. Both Willy Stone and Joe N. LaClaire (Joe W.'s son) told me about Bill Stratford. According to Stone: "[Bill Stratford] . . . could cut and split and pile three cord of wood a day. And I used to do it. I could cut and split and pile about one cord. . . . That was unusual. . . . Most of the real good men would cut a couple cord a day. But he was the champeen. . . . He was a great chopper. He won a lot of, they used to have chopping contests, always at the fair, Greenfield fair. And he was most always the one that could win it. He had a number of nice wide-bitted axes, and he'd have it sharp as a razor and he could, he could swing it. They had to see who cut through a log fastest, you know. He was the champeen in our area." Men like Stratford undoubtedly were sources of regional pride. But even a razor-sharp ax and a powerful physique could not shield a woodsman from the decline of the local logging industry.

Remembered for his physical prowess as well as for his legendary ability to calculate board feet as he surveyed an entire woodlot,[4] Walter Carey is another example of obsolescence. The record of his accomplishments, as well as his physical attributes, indicates that his type had all but disappeared from the regional milieu when stories about him were first "hatched." "Walter had some brothers," says Clifford LaClaire, "which I never met. They say they were huge, powerful men. Used to have hands on them like an elephant foot, they tell me."

"They [the Carey boys] were all big, rugged guys," Willy Stone remembers. "And they'd tell about the different stunts that they could do. They told about [how] Walter Carey come along and there was a Model-T Ford tipped over in the brook over up in Wendell. And he could get, he got down in there and tipped it back up on his wheels. Tremendously strong people. There's no comparison in how strong they would be."

Willy Stone's suggestion that Walter Carey has no contemporary equivalents is part of his story's appeal. Strong-man stories and tall tales that relate to woodcutters represent life as it once was, life before the coming of the powerful machines that have ended the need for superhuman strength—and, consequently, for regional self-sufficiency. The classic strong-man story pits muscle against machine, as in the case of Walter Carey and the errant Model T. But when muscle wins, as it always does in these tales, usually it is for the last time. John Henry, a well-known case in point, outdoes the steam-drill but dies of heart failure in the process (Dorson, *American Folklore* 231). Moreover, the age during which the John Henry legend saw its greatest popularity was an age in which the power of the steam drill did in fact supplant the power of muscular men.

In one of the many personal legends that local tradition has attached to Walter Carey, a portable sawmill provides the setting. Vernon Aiken heard this story from his father:

> They would find a place on the timber lot that they were cutting where [they] could be near the water. And then they could, they'd burn the slabs from the logs they were cutting and they'd make steam and run the mill on steam power. And . . . they had a whistle. And if the mill could saw all the logs before they got the next load in there, they'd blow the whistle. And that was quite a, quite [a] feat with them, to do that [i.e., deliver the next load in advance of the whistle]. And Mr. Carey was doing the logging, Walter Carey. And the boys, some of the boys

> were driving the horses and they had a pretty big load on. Just before they got to the mill, it was kind of muddy, and they got stuck. And he heard the commotion down there, and he run down there and said: "What's the matter?"
>
> "Oh, he says they're going to blow the whistle on us, they're going to blow the whistle on us." So he took a huge log right off top of the load on his shoulder and walked over and dropped it on the skids so they couldn't blow the whistle. And then he went back and he grasped the wheel, spoke and the wheel, and spoke to the horses the same time. And he lifted up on that wheel and brought the load of logs up to the skidway, so they weren't able to blow the whistle. . . . I wasn't there but my dad told about it. . . . He [Walter Carey] was a real strong man.

Like other strong-man stories, this one features a confident, capable, and ultimately successful laborer. Like some of the other strong-man stories with heroes like Walter Carey, this one involves a contest between human will and the relentless power of machinery. The pressure applied by an insatiable extraregional market's demand is the force which threatens to "blow the whistle" on the already overworked woodcutters and sawyers of the Sawmill Valley. Walter Carey, the region's "champeen" in all things woods-related, triumphs because his strength and will (and also his literal silencing of the whistle) enable him to win the race with the clamorous, all-consuming portable mill. A question must be asked, however. Isn't Carey's triumph also a capitulation to the impatience and voracity of an insatiable market? Like John Henry and the heroes of other stories pitting strong men against machines, even a man like Walter Carey can win only in the short term.

Within the Sawmill Valley's oral tradition, unusually strong men are not always depicted as invincible. Vernon Aiken tells one anecdote about a regional woodsmen's pastime called "pulling the broomstick." In this story, the main consequence of great strength is folly: "The Williamses—Herman, Bill and Ray—they were all pretty rugged. . . . Bill Williams and I . . . were pulling the broomstick. And you'd sit down and face each other, put your feet against each other's feet and have a broom. And the thing of it was to try to get the other fellow up off the floor. And Bill and I hung to that and finally broke the broom handle. That was the end of that. I had managed to get him up just a little bit and when that broom handle let go he went—splat—right back onto the floor."

A similarly comical result awaited those uninformed men who took their chances "pulling fingers" with that pastime's local champion. Wayne Howard explains finger pulling:

> If you take your fist and make a fist and then your middle finger, extend it and make a hook, each one of you. . . . And try to pull the other one off of a, over a line or off balance. Well, there was one fellow that worked in the sawmill that had got a bad cut on his arm and it damaged the cord in his hand, or wrist. So his middle finger was permanently hooked. There's no way you could straighten it out. Well, if a new man came in, [he'd] pull fingers with him and they always lost. He got sort of arguing one day with a fellow and the fellow started to run away and he reached and grabbed him on the back of his coat while his finger got hooked in his coat. And the more the fellow would run, of course the harder his finger hooked there.

Contests such as these had a good deal of entertainment value. The wise woodsman knew better than to rely on his physical prowess for survival, however. Too much attention to this standard of measurement, at least on the part of the average woodsman, never was a good idea. It was "kind of an honor if you could pick up a bigger log than the other guy," says Vernon Aiken, but knowing the limits of one's strength also was important:

> I worked, I don't know, a number of winters with Jess Richardson, [who] used to live down below here. Boy, he was . . . strong. Of course, being a kid, you know, I didn't want to get beat so I'd do my best. But of course I couldn't anywhere near keep up with him. We fell[ed] a tree one time in the back, in the brush, it was two eight-foot logs—the last two logs were eight-footers. So, just joking, I says: "You take that one, Jess, and I'll take the other one"—never thinking he'd do it. So he just ended that log up, . . . and got it on his shoulder and out he went with it. Well, the other wasn't so big, but I ended that log up, I got it up on my shoulder. And I got out by the sled, and I said to myself, "You dummy, don't you ever say that again." 'Cause he was, he was strong.

For all the muscle power they could muster up, the woodsmen of the Sawmill Valley could not rely on physical strength to shelter them from the changes that the rise of large-scale industrialism was bringing to the region. In order to compete successfully within the New England and North American economy, the woodsmen of the Sawmill Valley had to *participate* in these changes, not be swept up by them.

Becoming Yankee: The Impact of Immigrant Labor and the Process of Regionalization

The circumstances of life in the Sawmill Valley, at least by 1890 or so, ruled out regional self-sufficiency. Even with its population of energetic native-born woodcutters, the Sawmill Valley could not produce what the New England economy demanded of it without hiring non-Anglo immigrant labor. Today's oral narratives contain few overt references to the rivalries that this new immigrant presence within the Sawmill Valley must have brought about among woodsmen. The immigrants either disappeared shortly after their arrival in the valley or, as we shall see, allowed their ethnic allegiances to fall by the wayside as they adopted the regional work ethic. With few exceptions, the narratives that record the coming of non-Anglo immigrants to the woods of the Sawmill Valley—whether they are supplied by the descendants of those immigrants or by the descendants of the "Old Yankees" who received them—make reference to hard work as the regional standard of excellence among woodcutters.

The first large group of non-Anglo immigrants who came to the Sawmill Valley did not stay long enough to leave any sort of imprint upon the landscape. Consequently, I was able to find only a few traces of their presence in the valley's oral tradition. During Washburn Ripley's days as a lumberman in the latter decades of the nineteenth century, many woodcutters in the Sawmill Valley were actively engaged in one form of commerce that was turning Greenfield into a busy regional market. Robert Ripley describes his father's participation in the trade: "Everybody had a team of horses and they drew wood . . . to Greenfield for brickyards. They would cut . . . hundreds of cords in the winter and . . . then they'd have it a year's drying and then the next winter, father would draw it over to Greenfield with a team of horses."

Apparently the brickyards' constant demand for wood outran the ability of local Sawmill Valley woodcutters to supply it. According to Vernon Aiken, who heard about the trade from his father,

> It took a tremendous amount of wood to bake the brick. . . . They needed woodchoppers, so these, this French family, moved down from Canada. . . . And there was a building down here that was probably about sixteen by twenty. And there was seventeen in the family. Seventeen all lived in that little building. And . . . anybody that was big enough to handle an ax went to the woods every morning. And they cut wood to for the, to go to the brickyard. . . . I have no idea what their name was, 'cause they were just people that just come and left, you know. They worked there for, you know, maybe less than a year and then they moved on somewhere else. . . . I guess all they had was something to cook on and it was wall-to-wall people, almost, when they laid down to sleep.

Intriguing as it is, this anecdote generates more questions than answers.

For example, was this particular family of French Canadian woodcutters one among many such groups in the area? And did their arrival in the Sawmill Valley cause any kind of a stir among the permanent residents, who may have felt threatened by it?

Notwithstanding its fascinating historical content, this account of a French Canadian presence in the Sawmill Valley is relevant primarily as a window on Anglo attitudes toward an immigrant presence in the valley. It says nothing of the *immigrant* perspective. Assuming that the French Canadian woodcutters were the cultural and linguistic outsiders that they appear to have been (why else, for example, would they have spent all their free hours in a one-room cabin?), it is something of a wonder that any record of their sojourn in the valley exists at all. For the most part, present-day Sawmill Valley residents—including those who are descended from other turn-of-the-century French Canadian immigrants—have discarded whatever traces of ethnic difference once existed within the folk consciousness. What makes Vernon Aiken's account so remarkable is its *retention* of the memory of ethnic difference, its description of a mysterious cultural Other within a regional milieu that seems to have eradicated all traces of ethnic distinctions.

Vernon Aiken's anecdote points to the seemingly unbridgeable cultural rift that must have existed between the immigrant woodcutters and the permanent settlers of the Sawmill Valley. His description of the family dwells almost entirely upon their material circumstances—the exact size of their house, what furnishings they might have had. The circumstances of the family's ethnicity are largely hidden. The anecdote's reference to the exact number of family members contained within the small dwelling suggests that the locals were observant enough to take note of at least one aspect of the family's ethnicity—the Canadians' (presumed) Catholicism. Aside from this one detail, however, it is only the description's points of silence that announce the fact of cultural difference. Those silences—regarding the family's name, its members' inevitable interactions with locals, the linguistic and religious gaps that surely separated these French-speaking Catholics from the English-speaking Protestants who surrounded them—are the most crucial indicators of how ethnic differences play themselves out in a regional folk milieu.

Because the woodcutters apparently were incapable of being assimilated, the local oral tradition could commemorate their stay in the valley only by means of telling silences. The permanent residents of the valley took shelter from the foreign incursion by remaining on the perimeter of their mysterious little dwelling. Doing so, however, did not insulate them from the ultimate effects of non-Anglo immigration. Even the most forbidding physical (or psychological) barriers do not necessarily create or reinforce uniformity within the regional folk group. If anything, the barriers imposed by topography and, in this case, architecture only cause the potentially conflicting folk groups within a given region to pay closer attention to one another than they otherwise might do. Even if only a handful of the Anglo-Saxon residents of the Sawmill Valley ever saw the immigrant woodcutters, the French Canadians managed—probably *because* of their perceived inaccessibility—to become lodged in the oral tradition.

For the most part, a book like this one depends for its value upon the degree to which descriptions like Vernon Aiken's—be they legends, anecdotes, or first-person narratives—echo one another. Even with all its silences, however, Vernon Aiken's description of the seventeen French Canadian woodcutters is the most extended reference to an unassimilated regional group that I encountered in my work. As we shall see, valley residents do remember immigrants who made the valley their permanent home; assimilated families like the LaClaires, Merciers, and Careys come to mind. But *unassimilated* immigrants took a limited—or perhaps an unconscious—hold on the local imagination. What little we can learn about them comes to us in fragments; of these, Vernon Aiken's account happens to be the largest.

For a period, at any rate, "outside" help was not a rarity in the Sawmill Valley's woods. Vernon Aiken's grandmother, in fact, was an Irish immigrant who arrived in the Sawmill Valley to take a job as a domestic worker on a farm in Montague. "She was a devout Roman Catholic," Aiken says, but, unlike the French Canadian family who lived in the tiny hut, she assimilated to the local culture. "She fell in love with a . . . Methodist minister's son. So, well, I guess they didn't have a tremendous amount of friction over it. I guess they just—I heard my aunt say that they just never, never talked religion at all in the house, all the years that they were married."

Aiken also remembers some of the other "outside" workers (some of whom did not adapt), as well as the families who hired them and the buildings that housed them:

> There used to be people that, you know, they'd come through, get a job. Mr. Watson, up to Moores Corner, he used to hire a lot of help. And Ethan Howard hired quite a lot of help . . . years ago they used to call them drifters. They'd . . . come in and work a while. Mr. Watson had a family of Stratfords. They came from England. . . . They came over and settled. . . .
>
> There used to be houses and tenements that they [the hired workers] could

> live in. . . . There was a big building, right on the left as you head up Church Road in Moores Corner. I remember their living there. And then there was a house just beyond the old Moores Corner schoolhouse where they lived. And then Vera Carey's place, over on Dudleyville Road. There was a house there where some of them lived. . . . I think there was two tenements in that old house that, you know, [Ethan Howard] rented out to people that worked for him. . . . I remember one French fellow that worked for Ethan Howard. . . . Louis Belanger [the "Frenchman" who worked for the Howards]. . . . [He] didn't stay around too long. He was here for a while. . . . He lived with another family. He lived with a family of Clarks. I don't know where they did pick him up, but he was with them when they come to town.

Corroborating accounts of a temporary immigrant presence in the forests of the valley are scarce, but they do exist. Ruby Hemenway remembers that Amos Howard, the original proprietor of the Howard charcoal kilns, sometimes hired groups of French Canadian woodcutters. In two separate interviews conducted by Audrey Duckert and Ruby Hemenway in the 1960s, both Maurice Glazier and Joe W. LaClaire indicate that, within their memories, immigrant woodcutters came to work in the valley on a temporary basis. Glazier remembers working "on two or three jobs where they had Polish people did the chopping." LaClaire, himself the son of French Canadian immigrants, agrees with Ruby Hemenway that, in her words, "French Canadians used to come down in the winter and chop by hand" until "they got so they could earn more in the shops."

As Joe W. LaClaire echoes Ruby Hemenway's reference to French Canadians as a distant "they," he shows us how fully assimilated he and a handful of his fellow non-Anglos had become. In the minds of Sawmill Valley locals, the French Canadians who worked on a *temporary* basis in the forests of the Sawmill Valley were merely representations of a contemporaneous, entirely urban phenomenon—the millworkers who settled in industrial centers like Turners Falls and Holyoke. We can only speculate about whether the "invisible" immigrants left the valley because they wanted to live and work elsewhere or because they had been made to feel unwelcome among the Yankee homesteaders. What is clear, on the basis of the valley's oral tradition, is that, in order to assume their places within the regional folk group, non-Anglo immigrants would have had to shed all psychological attachment to their cultures of origin. Their neighbors' willingness to accept them was based largely on their status as committed local woodsmen, as permanent participants in a community whose very existence precluded overt ethnic difference. For turn-of-the-century immigrants to a rural area like the Sawmill Valley, the most important aspect of assimilation was regionalization—the process of allying self and family to traditions that revolve around place, not ethnicity. Unless a new arrival was willing to relinquish former ties, he or she was likely to be rendered all but nameless in the local reckoning, which seems to be what happened to every last transient immigrant laborer in the valley. To the extent that an outsider sought admission into the regional group, his or her willingness to do hard work was always key. Indeed, in a 1945 celebration of pluralism as a force in American culture, the author Louis Adamic refers admiringly to New England's Polish farmers as "people [to] whom hard work is a religion" (Blejwas, "Inherited" 46).

By the turn of the century, the degree of a woodcutter's social acceptance within the Sawmill Valley was—at least in part—an outgrowth of how many cords of wood he was able to lay up against the specter of the Town Farm. The oral tradition has preserved the memory of a number of turn-of-the-century woodcutters whose fame was linked to their unusual productivity. Vernon Aiken remembers a number of these men. Among them was "a big, big old Austrian fellow, woodchopper, Ed Haufbar. And he, that's all he done was cut wood. Fifty cords a month, that was his stint. He . . . would work 'til he got fifty cords. And he done it all with a ax and, well, he had a pulp saw that he used some but mostly with the ax. And they were real cords of wood, eight foot long and four foot high and four foot long." When they are remembered within the folk tradition, the non-Anglo immigrants to the Sawmill Valley most often are remembered, as Ed Haufbar is, as powerful and productive workers. Here we find a telling convergence between oral accounts and literary ones. According to Thomas Gladsky, the "robust, vigorous and prolific" Polish characters in early-twentieth-century New England fiction suggest a "stark contrast to the withered and withdrawn Yankees who populate" the same novels (qtd. in Gladsky 438). In the words of a character from Francis Allen's tellingly titled *The Invaders* (1913), the newcomers "bring to us [Yankees] 'what we are in need of, and just when we need it'" (438). Likewise, in a strong-man story that he picked up at the blacksmith's shop in Montague Center, Willy Stone tells of a Polish man whose physical prowess might have matched, or at least reminded listeners of, the faded glory of Walter Carey: "One of our Polish fellows from down on the meadow was in the blacksmith's shop in Montague there. And they were trying to take the front wheel . . . off of his truck, so the blacksmith could do a little work on it. . . . And this guy, the blacksmith told me about it, he leaned on his, on his knee [and] took one hand, picked the front end of the truck right off the ground with the wrench. Quite a difference in the strength of some people. That man was a, quite a big, fat guy, you know. He didn't look as if he'd be, but he was, awful strong." Immigrant workers helped old Yankees not only to redeem their desiccated birthright, but also to remember what it meant to be a Yankee.

We might ask whether these men have been celebrated because, eager to be accepted into the regional group, they actually did lift heavier things and cut more cords of wood than their Anglo neighbors. Like Ed Haufbar, Old Joe LaClaire, whose family is still well represented in the Sawmill Valley, is remembered for his enormity and strength. According to Clifford LaClaire, his grandson, "He was a big man, big broad-shouldered man. He would carry two bags of grain with snow way up to his knees, and carry them for a mile. I know he used to carry them up the hill where we used to live and never set them down. One on his shoulder, and one under his arm. Two hundred pounds of grain. Nobody could do that today." Partly on the basis of feats like the one described by his grandson, Old Joe LaClaire evidently attained uncontested status as a local, despite the fact that he had been born in Quebec and not Massachusetts. Only one of my informants—Gertrude Carey—suggests anything to the contrary. Her description of LaClaire indicates that he was not only "real Frenchy" in appearance, but "dark" as well. Apparently, her neighbors were either oblivious to such otherness or more guarded in their observations. Indeed, Clifford LaClaire, Joe N. LaClaire, and Marian LaClaire Norwood all concur that their grandfather Old Joe never spoke of his days in Canada, retained no French customs, and never spoke any French. In other words, Old Joe seems to have regionalized himself by yielding up whatever attachment to his ethnic heritage he once might have had. His wife, who was reputed to be of Native American as well as Franco stock, must have done the same.

Loyce Glazier Dunbar remarked that, until I mentioned it, she had "forgot[ten] all about" the fact that the LaClaires were of Franco heritage. "They were hard-working woodsmen, that's what they were," she says. According to Wayne Howard, the LaClaires are "an old family that have been there [the Sawmill Valley] for years. . . . They didn't have an accent or anything. . . . Typical Yankees, I'd call them." Marion LaClaire Norwood has done genealogical research on the LaClaire family; her information also points to the family's degree of assimilation. Based on what she has been able to find, it seems safe to conclude that the LaClaires had discarded whatever French Canadian cultural ties they once had well before they reached the Sawmill Valley. The LaClaires lived in Vermont for a number of years before they moved to the Sawmill Valley. Norwood has documented a LaClaire presence south of the American border from as far back as the 1860s. The family apparently shed its Catholicism somewhere along the long journey from Quebec. "My . . . great-grandfather was married in a Methodist chapel," she says. "I have no indication of the Catholic religion, although . . . it makes sense that they would be."

The combination of the LaClaires' own assimilating tendencies and their reputation as hard workers enabled them to take their places within the community. "They became Yankee," says Bill Fleming. "They had all the Yankee traditions and everything else." Like his Anglo neighbors, Clifford LaClaire says, Old Joe "was a log-cutter most all his life. Cutting logs and cutting cordwood." Unlike the nameless French Canadians who appear in Vernon Aiken's account, a permanent settler like Old Joe LaClaire, by virtue of his having shed most, if not all, ethnic traditions, is looked upon as a genuine Yankee and not as a mysterious interloper. If nothing else, he did not move on from the valley, like many of the temporarily resident French Canadian laborers, to work in one of the urban mills. For whatever reasons, he cast his lot with the impecunious, landlocked woodcutters of a rural upland, decided upon them as his adopted (and adoptive) neighbors, and also decided upon the valley as his *place.*

Henry Mercier—the man who, in Vernon Aiken's story, defied the head of the town welfare board—was the son of a French Canadian man. Willy Stone remembers him as being renowned among local woodcutters for his athleticism. "One of the stunts they used to do was jumping over a broomstick handle, you know. He could do it, he was the champ at that. He was a small man." Dave Mercier adds literal weight to his father's accomplishments, indicating that the broomstick jumping was made all the more challenging, owing to the fact that a sack of feed weighing one hundred pounds would be tied to the jumper's feet. For whatever reason, Henry Mercier's agility came as a surprise to many of his neighbors. Willy Stone remembers that "they used to be amazed. . . . Most of the lumber fellows—the Careys and Williamses—was all big men, you know, strong. And he [Henry Mercier] could beat them all at some of them things." Whether it was to compensate for his small frame or for his French Canadian roots, Henry Mercier achieved enough notoriety as a local "champeen" during his career as a woodsman to have been accepted as a local. Since he could prove himself according to the local woodsmen's standards of strength, he is treated in the oral tradition as a "Yankee" like all the rest. By adhering to a local work ethic and by mastering the rituals required of those who drew their sustenance from the woods, Mercier earned the right to call himself a native.

For all the indications within the oral tradition that Henry Mercier was thoroughly assimilated to the Sawmill Valley's version of "Yankee," evidence exists that his *father* had remained essentially an outsider. According to Henry's son David, it was his grandfather Andrew and not Henry Mercier who first came from Quebec. Evidently, Andrew Mercier was sufficiently different from his neighbors to be remembered primarily as "the old Frenchman." In fact, Wayne Howard, whose own grandfather ran the charcoal kiln at the time of Andrew Mercier's employment there, does not even remember ever having heard the charcoal burner's proper name. Whenever the old-timers recalled Andrew Mercier to Wayne Howard, they referred to him by invoking his ethnicity: "The old Frenchman, they would say." Perhaps due to his status as a foreigner, Andrew Mercier was surrounded by an aura of mystery.

Because his arrival and career in the Sawmill Valley seems to predate the births of all my informants who are still alive at the time of this writing, Andrew Mercier does not appear in any of today's oral narratives. But a handful of sketches of the "old Frenchman" do exist in print, in newspaper and magazine articles by and about one of the Sawmill Valley's most prolific repositories of folk memory, the late Ruby Hemenway. Ruby Hemenway's recollections do more than merely corroborate Dave Mercier's and Wayne Howard's threadbare accounts of "the old Frenchman." Their most distinctive feature is their placement of Andrew Mercier within a particular landscape, their attribution of almost earthen qualities to his body.

Woods-related Manufactures: Heterogeneity and Tension within the Regional Landscape

In one of her columns in the *Greenfield Recorder,* Ruby Hemenway sketches the elder Mercier: "When I was a girl in North Leverett there was only one coke kiln . . . just before the Meadow Bridge. An old Frenchman who was yellow and wrinkled as if smoke-preserved burned the charcoal kiln." In January 1984, after she had become a locally renowned newspaper columnist, Ruby Hemenway was the subject of a profile in *Yankee* magazine. Here Hemenway describes the charcoal burner again. As she and her interviewer walk down the old Coke Kiln Road and across the Meadow Bridge over the Sawmill River, she says, "There was an old Frenchman that lived down here in this boggy place. When I was a child, there was just one old coal [charcoal] kiln down across the way. . . . That old Frenchman used to run the kilns. He was puckered up, looked as if he'd been dried in smoke. His name was M-e-r-c-i-e-r but they always called him 'Mercy'" (Clark 109–10). One town clerk corroborates the common view of the Merciers as foreigners, at least initially. The record of young Henry's birth in 1887 spells the surname "Mercia," in accord, presumably, with local attempts to "Yankee-fy" the pronunciation. Ruby Hemenway's accounts of Andrew Mercier are similar enough in content and language to suggest that, at least in her memory, "the old Frenchman" was a veritable local "character."

Ruby Hemenway's descriptions of Mercier are particularly effective because they evoke visual images of both the man and his surroundings. Within her accounts, character and landscape are linked. In the second description, which apparently was recorded while Hemenway and her interviewer were walking, it is the direct experience of the landscape which leads her to describe the man. For Ruby Hemenway, the Meadow Bridge is virtually synonymous with the "old Frenchman." Unlike his son Henry, Andrew Mercier appears not to have shed his ethnic identity, at least in the eyes of the men and women who lived around him. Unassimilated as he was, however, Andrew Mercier did achieve a form of regionalization. "The old Frenchman" occupied a psychological space halfway between the mysterious anonymity of the seventeen French Canadian woodcutters and the thorough assimilation of Old Joe and his LaClaire descendants.

As if to underscore this folk region's permeability, it is Andrew Mercier's French Canadian heritage—his apparent Otherness—that earns him the status of a landmark. More than anything, the presence of the grizzled charcoal burner, coupled with the fact of his foreign origins and his unusual appearance, set the boggy area adjacent to the Meadow Bridge apart from the rest of the landscape within the local memory. Had he been just another "typical Yankee," the charcoal burner might never have achieved a distinctive place within the region's oral tradition. As an apparently unassimilated "Frenchman," however, Mercier stood out among his neighbors; both he and his shanty next to the Meadow Bridge became objects of curiosity. His mysterious legacy illustrates the power that the slightest evidence of cultural difference can have in even the most homogeneous-appearing communities.

Moreover, Mercier's "smoke-puckered" face and the charcoal kiln that he fired reminded locals that their landscape had distinguishing physical features, noteworthy departures from the rural norm. Built in 1881 by Amos Howard, the charcoal kiln routinely sent billowing clouds of smoke as far down the Sawmill Valley as Montague Center. The grime was thick; men who worked in the kiln were more than just "smoke-puckered"; they turned black. According to Gertrude Maynard Carey, "The ones who worked there looked like Negroes." The kilns were also a source of loud noise; every now and then a gas buildup would lead to a colossal explosion.

Wayne Howard, who ran the kilns that his father built in the 1930s, explains the process of burning charcoal. Such a facility's effects on the local landscape was considerable:

> With the charcoal kiln, brick kiln, you put, it held about seventy-five cords of wood. You put it in, filled it right up to the top. And you lit the fire in the center of the kiln, but you . . . had a small opening about two foot of, sort of, we called it a runway. An opening back into the center because the wood was piled right up to the door. You put the iron doors on and through the center of the top door you could take, we used an old burlap sack, put a little kerosene in it, and with a long pole pushed it to the center of the kiln and started the fire that way. It would spread out, burn up to the top of the kiln, and by controlling it you brought the fire down to the bottom. If you did it right, you had charcoal. And then, around the bottom of the charcoal kilns was vent holes. And you sealed up, shut off all the air, and smothered the fire. And that took about a week to ten days and then you could open up. Burning it could take anywhere from five to eight, nine days . . . and about a week to ten days for the fire to go out and cool it off. Then you could open up and get your charcoal out.

Robert Ripley recalls the care that the kiln burners had to take in order to prevent catastrophes from occurring: "You had to . . . start the coke kiln and then you had to watch it and shut it all up tight at a certain time and keep it that way. And you had to watch it so you wouldn't get a fire. And they had somebody working, one of 'em, and they got a fire on 'em and they burned the kiln down, couldn't put it out.. . . . You couldn't let it get going only so much and then you had to put up all the holes and it smoked there for so many days and smoke would come out of there and sometimes it would come down this way and sometimes it'd go that way." As a result of the impact that they had on the valley's landscape, not to mention its inhabitants, the charcoal kilns were mentifacts of place, crucial to valley residents' collective sense of regional identity. The existence of the kilns (as well as of other industrial sites in the Sawmill Valley) was an indicator of the region's physical, if not cultural, heterogeneity.

Apart from instances in which the wood was used as heating fuel, the greater portion of the logs that woodsmen cut and hauled out of the Sawmill Valley's woods ended up in one of the region's many industrial sites.

Many residents derive a sense of regional pride from the existence in their midst of so many sawmills, as well as the varied uses to which those mills were put. Among the mills remembered most fondly, Bourne's mill—which was located at the Moores Corner end of Rattlesnake Gutter—figures prominently. Marion LaClaire Norwood recalls: "My mother [Harriet Bourne LaClaire] was often talking about grandpa's [Frank Bourne's] mill and the kinds of things they made there. They even made coffins there. . . . He [Frank Bourne] also ground grain, as well as cutting logs and making shingles and things like that." In an audiotaped interview with Ruby Hemenway and Audrey Duckert, Harriet LaClaire and Joe LaClaire's enthusiasm in describing Bourne's mill corroborates their daughter's memory:

> HBL: It [Bourne's mill] was a two-story [structure], and there was a grist mill in it. . . . And they sold grain, and they made tobacco lath and they made shingles. . . . And their power was through a water-wheel, through a big iron tunnel, you know, down through . . . what do you call it, a flume?
>
> JL: Yeah, a flume and a water-wheel. . . .
>
> RH: Well the water-wheel wasn't on the outside as you see pictures of it. . . .
>
> JL: No, down in under, down in under where the water come down to it, see, you run it from the dam. . . . There's more power there than there was in the regular mills nowadays.
>
> HBL: I guess it's about the best power anywhere around, I think. . . . You know . . . they made coffin boxes there. We had two of them and the kids got in there and took them and used them for boats. . . . Everybody done so much more than they do nowadays. It's one man for one job today. And it used to be a dozen different jobs for one man, you know. We worked right in the mill. . . . We worked in the mill. I sawed lots of shingles and lath and all that stuff, you know.

The LaClaires' pride in the force of Bourne's mill is matched only by their assessment of its versatility. Like many of their neighbors, the LaClaires look back with a measure of pride at an era when adaptability was the rule, among people as well as among mills.

If the valley's woods-related production had been restricted to cutting down and hauling wood, the likelihood is great that it never would have attracted any settlers beyond the handful of woodsmen necessary for such a task. Its attraction of a broader population was a direct outgrowth of its importance as a milling and manufacturing site. While the valley's largest industrial sites did not approach the size of those in nearby urban areas such as Turners Falls, they did draw members of some of the same ethnic and social groups who were employed in such numbers in the urban shops. Quite often, itinerant laborers would come to work in the Sawmill Valley. Typically, Loyce Glazier Dunbar says, "A man would know how to saw lumber, and he might work for one mill and move on to another." Some of these men stayed for relatively long periods of time. "There'd be a man that would come through," Marion LaClaire Norwood recalls, "And he would . . . have a little shanty somewhere. And he would live there for ten, maybe, years. I remember one especially that used to drink a lot, and he finally burned himself up in his little cabin, you know, from drinking." More often than not, local folks' recollections of the itinerant laborers who sought and found work in the valley's sawmills are as sketchy as Norwood's memory of the man who "burned himself up." Having come to the area without families, it was difficult, if not impossible, for such workers to be drawn into a regional social sphere that was rooted almost entirely in the interaction of one family with another.

Some outsiders were recognized more easily than others when they came to work in the sawmills. A new sawyer had to become familiar with each type of wood that passed through his mills. In order to become an accepted member of the regional group, a given millworker had to have the wood-types inscribed in his mind. "Maurice Glazier was telling me . . . about some man who came to work in a mill and he'd come from the city," Ruby Hemenway says. "He didn't know anything about lumber and things like that at all, but he worked in the mill. And when they took the lumber away, they were sawing several kinds, and they wanted it sorted. And the men who were used to it could tell by the looks and the smell and the grain and so forth which kind was which. And they'd sort it, you know. And this man was utterly bewildered. And then they asked him—well, I guess his language wasn't very good. How they knew, what kind of boards it was. How could they tell what it was? He couldn't see." Within the anecdote, the city man's language difficulties pale in comparison with his bewilderment concerning the types of wood he was expected to distinguish from one another.

Joe LaClaire laughs as he listens to Ruby Hemenway's anecdote about the urban sawyer: "Well, you can tell [tree types] by the smell even if you was blindfolded, a lot of them. . . . If you knew. If you didn't know, you don't know." LaClaire's answer implies that, like any other taxonomy, the sawyers' familiarity with local trees is predicated upon a grammar of sorts, a system whose rules transcend simple explanation. Based on what LaClaire says about other aspects of sawmilling, it is no wonder that none of the local millers was able to explain the tree types to the city man. Anyone but a local sawyer would have been challenged by an explanation like this one, which LaClaire provides when his interviewers ask him for a definition of "board feet": "You got to take the width, see. How wide it is. And if it's one inch, if it's six inches wide and four foot long, there's six feet in it. And if it's eight feet, it's two-thirds of six, it's four, see. . . . It's simple, but if you don't know, it isn't. And even when you do know." Given "explanations" like this one, it is easy to see how bewildering the adjustment period might have been for outsiders who were not already familiar with the sawmilling trade. On the other hand, by the 1890s, at least the most determined newcomers to the Sawmill Valley were being accepted into the regional fold. They had arrived at a time when the natives no longer were in a position to offer any true resistance to an "outside" incursion that, perhaps unbeknownst to them, had been under way for quite some time.

Chapter 4

Life in "Sweet Auburn"

Baker Whipple's monument, from the Mount Hope Cemetery on Chestnut Hill Road in North Leverett, March 1999. Photograph by Janice Sorensen.

Village (Self-)Consciousness in the Sawmill Valley

Village Traditions

Not many years before automobiles put an end to the Sawmill Valley's sense of autonomy, author Rollin Lynde Hartt settled in Leverett Center. As Loyce Glazier Dunbar describes it, the writer's tenure in the town caused quite a stir, even after he left to pursue his career elsewhere. Rollin Lynde Hartt

> was a minister in Leverett for a short time. . . . He wrote a book, *Sweet Auburn.* After he wrote that book, I don't know, when it was published, he left town. He had written some things about some rather prominent people in town. They weren't always the best. Anyway, they didn't like it, and these people he wrote things about had given money to the town for the library. And they used to own the big tavern down here, one of them was a businessman in Chicago. Well, that book was in the library for a while. I have read it, I was quite young when I read it. But at that time I guess libraries weren't taken so good care of as they are now, and that book disappeared, along with *The Boy Captive of Old Deerfield.*
>
> Well, at this time that this *Sweet Auburn* was written, my grandfather used to live in North Leverett. And he rode a bicycle to Springfield. The police stopped him and said, "Don't you know you're supposed to have a bell on that bicycle?"
>
> Grandpa says, "No, I don't know very much of anything. I came from 'Sweet Auburn.'" . . . So that was his venture into town.

"Sweet Auburn," Hartt's poorly disguised version of Leverett, evidently had a reputation for insularity, for the countrified naiveté of its inhabitants. But, as Dunbar's story about her grandfather suggests, that reputation also supplied locals with a ready retort to such exemplars of urban quick-wittedness as the Springfield police—or, for that matter, writers like Rollin Lynde Hartt. As Sweet Auburnites set themselves and their village apart from nearby urban enclaves, they gave voice to a form of exoteric, or outwardly directed, awareness and savvy.

Loyce Dunbar's story does not tell us whether or not her grandfather actually avoided the logical consequences of his encounter with the Springfield policeman. What it *does* tell us is that Sawmill Valley residents were well aware of their reputation for rural ignorance and knew how to make rhetorically advantageous use of that reputation. In Loyce Dunbar's "Sweet Auburn" anecdote, "city people" such as the policeman and the itinerant writer are outdone by a seemingly self-effacing hayseed. Loyce Dunbar's grandfather, and the village life he represents in the anecdote, exemplify traits which Richard Dorson, in his discussion of "Yankee Yarns," describes as vital aspects of native New England wit. On the one hand, the grandfather can be said to play the role of a greenhorn, or, in Dorson's words, "a fool, an ignorant countryman, baffled by urban ways" (*Jonathan* 70). "On the reverse of the shield," as Dorson puts it, a man like Dunbar's grandfather also can be considered a self-deprecating version of the Yankee trickster, "A scheming knave and a fertile prankster who matche[s] wits against a suspicious world" (78).

Like Dunbar's anecdote, the folklore of the Sawmill Valley villages is the product of a dynamic convergence of seemingly contradictory regional mentifacts. On the one hand, Sawmill Valley villages undoubtedly *were* less advanced technologically than places like Springfield; their lack of urban amenities made locals feel that they lived at an enormous remove from the complications of town and city life. But distance from such things as traffic laws did not prevent valley residents from being self-consciously aware of the faster pace of life in certain surrounding communities. By the turn of the century, at any rate, the conditions of village life may have given valley residents a sense that their rural "isolation" was something of a badge of distinction. Self-consciousness of this sort is not the result of insularity *per se,* but of interaction and engagement with the "outside." In combining the "greenhorn" and the "trickster" tendencies of the village Yankee, Loyce Dunbar's grandfather manifests seemingly opposed qualities. Yet, as these qualities coincide, they create the terms of regional identity in the folklore of the Sawmill Valley.

As we have seen, the folklore of village life in the Sawmill Valley at the turn of the century was predicated upon the relatively widespread perception that informants' particular settlements were small worlds unto themselves. This perception certainly had some basis in historical actuality. Each of the valley's settlements did have its own school. Two of the villages—Moores Corner and North Leverett—had their own general stores and post offices. To the extent that this separateness came to be deployed in an exoteric context, as an ironic and ideologically charged witticism ("I don't know much of anything. I came from 'Sweet Auburn'"), however, it was essentially a construct, a rhetorical strategy.

As if to point to their perceived singularity, Sawmill Valley residents often drew a sharper distinction between their own villages and the other settlements within the town of Leverett than they did between their region and the towns surrounding it. Because of impediments to transportation created by topography, valley people felt that even the townspeople in the southern part of Leverett lived lives entirely separate from their own. "In those days," according to Clifford Blinn, "people didn't travel very much. And if they went anyplace they had to go by horse and buggy. And so there was, you know, local schools. Each little district had its own school. Each little district had its own store."

As Clarissa Truesdell LaClaire and her husband Clifford LaClaire discuss Leverett's degree of decentralization, they underscore the local conceit:

> CTL: Leverett used to be a very separated town. . . . North Leverett and South Leverett, or, it's now called the Center, we didn't know anything about each other. . . .
>
> CL: Well, years ago they was separated because they had no transportation. The only thing you had was a horse and buggy, or horse and sleigh. North Leverett had their own school, Moores Corner had their own school, East Leverett had their own schools, and they were more or less separated, you know. . . . Kids didn't associate with one another. . . .
>
> CTL: I've heard Forrest Briggs [a nonagenarian former resident of the Sawmill Valley at the time of this interview, now deceased] say many times that he didn't know anything about people in Leverett when he was growing up.
>
> CL: People didn't travel so much. Her father [Rev. Arthur Truesdell] did more traveling on foot than any man probably living. Unless it was Abraham Lincoln. He . . . used to go up over the mountain all the way from Leverett, over Brushy Mountain to Moores Corner. Loved to go through the woods.

Arthur Truesdell apparently was a notable exception to the regional norm. Most of the men and women who lived in the Sawmill Valley, according to local lore, were disinclined to travel more than a few miles from their villages.

Vernon Aiken, who has lived all his life in North Leverett, tells an anecdote reflecting the Sawmill Valley's self-conscious attitude toward its own separateness: "I remember my dad coming home from Town Meeting [in Leverett Center] when they first talked about plowing the roads—they never used to plow the roads, you know. And this fellow up to Moores Corner said that they wanted to appropriate some money to plow the roads, and some of them was against it. He said, 'Well, . . . I think you ought to plow the roads,' he says. Says, 'We pay taxes same as you do in Leverett Center. We'd like to come down there and see what's going on.'"

For all the townspeople who, like the man from Moores Corner, felt strongly that the roads linking the northern and southern sides of Leverett should be kept open, there probably were as many who were entirely content that the distance be maintained. The space separating one village from the next occasionally was a hindrance to smooth travel and commerce, but it also was a basis for honor, at least for those who lived on the northern side of town. Separate villages connoted full autonomy and at least the trappings of self-sufficiency. The short distance between one end of town and the other had a considerable effect on valley residents' sense of regional boundaries. "When I was a child," says Loyce Dunbar, "North Leverett was another country."

Even *within* the Sawmill Valley, where no equivalent of Brushy Mountain stood between the main settlements of North Leverett and Moores Corner, residents drew clear distinctions between the two villages. Loyce Dunbar, who spent her early childhood in North Leverett, remembers clearly delineated parameters: "See, all I remember about Moores Corner, I used to walk up to my grandmother's. I'd stay overnight and go to church up there with my aunt. . . . Dad and some of us children would [usually] go to North Leverett church. . . . [But] my grandparents, the Glaziers, lived there [in Moores Corner]. You see, after you crossed that brook there by where the old Richardson Road comes down . . . anybody who lived on the other side of that brook lived in Moores Corner, and that's where the children went [to school]. And then anybody this side of the brook, [their children] went to the North Leverett school."

Village allegiance almost always was stronger than any other form of geographically derived identity. For better or worse, most residents of Sawmill Valley villages paid relatively little attention to the fact that they were citizens of particular towns, too. Willy Stone and Robert Ripley, whose family homes on Chestnut Hill happened to be on the Montague side of the town line, thought of North Leverett as their village. Robert Ripley went to school—as the law required—in Montague Center. But he was a member of the North Leverett church for years and left that church only when he became a member of the Moores Corner congregation, which was even farther away from Montague than North Leverett was. For these two families, their affiliation with upland culture and topography was more important than any connection they had with the mostly low-lying town of Montague.

As centers of regional commerce, education, and social life, the villages of the Sawmill Valley were sources of a sizable proportion of local lore. Decentralization, as residents of turn-of-the-century rural New England practiced it, helped to create strong village institutions and traditions. Villages were small enough to promote a high degree of social interconnectedness among residents. "When I was a child, they were quite close-knit communities," says Loyce Dunbar, speaking of North Leverett and Moores Corner. "You knew everybody. You'd see a horse go by and you'd know [if] it was new, or a new wagon." Under such circumstances, it comes as no surprise that each village, and the valley as a whole, cultivated a lively set of oral traditions centered on village life. In a community where every family knew, interacted with, and, often enough, intermarried with its neighbors, storytelling tended to focus on so-called "town characters," whose perceived eccentricities served as starting points for the bulk of village oral traditions. Other village traditions revolved around local institutions and pastimes that helped create and uphold the sense of kinship and community to which so many local residents refer.

Village-centered traditions underscore the distance (both psychic and geographical) of valley villages from neighboring communities and so reflect informants' collective sense of autonomy and removal from the outside world. The plethora of stories about town characters, as well as about aspects of a highly *localized* social life, suggests that valley residents of the early twentieth century cultivated a view of themselves as unmindful of events and trends beyond their immediate boundaries. Even so, the self-conscious construction of these same traditions, and their dependence upon the existence of an extraregional Other as a basis for comparison, suggest that the regional mindset was as much the product of a strained engagement with the conditions of modernity as it was the outgrowth of local residents' belief in their own self-sufficiency.

"Some of the Town Characters We Had Around": Notorious Village Eccentrics

Two or three weeks into my field research in the Sawmill Valley, I discovered an interview question which almost always elicited prolific responses and, as it happened, also brought smiles to the faces of my informants. Seeking stories about people who lived on the margins of regional social life, I chanced to ask Loyce

Dunbar and her niece, Charlotte Glazier Abbott, if they recalled any "town characters" from their childhoods. The list that poured forth provided me with more than a series of accounts; it also equipped me with an indispensable list of questions and starting points for future interviews with other informants. All I had to do was to mention a particular name to an informant, and I would be regaled with all manner of stories and anecdotes pertaining to village life. By the time I had completed my interviews, the list of town characters had grown to considerable length. Moreover, each of these characters gradually took shape as an accretion of the storytellers' diverse perspectives, experiences, and interpretations. If the broad variety of stories about individual town characters prevented any final picture from emerging, it also provided me with an important lens for taking the measure of regional lore as a whole. The oral narratives associated with town characters, spun as the result of countless personal encounters, second- and third-hand accounts, familial traditions, and general-store bench yarns, comprise a significant portion of village-centered lore in the Sawmill Valley.

Presumably, the stories that a given community tells about its inhabitants have some bearing on that community's sense of itself and of its boundaries. New England folklore has featured eccentrics and "originals" as far back as the seventeenth century. Published collections of New England folklore, such as B. A. Botkin's *Treasury of New England Folklore* and Richard Dorson's *Jonathan Draws the Long Bow*, devote entire sections to the idiosyncratic characters who, over the years, have formed the basis for a broad assortment of localized anecdotes, legends, and tall tales. On the one hand, such characters clearly represent deviations from the accepted regional behavioral norm; in so doing, they "present residents with a real dilemma," as folklorist Diane Tye puts it (194). On the other hand, because their departures from communal practice appear to be not only widespread but also integral to the life of rural New England villages, eccentric town characters can be said to comprise the regional *standard.* According to Botkin,

> New England localism bred "characters" and a distinct feeling for "characters." New England provincialism (in the best sense of the word) rests on the twin pillars of family tradition and the tradition of the New England town or village and self-government (symbolized by the town meeting). Both traditions, especially in rural communities, foster respect for strong characters and distinctive traits and talents, which became part of the social heritage. . . .
>
> New England also had its rebels and non-conformists who carried the Yankee spirit of self-dependence—the right to be one's self—to extremes. Violating the sense of order inherent in the neat, tight pattern of New England farm and

> village life, their revolt broke through the surface of New England constraint to give us . . . a host of minor recluses, cranks, self-constituted prophets, reprobates, vagrants and ne'er-do-wells (103–4).

In their apparent violations of the village order, town characters like those found in the Sawmill Valley make regional stasis an impossibility. Whether their deviations come as the result of "outside" influences or "internal" implosions, town characters speak to the fact that village life in rural "pockets" like the Sawmill Valley was the result of struggle and inequity, as well as consensus. The reputations of eccentric and alienated town characters often evoke what Tye refers to as a fear of strangers on the part of local residents (195). Town characters present a challenge to regional homogeneity. They threaten the *status quo.*

Crucial to the existence of such characters in folklore is the fact that their lives, as we know them, actually are the sum of *other* people's impressions of them. Within the oral tradition, town eccentrics were the products of their neighbors' efforts at typecasting. In this sense, the town character, like other aspects of the region's folk heritage, was essentially a fictional construct and, as such, a product of his or her neighbors' projections. Whether or not the stories told about them are factually true, town characters reflect the existence of certain *communal* truths. In their tendency jointly to ridicule and to celebrate various town characters, local tradition-bearers betray a telling ambivalence. They enunciate the yoked self-consciousness and pride that is the defining feature of Sawmill Valley folklore.

Local exemplars of eccentricity and deviance owe their existence to a self-perpetuating cycle of hearsay and personal experience. Some local-character anecdotes exist independently of their tellers' first-hand experiences; such anecdotes have their origins in a cycle of telling and retelling which established the character as an aspect of communal, rather than purely personal, imaginative property. Clifford LaClaire's own recollection of a town drunkard is rather dim, but this does not stop him from recounting dialogue:

> Used to be a man by the name of Cutter, lived up there in Dudleyville. . . . He was a huge man, they tell me. I can just about remember seeing him out in front of the house on a stone step. But anyway, he used to go to Wendell Depot to get his groceries. And they sold alcohol down there, I guess. But anyway, he'd come home—he'd be gone all day long—he'd come home with no groceries. And Mrs. Cutter would say to him, "Jerome, where are the groceries?"
>
> He'd say, "One man can't remember everything."

> But sometimes, I've heard the story [told], they found him in a ditch. His hair would be frozen in the ice. They'd take a jackknife and cut his hair off and put him in a sleigh and take him home. Those are stories, you know, hearsay. I don't know, I wasn't there. But evidently, he liked his booze. The only place they had any alcohol was in Wendell Depot. So he hooked his horse up to the sleigh, go to Wendell Depot, spend the day, forget the groceries.

Within the relatively restrictive cultural milieu of the Sawmill Valley at the turn of the century, irresponsibility of the sort enacted by Jerome Cutter appears to have been relatively rare. In my interviews, I heard of only two other reputed drunkards—the resident of a Moores Corner "tenement" who, according to Joe N. LaClaire, was fond of boasting that he never had spent a single Thanksgiving out of jail, and the immigrant, recalled by LaClaire's sister Marion, who "burned himself up." Nonetheless, the drunken exploits of these three men evidently were a reliable source of entertainment for their less carefree neighbors.

Based on what Gertrude Carey remembers about him, Jerome Cutter's trips to Wendell Depot were more than sources of comic relief for local residents; like Pap Finn and a host of other town drunkards, Cutter could be brutal as well as funny. According to Carey, Cutter "had his little horse and buggy, and he'd be away drinking. And he'd come back and he'd find one of his boys in the [Moores Corner] store. And he would grab . . . one of those ropes that they hitch a horse to. And the metal, you know that you hitch it with. He would give that kid an awful licking. That was hard to see."

It is the combination of comedy and terror, as well as of hearsay and eyewitness report, that makes Jerome Cutter into a veritable town character. Because we know nothing of his own perspective, these accounts of the drunkard's deviations from the regional standard of acceptable behavior tell us much more about the ways in which local-character anecdotes are fashioned and what they mean to the community than they do about the actual individuals being described. To his more controlled neighbors, Jerome Cutter represented a dangerous departure from the rigors of regional and familial self-sufficiency. More responsible and enterprising citizens would not have squandered their families' small holdings of cash on store-bought liquor. Nor would they have disciplined their children in public and, in so doing, displayed their lack of control over themselves, their families, and their circumstances. The character of Jerome Cutter manifested the local oral tradition's fascination with men and women who violated the valley's strict codes of behavior concerning liquor and proper control of "one's own."

Like those about Jerome Cutter, anecdotes about Fred Cole, a Moores Corner blacksmith, also combine hearsay and informants' own personal experiences. "Did you ever hear of Fred Cole?" Gertrude Maynard Carey asked me.

> He had a blacksmith's shop . . . on the Gutter Road. . . . He was kind of a town character. He always lived alone. He was kind of a short, little man. He used to do the clog dance when we'd have . . . a social or something. . . . He always had [on] a lot of shirts and coats and things. One would be below the other. And he'd have safety pins all down the front, no buttons. I don't know if he had any relatives or friends—he was always just alone. . . . They said when he was young that some of the fellows—I don't know whether it was in this town or where—but they had, they were cutting his hair and they cut his ears. There were . . . little strips there. . . . I don't know where that happened but I hope I didn't know the ones that did it. . . .
>
> On . . . Fourth of July . . . they would take signs, put them down on the place where he had his [shop] . . . and mix the signs all up. . . . But we always liked to have him go to the things, though. He'd walk along, kind of a shuffle, he didn't stand up very straight. He had a long beard, and he was always carrying a lantern everywhere he went. He was the town character.

Fred Cole's eccentricities—particularly his torn earlobes—had a notable impact on Moores Corner's oral traditions. Four other informants provide anecdotes concerning his presence in the community and his status as a tragic victim of Fourth of July pranksterism.

For all his apparent oddity, Fred Cole would not figure as prominently as he does in the local lore if he were merely an anomalous exception to the overall regional pattern. If he had been the sole representative within the Sawmill Valley's village lore of what Richard Dorson refers to as "general eccentricity" (Stahl 285), it is unlikely that people would have paid such close attention to him. In fact, his outward strangeness provided his less eccentric neighbors with a springboard for expressing their own inner departures from the perceived local norm. As Diane Tye suggests in her study of local-character anecdotes from Amherst, Nova Scotia, eccentric men and women offer residents of close-knit rural communities a sanctioned means of accommodating—even welcoming—the Other in their midst (195). Despite her or his apparent oddity, the nonconformist who becomes a town character is incontrovertibly a *member* of the regional group.

Loyce Dunbar remembers seeing Fred Cole in Moores Corner, but one of her most vivid "memories" of the blacksmith actually is something she remembers her mother's saying to her about him:

> At that time they [the Moores Corner church] had just a big cup and they passed it around. . . . Everybody would drink out of the same cup and take a little sip. My mother says: "I'd never go up there and drink out of the same cup [that] Fred Cole drinks out of." He was a dirty man. . . . It's too bad—he was kind of simple. He . . . lived alone. He didn't keep himself too clean. His ears, the boys caught him one Fourth of July night—I can remember my father telling about some kids that did it—and they took shears or something and cut his ears. So his ears hung down like little fingers. I can remember . . . he was an old, old man when I remember him. And I can remember asking Dad how it happened. He says that was what they told him, that that was what happened to him.

A significant portion of Dunbar's account is the result of her own experiences and, in particular, her memory of the blacksmith's mutilated ears. For all her description's relevance as a personal narrative, it nevertheless relies most heavily upon an oral tradition that predates her. Both her parents were sources for her account of Fred Cole's place within the village life of the Sawmill Valley. This suggests that, at least by the time Dunbar was born, the blacksmith was not merely an unusual neighbor; he had become an integral aspect of the region's orally transmitted repertoire of folklore.

If the people who told stories about Fred Cole did not agree on every detail of his role as town character, they reached a consensus of sorts on his apparent lack of "brightness." Harriet Bourne LaClaire remembers that children were much taken with the blacksmith's unwitting status as an object of ridicule. "We as kids used to get quite a kick out of Fred Cole," she says. "We had to go down there every day. And he'd always write on his door: 'I hare gone a hay.' He couldn't spell *have* and *away.*"

Vernon Aiken's account does not refer to any misspellings on the blacksmith's part; to Aiken, the note's pronouncement of the obvious was clear enough manifestation of Fred Cole's abnormality. Cole "was . . . kind of an odd character. . . . He'd leave a note on the door—he says: 'I'm not home, I've gone away.'" The question begs asking: what could be so remarkable about the blacksmith's inability to spell properly or his habit of posting redundant notes regarding his whereabouts as to inspire such a level of detail among those who remember him? How could such a character and his perfectly benign deviations from local standards of "brightness" come to occupy such a considerable position within Moores Corner's local lore?

Like their counterparts in many other areas of the world, young people in the Sawmill Valley derived amusement and adventure from tormenting the people within their communities whose behavior and bearing diverged from the accepted norm. I asked Loyce Dunbar and her niece, Charlotte Glazier Abbott, about the people picked on by two generations of valley children. The ensuing dialogue between the two of them suggests that, considering the community's relatively small size, village oddballs accounted for an exceptionally large proportion of the valley's personal anecdotes:

> CA: Dave Nichols . . . lived . . . not too far from where Rob Ripley, in the area, lives, only out toward Montague way, on the upper side of the Sawmill River there, down through Montague woods. He had a little camp. . . . Dirty Dave, they called him.
>
> LD: Wasn't that the one that ate the rats?
>
> CA: He ate ants. He used to try to get us to eat ants, chocolate covered ants, or just ants. . . . And then there was Clestin Torrey. He lived down across. . . .
>
> LD: Well, Clestin—of course, when we were children if a person wasn't normal we just said they were stupid. Well, a lot of these people, like Clestin, I wondered, they might have had a shock in their life sometime and something could have happened.
>
> CA: We didn't know that then. I don't think we knew that then.
>
> LD: He was a strange character, I remember that.
>
> CA: We used to pick on him. And Harry Wentworth was another one they used to like to pick on. This is as kids.
>
> LD: Yes, that's right. Harry Wentworth and Sam Graves—they were kind of mean to some people anyway. They really were.
>
> CA: And then there was "Psych." And I can't remember his name. . . . He was real mean. . . . They were some of the town characters we had around here when we were kids. And we used to get milk at Vernon [Aiken]'s and they would come and get milk. And as kids we would pick on them and throw snowballs or run and hide. That kind of thing.

The *number* of town characters who appear in this relatively short exchange is not the only noteworthy aspect of the discussion. Even the dialogue's seemingly innocuous discrepancy—the question it raises of whether Dave Nichols ate rats or ants—suggests that the valley's repertoire of character anecdotes was as much the product of rumor and imagination as of first-hand experience. Town characters were no mere individuals; their lives within the local lore were—for better or worse—the property of the community at large, with its telling fixation on deviance.

Indeed, for all the tormenting they received at the hands of local children, town eccentrics like Fred Cole, Clestin Torrey, and Dave Nichols often were viewed by their neighbors as integral members of their respective villages. In the days before large-scale institutionalization of the mentally handicapped became common in rural areas like the Sawmill Valley, local pride had a good deal to do with the locals' self-proclaimed ability to take care of their own. In the Sawmill Valley, the existence of eccentric characters helped local residents to cultivate a sense of themselves as autonomous. The fact that the valley supported its town eccentrics enabled locals to keep outside incursions to a minimum.

Robert Ripley fondly remembers one "deaf and dumb" man, whose habits always struck him as odd: "He could never talk nothing [imitates grunting]. He used to go back and forth on the main road with a shotgun all the time. . . . I don't know if he was hunting or just carrying it. [You'd] see him going down, he always had a shotgun with him. [If a] dog would bark out at him he would swing right around and point his gun, but I never heard him shoot it or anything. Oh boy, he was a nice old chap."

Sil Glazier, a deaf and dumb man recalled by Harriet LaClaire and Joe W. LaClaire, as well as by Ruby Hemenway, was well known throughout the valley, not only for his eccentricity but for his ability to exceed the normal boundaries of knowledge and awareness. "If he went anywhere," Ruby Hemenway says, "he would sign and shut his eyes or put his fingers on his eyes." In any case, he was looked upon as a local, not an outsider.

As long as a given eccentric could participate productively in some aspect of the region's economic life, he[1] was—according to the local lore, at any rate—happily tolerated. Despite his lack of "brightness," for example, Fred Cole as a blacksmith earned his neighbors' approval. At the very least, Cole was a sufficiently valuable member of the community to have been taken care of in "his last days" by local resident Farley Glazier. Glazier evidently was a devotee of local self-sufficiency and of caring for one's own. "He used to take in a lot of the town poor," explains Vernon Aiken, ". . . after they didn't have a poor farm." At the Aiken home, Dave Nichols—the reputed rat- or ant-eater—often was welcome. "He was a good old guy," Aiken says, and a man not too proud to accept a free lunch from time to time.

Local eccentrics apparently elicited their neighbors' charity, as well as their cruelty. In a paternalistic form of proprietorship, the valley's farmers and householders did more than poke fun at the region's behaviorally errant residents; in many cases, they helped support them. Ultimately, the coexistence of affection and ridicule within the oral tradition's treatment of the valley's eccentrics bespeaks an overall ambivalence that local people felt in regard to their own relatively strict codes of behavior.

Vernon Aiken's story about another town eccentric brings the community's paternalism to bear on Clestin Torrey's humorous display of an embattled, if not entirely astute, business approach. In my view, the anecdote underscores the relationship of stories about local eccentrics to regional beliefs concerning economic, as well as social, self-sufficiency. The anecdote views Torrey as an unfortunate in need of his neighbors' protection, a man whose mental deficiencies necessitated that he be supported by the valley's more competent citizens. Even so, Torrey *attempts* to appropriate the quick-witted trading tone that he hears all around him. Despite his neighbors' helpful ministrations, he possesses a jagged edge that resists easy encompassing. I had asked Vernon Aiken my "town character" question. "I could tell you about one of the fellows that lived down below here," he responded, "Clestin Torrey."

> He, poor fellow, he was kind of retarded. But you know, he was never put away anywhere, he always, his folks took care of him. When his folks died he kind of took care of himself, self-supporting, you know. But he didn't always know all he should. He worked with Rob Glazier and . . . Rob used to sell him ice for his refrigerator. So he come down the road one day, a piece of ice on the wheelbarrow, and he come up in the yard and my dad was out there and he says, he says: "You haven't got a very big refrigerator, have you, Cles?" He says: "That isn't a very big piece of ice."
>
> "Oh," he [Clestin] says, "sixty pounds."
>
> My father says: "That don't weigh sixty pounds. Where'd you weigh it?"
>
> "Oh," he [Clestin] said, "Rob guessed at it."
>
> My father says to me, he says: "Go get the ice tongs." He says: "Weigh that." So I weighed it—thirty-five pounds.
>
> I says, I says: "Thirty-five pounds," I says, "take out five pounds for the tongs."
>
> He [Clestin] kind of looks around, making sure nobody was around. Says: "I ain't going to take out nothing," says, "he cheated me all summer."

"They Had All the Money in the World" (But Never Spent It): Village Misers

In the case of an "oddball" like Fred Cole, a well-regarded attribute—determination, for example—apparently had given way to what Dorson calls "general eccentricity," turning an otherwise "normal" person into a town character, a subject for local storytelling. In this sense, the Sawmill Valley eccentric represented a logical extension of the regionally sanctioned pattern of individualistic self-reliance; he or she was an apotheosis of the same pattern that impelled a crippled man like Old Mr. Miller to cut cordwood for a living and inspired Loyce Dunbar's Grandma Hemenway to use her spare time to make Panama hats and sell blueberries.

Stubborn individualism, however, was not the only means by which a person could distinguish herself or himself within the community and achieve town-character status. In the folk tradition of the Sawmill Valley, good business sense—or lack thereof—was an indispensable index of good character. The regional ideal of self-sufficiency required local men and women to live frugally, trade skillfully, and be wary of threats to their financial integrity. Much as determination could be extended to become "general eccentricity," a particularly frugal householder or shrewd trader easily could evolve, within the community's oral tradition, into another type of town character, the miser. Thus, "stinginess"—another of Dorson's behavioral categories defining local characters—was an attribute that repeatedly evoked village-centered storytelling in the Sawmill Valley.

In some cases, an entire repertoire of personal anecdotes exists concerning particularly miserly or frugal town characters. In other cases, the anecdote's traditionalism has more to do with the way its subject matter conforms to a regional standard than with the number of tellers who can repeat or reinterpret it. The latter form of traditionalism applies to the following anecdotes about a North Leverett woman, provided by Loyce Dunbar:

> I think Mildred Rice was a character in our end of town. She had . . . three boys and a girl. She'd be over to the neighbors'. Buster'd come leave their kids off, and she'd say, "Oh, I got to go home, I got to go home, I made some doughnuts this morning [and] I didn't lock the pantry door. If I don't get home the kids'll have the doughnuts all eaten."
>
> She owed old Muriel Bourne five dollars for some groceries she had bought. She come down [and] she told Muriel: "I can't pay you. I lost that five dollars I was going to pay you and don't know where it is. When I find it I'll pay you." Two, three months later she found it in the bureau drawer. They had all the money in the world, but after they put a penny in their pocket, they didn't want to take it out.

Because valley residents placed such a premium on a family's ability to support itself on relatively minuscule earnings, it could not have been easy for a given individual to know how far to take her or his frugality. Given the tenuous distinction between business acumen and stinginess, the transition from acceptable to forbidden behavior probably was seamless. Overly zealous adherence to the regional standard of self-reliance could work to an individual's disadvantage and quickly turn him or her into a subject for storytelling.

Among the Sawmill Valley's notorious misers, Baker Whipple certainly was the least materially advantaged. Whipple, who lived by himself and had no immediate relatives in the vicinity of the valley, was by local accounts a victim. His eccentricity certainly made him ready fodder for village storytellers, but it was his apparent reluctance to spend money which created the greatest stir among the residents of North Leverett and Moores Corner.

Robert Ripley's anecdotes about Baker Whipple are, for the most part, based upon personal experience, although they undoubtedly are the products of the storyteller's participation in a communally based code of behavior as well. Baker Whipple took frugality to unprecedented extremes:

> He had a little shanty . . . and he owned a house there [at the corner of North Leverett and Richardson roads]. When I knew him and got old enough to know who he was, he lived in this little shanty. And Baker Whipple had more money than anybody around. And he lived there alone in the little shanty. He'd go to Greenfield on the train . . . or electric car and buy bread, a whole bag of it. Stale bread—he didn't buy new bread—stale bread, day or two old bread. And cookies and other stuff, same thing. And he'd take it up there. . . . In 1919 there I used to run a grocery cart. Some day[s] I'd come this way and I'd go in there and he'd be there in a room full of smoke. He . . . burned his fire with the lid off. Said it didn't use so much wood that way.

Unable, for whatever reasons, to determine the proper boundaries of frugality, Baker Whipple evidently had taken leave of his senses by the time Robert Ripley encountered him in his smoke-filled shanty. Whether he "had more money than anybody around," however, is difficult to ascertain. Like Mildred Rice, Whipple was presumed to be well off, for the simple reason that few of his mystified neighbors ever saw him spending money. The lengths to which he went in order to avoid expenditure apparently indicated that he had large—albeit invisible—holdings of cash. Again, the pattern that holds sway in the Sawmill Valley seems to replicate one that Tye locates in her Nova Scotian community, where solitary eccentrics within the regional group were reputed to be sitting on large amounts of inexplicably attained cash (193–94).

Baker Whipple's frugality was perfect subject matter for local storytellers. As with Robert Ripley's set of anecdotes, personal experience figures in some people's descriptions of Whipple, but such experiences almost always are informed by second- and third-hand accounts, too. Vernon Aiken heard about Baker Whipple's habits from an older relative of his: "My grandfather bought a house down in North Sunderland. Baker said he didn't have no place to go. My grandfather was alone, so he let him have a room down in the basement.

But there was a pantry down there, and the baker used to come along with a horse and wagon. And so Baker would buy the day-old bread and he'd slice it right up and he'd lay it up on the pantry shelves. And see, if it dried up it wouldn't mold, so he'd leave it there for a day and then he'd turn it over and he'd eat that stale bread and drink tea. That was his living a lot of the time."

The fact that Baker Whipple subsisted on dried bread and tea was viewed, by and large, as a perfectly harmless eccentricity. His frugality and solitary life were, at the very least, logical extensions of the premium placed upon self-sufficiency by the entire regional group. As for Baker Whipple's idiosyncrasy, Vernon Aiken says, "Seems like my uncle said once that he had a bad fever one time that affected his mind." Loyce Dunbar speculates as to whether "he was an educated man and might have had a shock." Dunbar continues: "He was harmless. I don't ever remember hearing him say a cross word or anything."

At least one resident of Moores Corner *did* take offense at Whipple's laying up of free food, however. Because "he was real tight with his money," Vernon Aiken says, Whipple would "go to every auction there was, because back then they'd give you a little bag. Usually it had a doughnut in it and some crackers and cheese. And he'd go through the line, you know, two, three times, you know, stuff his pockets full. And he'd eat plenty when he was there. And so Cliff LaClaire's father [Everett LaClaire] was there at the auction. I was there, I was just six years old, I guess. . . . And he got his pockets full and Everett slipped up beside of him with a cup of coffee and he poured it right in there, [in] his pocket, on top of the crackers and cheese."

"What a cruel thing for anybody to do," says Loyce Dunbar about the auction incident, which she had not seen but had heard about. "I do remember him coming to auctions and putting the food in his coat pocket," she explains, but so did other people who happened to be hungry.

The likelihood that Baker Whipple was imposing a form of impoverishment on himself "by choice," rather than by necessity, seems to have fueled Everett LaClaire's unfriendly prank. Indeed, the notion that Baker Whipple's outward display of frugality may have masked enormous wealth never has been put to rest among Sawmill Valley informants. Because he was not seen laboring in the woods or farming a plot of land (in other words, practicing the regionally sanctioned code of hard work), Baker Whipple's survival was an enigma. It was the thought that he might be getting something for nothing that fed the rumors that circulated about his freeloading.

In and of itself, wealth was not looked upon as scandalous in the villages of the Sawmill Valley. People like Mildred Rice and Baker Whipple—who seemed to subsist on less than their neighbors did—were far more likely targets of rumor-mongering than the valley's one *outwardly* prosperous couple. The Bournes of North Leverett (who apparently were unrelated to the Moores Corner Bournes) were *different* from their neighbors, but no one ever would have accused them of concealing their wealth. Loyce Dunbar remembers them:

> Every morning he'd [G. V. Bourne] walk up by the house, you know, leisurely. He had a gold-headed cane. Always looked dapper. Had, you know, a hat and she had a big hat on. Then in the afternoon you'd go by, she'd be sitting in that swing out on the porch. And I went over to her house once because . . . Mrs. Bourne said she had a saddle that she would like to sell me. And so I says [to my father]: "Come over with me and we'll go look and see what the saddle looks like." So Dad went over. Wow.
>
> We got in that house. They had a spiral staircase. She took me upstairs. Oh, it was a very elegant saddle. It was a sidesaddle. Dad says: "You'd never like a sidesaddle, you don't want that." So we never bought it. That's about as close as I ever got to her. But they made quite an impression on the North Leverett people. Because they were different, you know. They were people that had traveled. And she of course had a maid. And I think she was a live-in maid, which very few people had at that time.

People who regarded reputed misers such as Mildred Rice and Baker Whipple suspiciously and simultaneously turned an amused but accepting eye on outwardly prosperous citizens like the Bournes evidently had failed to resolve their own doubts regarding the place of money in an ostensibly self-sufficient community.

The wealth of the North Leverett Bournes certainly was not derived from farming or from lumbering; for better or for worse, it had to have come from "outside" the immediate boundaries of the Sawmill Valley. Neither the Bournes' "leisurely" approach to life nor their elegant furnishings were attributable to the landscape-based occupations pursued by so many valley residents. Nonetheless, the couple was held in awe by local people and exempted from the region's dominant code of behavior. More than anything else, G. V. Bourne is remembered by those valley residents who recall his presence in North Leverett for having been the first local inhabitant to welcome the technological advances of the twentieth century and buy an automobile.

In contrast, "town characters" for whom the valley's reverence for frugality had become a sort of compulsion were held to be "different" enough to warrant gossip at best and outright persecution at worst. The crucial difference between the Bournes and characters like Baker Whipple or Mildred

Rice was that the latter could not be dismissed as imposters. Despite his lack of blood relatives in the valley, no one could deny that the austere Baker Whipple *belonged* in the community. If his frugality posed a threat to local residents, it was because it mirrored—albeit in an exaggerated way—their own obsession with subsisting on next to nothing.

"Skinflint" Watson, Village Tycoon

The ambivalence characteristic of valley residents' attitudes toward wealth (or reputed wealth) is nowhere more evident than in the case of Moores Corner's foremost trader at the turn of the century, J. Wesley Watson. To his friends and relatives in the community, J. W. Watson was a model of energetic entrepreneurship, as well as of morally upstanding and philanthropically generous citizenship. To his detractors (who to this day exist among my Sawmill Valley informants), however, Watson was a cheapskate and a swindler, a man whose pennies were saved at the direct expense of his less successful neighbors. Friends and enemies of the trader agreed on one thing: Watson was the "kingpin" of Moores Corner. His character plays a pivotal role in the folklore of the Sawmill Valley, because it speaks directly to local people's often contradictory views concerning the accumulation, possession, and expenditure of money. Within a regional milieu where self-sufficiency gradually was giving way to satellite status, an unquestionably successful man like J. W. Watson represented flux, adaptability, and—to some—exploitation.

It is difficult to find an informant whose account of J. W. Watson is not marked by some form of judgment. The most "neutral" report I collected came from Clifford LaClaire, but even his description evinces a sentiment that could pass as irony. Watson, according to LaClaire, "was a very strict businessman. If you owed him a penny, he wanted the penny. But if he owed you the penny, he'd pay you. That's the kind of man he was. He didn't—he trusted people. People used to come to his store there at the gristmill, right by the bridge there in Moores Corner. He would trust them, 'cause they all worked for him anyways."

Marion Watson Fleming, Watson's granddaughter, relates a specific episode from her family's lore which pertains to the trader's reputation for taking pennies seriously. Her story also echoes LaClaire's account: "Somebody paid grandpa, and it was, I think, one cent too much or something—he didn't have change. So he walked, came all the way home, he walked all the way down the hill to give them the change of one cent. He didn't have to do that. He said: 'If I owe it, I want to pay it. If you owe it, I want to be paid.'" If nothing else, the consistency of both LaClaire's and Fleming's versions of the penny anecdote speaks to Watson's prominence as a town character, one whose very identity in the Sawmill Valley was an outgrowth of his reputation as a businessman.

In the eyes of many of his neighbors, Watson was almost equivalent to money itself; every one of the quotations that the local lore attributes to him is in some way related to a business transaction. Bill Fleming, who married into the Watson family in the 1940s, recalls having been told this story by his neighbor, "Uncle" Henry Blinn, who—like many other local men—once had worked for Watson. The anecdote's "punch line" points to the centrality of cash as the basis of John Wesley Watson's relationships with other people. Blinn was helping the "kingpin" move a sawmill. Watson "said to Henry:

> 'I want to cut this place in half, so what we're going to do . . . we're going to start up on the roof. And I want you to get up there and take a saw and start sawing down. . . . '
>
> "So Uncle Henry got up there, and he was sawing away, and Mr. Watson was down there watching.
>
> "'Mr. Watson,' he [Blinn] says, 'I think that if we—'
>
> "Mr. Watson says, 'Henry, I'm paying you to saw, not to think.'"

Over the years, Watson's character has absorbed the lion's share of the valley's commerce-related lore. Even for his own family members, J. W. Watson's business dealings seem to have formed the core of his every act.

The Watson family itself always had stood out among its neighbors in Moores Corner. Unlike most of the village's inhabitants, the Watsons remained "up on the hill" far past the period of initial settlement; indeed, Watson's granddaughter, Marion Fleming, with her husband Bill, still lives in the old family house on the edge of Brushy Mountain. Bill Fleming, who heard many family stories from his mother-in-law, Verdie Watson, is a repository of Watson family lore. Bill Fleming provided some interesting details concerning John Wesley Watson's father, as well as the Watson house and property itself, as he and his wife talked with me in the old house's living room. Evidently, the elder Watson was no less an astute trader than his son, even when it came to money matters within the family:

> [John] Wesley Watson was the son of Amos Watson, who bought this area . . . in 1795 and built the first house within several years of that. That house is a little section in the middle of this house. The room that we're in now was built in 1880 by J. Wesley Watson. And an interesting thing is that Amos Watson,

> his father, turned over the house that was there and the land to J. Wesley Watson with a stipulation that he would have a room, with an outside entrance and a fireplace, and that J. Wesley Watson would supply him with all his needs, foodwise, medical and everything else, until he died. This was all great. But you know how long he lived? He was 97 years old when he died. . . . So we have five doors on the house because of things like this.

For all his apparent prominence as the patriarch of the Watson clan in Moores Corner, Amos Watson's reputation within the regional tradition pales beside that of his son. Amos seems to be an important figure in Watson *family* lore, especially as a precursor to his even more money-minded son. But John Wesley Watson and his exploits permeate the spoken traditions of the entire Sawmill Valley.

As Vernon Aiken tells it, J. W. Watson is remembered because he had more business initiative than any of his neighbors. While most of the settlers in the Sawmill Valley were content to farm their small plots of land and participate in some way in the region's lumbering industry, Watson saw fit to be a speculator. He aspired to manage the entire region's economy and a portion of its religious life as well:

> He was quite a . . . businessman. He had a big, big store in Moores Corner. . . . Of course he had quite a little property. . . . And he had a mill just beyond the old Moores Corner schoolhouse. . . . He had a sawmill down there. And he had a lot of acreage of land. I guess he farmed some and he had the lumber business and he had the store so he was quite a busy man. And he gave the land where the Moores Corner church is, 'cause he could look right from his house—back then it was clear and he could look right over and see the church. . . . He give them the land and nobody done anything about it. So he took one of his men, and they took one of these old scoops, that they used to dig cellar holes with, and his horses. And they started digging the cellar hole. Then people got interested.

It is difficult to know exactly why Watson had such a hard time building interest in the new church. But perhaps the trader's overall reputation as an imperious pretender to the village throne had something to do with local people's reluctance to join in his schemes.

Loyce Dunbar's version of J. Wesley Watson is not as even-handed as those of her neighbors. Watson's initiative, her account suggests, was the product of nothing less than greed. When I asked her what she knew of the village "kingpin," her response was an immediate indication that even the years that have elapsed since Watson reigned as Moores Corner's foremost town character have not erased the scorn which some local residents view him. When I mentioned Watson's name, Dunbar provided me with an energetic interpretation of the man's entire career: "Oh, 'Skinflint Watson!' . . . I can remember my grandfather talking [about him]. He owned all of Moores Corner once upon a time. I guess he cheated everybody that he could. . . . Maybe he did [donate the land for the Moores Corner church], maybe he was getting old and he wanted to be sure he went to Heaven or something, he might have given the land. . . . Now he owned mills up the river here, he owned houses, stores. . . . He was a very wealthy man. . . . That's all I know about Mr. Watson. I used to hear people say 'Old Skinflint Watson' did this and that."

Joe W. LaClaire's account of his father's tenure as one of Watson's employees affirms Watson's reputation as an exploiter: "My father worked there [in Watson's mill] thirteen years for a dollar and a quarter a day. . . . Ten hours. He done chores in the morning and milked the cows and took care of the horses night and morning besides. A dollar and a quarter." Taken together, Dunbar's and LaClaire's accounts are noteworthy for more than their completely unguarded indictment of Watson's motives. "Skinflint," the sobriquet that lies at the heart of Dunbar's description, points to the problematical operation of the regional ethic in the town-character anecdotes about Moores Corner's chief speculator. For valley residents, the character of John Wesley Watson evoked some of the same tensions and double standards elicited by far less ostentatious figures, such as Baker Whipple and Mildred Rice. While Baker Whipple and Mildred Rice, by reputation at least, held tightly to their money through frugal habits, J. W. Watson did the same by investing widely, pursuing varied financial schemes, and, at least by some accounts, swindling his neighbors. All three characters enacted the principles and tested the boundaries of regional self-sufficiency.

Even in the years before John Wesley Watson inherited the Watson property from his father, full-fledged self-sufficiency had ceased to be a viable option for the Sawmill Valley region as a whole. Valley farmers, householders, woodcutters, and sawyers who wished to cultivate and harvest only what they could use in their own communities may have outnumbered speculators like Watson; but, in the face of an increasingly market-oriented economy, they had little choice but to participate—as employees, primarily—in large-scale operations like the Watson mill. On the surface, J. W. Watson's initiatives and investments of capital seemed to fly in the face of local fealty to subsistence as a way of life. Ironically, however, they provided the only means by which valley residents could forestall their ultimate fall from economic autonomy. Whether or not the speculator actually cheated his neighbors is impossible to determine solely on the basis of local oral traditions. To the extent that his entrepreneurship was a controversial harbinger of economic and social change in the valley, though, it is easy to see how his character became a receptor for local misgivings about the region's participation in a market economy. Despite seeming to contradict the local ethos, Watson's scheming—like Baker Whipple's and Mildred Rice's frugality—actually epitomized the ideal of regional self-sufficiency. Without Watson's mill and Watson's store, the Sawmill Valley very well might have undergone economic eclipse sooner than it did. Local accounts which attribute virtue and good business sense to Watson speak to the community's approval of his enactment of such regional values as thrift and clarity of purpose. The recollections and accounts which depict Watson as the embodiment of selfishness and grandiosity, on the other hand, point to the tenuous nature of self-sufficiency as a regional standard, as well as to the direct effects that modernization has had on the regional group.

Watson's imperiousness reached its acme when the speculator reportedly made a proposal that Moores Corner be named for him instead of for the Moores, who had built the original millsite in the village center. Watson "wanted . . . to call Moores Corner Watsondale," according to Marion LaClaire Norwood. "And it even came out in the paper that the name was going to be changed, but for some reason it never was. . . . He practically run the town. . . . He had a lot of power, really. . . . Things were different then. You didn't go to Town Meeting to make all these changes."

"Oh yeah," says Watson's granddaughter, "he thought that [Moores Corner should be renamed Watsondale] at one time. . . . But he owned a lot of land around. . . . So I guess he figured he ought to have the whole place named after him."

Resistance to Watson's name-changing scheme apparently was sufficiently widespread to prevent it from taking place. The businessman's proprietorship of a large portion of village real estate, as well as his role as the employer of many of its male residents, failed to translate into complete ownership of the village's sense of identity. Watson's questionable stature in the eyes of the community caused his proposal to seem even more pompous. For all his power and influence in the community, J. W. Watson's character seems always to have had a pathetic quality, a predisposition to unpopularity, disappointment, and failure which was incommensurate with his imputed status as "kingpin." Since his character, as depicted in the oral tradition, was the product not of his own words but of local people's recollections and anecdotes, it probably is safe to say that Watson's two sides were acute projections of his neighbors' ambivalence concerning their region's social and economic fate.

Midway through his career, Watson was profoundly affected by an accident that—according to the local lore—changed the course of his life. Bill Fleming provides the most detailed description of the event and its aftermath. Like other local residents, the Watsons

> had horses and cows and whatnot, so they did their own haying and whatnot. And he [J. W. Watson] was haying and he was missed and Marion's mother, who was a little girl at the time, went down in front of the house, and the horses were there and he was laying on the ground. And something had happened and he had bent over, and one of the horses kicked him in the head. And that fractured his skull—in fact, we have a little bottle, they say, that the bones that they took out of his head [are in]. And from that time on—up until then he was quite an industrious and a go-getter of a man—from that time on . . . he had periods of being depressed and periods of elation. And in these good periods, he did great things; and in the depressed periods, he just didn't do anything. So . . . that was one of the things [that] led to his—well, it wasn't a downfall, because he still owned all of this land and stuff.

The Watsons themselves were not the only local people to attribute John Wesley's increasing fickleness to his "horse-kicking"; the entire community participated in telling that story. "They said that when he was kicked by a horse that he . . . would have these spells that he was going to do this, and he'd switch right around," Harriet LaClaire told her interviewer in 1967.

"I do remember them telling about that," Ruby Hemenway says in the same interview, after having described one of many ill-begotten schemes of Watson's "later" period. Watson "at one time bought up land, a lot of it . . . around Lake Pleasant up on Montague Plain, and set up a lot of catalpa trees, didn't he? . . . [And] they pretty nearly all died. You would have thought they would have grown. They were set up like a big forest. Oh he had acres. He had some scheme, I don't know what, and all the trees pretty nearly all died."

"So many of his plans fell through," explains Marion Norwood about the period after the accident. The lesson to be learned from the stories about Watson's accident and its aftermath seems to be that arrogance and greed must meet with folly and disaster. Unfortunately for the less daring residents of the Sawmill

Valley, the small, subsistence-level endeavors that posed the only local alternatives to Watson's scheming were due for a period of decline as well.

Cultivating "Stick-to-it-iveness": The One-room Schoolhouse

Sawmill Valley residents' descriptions of the roles that the village schoolhouses once played in the lives of valley children suggest that the area's schools once provided training that was not only rigorous, but also highly practical. Moreover, these schools saw to it that their students completed what few years of formal education they received well prepared to serve, among other things, the cause of regional self-sufficiency.

Such a view contrasts markedly with what valley dwellers perceive as present-day educational degeneration. In response to Audrey Duckert's question as to whether "one teacher had all nine grades" at the Moores Corner school, Harriet LaClaire and Joe W. LaClaire elaborate upon the local conviction that small, decentralized schools were better than large ones. Children in the one-room schoolhouses "learned more than they do today when one teacher has just one grade," says Joe W. LaClaire. Harriet LaClaire tellingly compares her own generation with that of her children: "You know, some of my children come home and some of them can't spell. They can't write a sentence." In conjunction with such nostalgic glosses, some local descriptions suggest that the one-room schoolhouse had its shortcomings, among them the fact that teachers in such schools rarely had enough time to attend to all their students' needs. Nonetheless, as regional permeability grew, due to such things as automobile travel and the urbanization of nearby Connecticut Valley towns, the one-room schoolhouse increasingly became a precious—and precarious—memory for local residents.

As if to underscore local faith in a decentralized cultural life based upon geographical locale, the settlers of the Sawmill Valley located schoolhouses at nearly every one of the region's major crossroads. Because transportation posed the greatest challenge to smooth functioning of a rural educational system, valley residents tried to minimize the distance that any given child had to travel to school. With schoolhouses located at Moores Corner, North Leverett, and (for a time) at the main intersection on Chestnut Hill, pupils rarely had more than a mile to travel for their education. There were exceptions, however; Robert Ripley, who lived not more than a few yards from the Leverett-Montague town line in Montague, had to spend at least half an hour traveling by horse and buggy each way to attend the Montague Agricultural School in Montague Center. Moreover, those few Sawmill Valley children who sought education past the eighth grade often had still greater distances to cover. Ruby Hemenway explains that, in her father's day, "if they wanted to go any further [than grammar school], they had to go to an academy." Upon completing high school in Montague Center, Hemenway attended the Normal School in North Adams; she was one of the few valley residents to do so. Education beyond grammar school was by no means a commonplace attainment for the young men and women who grew up in Sawmill Valley villages. "Most of the country people didn't go onto higher education," says Hemenway; "they went to work." Some, like Vernon Aiken, spent a short period at high schools such as the New Salem Academy and then quit: "I thought I wanted to go to work instead of going to school," Aiken says; "[there'd] have been plenty of work left if I'd finished my schooling."

Whether they went on to high school or not, almost all the children who grew up in the Sawmill Valley spent their first years of school in one of the region's one-room schoolhouses. As today's informants portray them, these schools provided crucial lessons in independence and self-sufficiency, giving pupils a sense that they had to rely on themselves for the better part of their activities. Local descriptions mention the teachers almost as afterthoughts. Gertrude Carey explains conditions at the Moores Corner school: "We probably had thirty-five, forty students. And they had nine grades then. All the grades and one teacher. . . . No helpers or anything." Typically, the older students (especially girls) were put to work as supervisors of the younger ones. "In our later years," recalls Marion Norwood, who also attended the Moores Corner school, "after, oh, like sixth, seventh, and eighth [grades], we mostly helped the younger children. And if we had time we read our own books. But the teacher really didn't have time for us anymore. She was busy with the younger ones."

One-room schoolhouses were run as microcosms of valley households. While the older girls were responsible for watching and teaching the younger children, the older boys often were held responsible for the physical maintenance of the schools. "We didn't have any of the modern things they have today," says Vernon Aiken. "She [the teacher] would assign two boys to see that there was wood in, for the fire. Two more boys were assigned to go to one of the neighbors and get a pail of [drinking] water." Clifford Blinn, who lived across the street from the Moores Corner schoolhouse, remembers having to "get up and start the fires in the morning." Willy Stone, who walked from his family's farm to the Chestnut Hill schoolhouse every morning, earned fifty cents a week as the school janitor. "I had to get there early," he remembers. "And if it was a really cold day, we'd all—rather than sitting on our seats—we'd gather around near the stove."

Pupils in the one-room schoolhouses were allowed to structure their own leisure activities as well as the time spent on lessons. "The children who stayed there [at school] at noon," explains Ruby Hemenway, "didn't have any teachers to come outside during play hour and supervise them. They went all over Kingdom Come."

"We used to play around in the woods," recalls Willy Stone. "We used to go quite a ways from the school sometime in recess or noon-hour." The pupils' high degree of freedom during recess had benefits, at least for those boys who went on to become lumbermen. As a result of all their wandering, Stone says, the boys at Chestnut Hill school "knew them woods pretty well."

In Ruby Hemenway's day, the children who went to one-room schoolhouses in the Sawmill Valley earned a collective reputation for self-sufficiency. In 1984 Hemenway gave an interviewer a particularly illustrative anecdote concerning her days at the Montague Center High School:

> A great many of the businessmen of that period had very little formal education. They depended on their own ability and their own stick-to-it-iveness to get what they needed. . . . They had to work things out for themselves. . . .
>
> Our principal Eva Tower . . . was known by a great many people and was an excellent person, a person of good moral worth and taught us children that way, and she was quite put out with some student in mathematics. Because they came to class and said no, they couldn't do their work, they didn't know how. And she was disgusted, she jumped on them. She said: "You don't know how! You don't work and dig in and try to solve your problems yourself. You just sit back and say you don't know and ask the teacher or somebody to show you how. When you come to class the next day you just say you can't." She said, "You ought to work the way the North Leverett pupils do." She said they have been in a school where they had one teacher for every grade, all the grades together. And if they couldn't do anything, she didn't have time to show them, as she wanted to. She said the pupils had to dig in and work and work and find a way themselves. And not depend on somebody else. Oh, she was so disgusted with anybody who gave up too quickly.

Whether or not children in the North Leverett school actually were able to "solve their problems" in mathematics or any other subject, the conditions under which they were schooled instilled in them and their families a sense of regional pride that grew out of their educational *disadvantages.* Like valley farmers who "preferred" their rocky pastures to rich holdings along the Connecticut River, the parents of children who attended one-room schoolhouses had convinced themselves that simplicity and "stick-to-it-iveness" were the keys to self-sufficiency.

Stirring Up the Neighbors: Serenades and Fourth of July Pranks

Even as they adhered to a regional standard based on hard work, many residents of the Sawmill Valley during the turn-of-the-century period did not hesitate to partake in their fair share of festivities. Marriages within the community often involved "serenading" a newly married couple or "stealing" the bride.[2] On the Fourth of July and during the preceding night, local people observed the anniversary of the nation's independence by, among other things, collaborating in pranks and traveling to a big community picnic and dance at Locks Pond [Lake Wyola].

Maintaining folk customs such as these allowed valley residents at the turn of the century to honor their collective identity as a tradition-oriented, predominantly Anglo-American region. When serenaders hounded newly married couples, they were doing more than simply having fun; they also were asserting the community's control over its individual members and their domestic lives. Likewise, when young men engaged in Fourth of July pranks, they were not merely testing the limits of their targets' patience. Pranksters occasionally chose as their victims men and women who, for better or worse, had trouble fitting the local mold. The Fourth of July prank, whether intentionally or not, sometimes called attention to the points at which the seemingly immutable terms of regional identity no longer could be taken for granted.

Despite at least one recent attempt to revive the practice, serenading, according to Robert Ripley, "gave out . . . after the automobiles came in" to the Sawmill Valley. As Jan Harold Brunvand observes in his *The Study of American Folklore,* "Noisy harassment of brides and bridegrooms is an old custom in the United States" (202). But the serenade *per se,* in which, according to Brunvand, "a crowd of friends would awaken the bridal couple with 'rough music,' shouting, subjecting them to various indignities, and pestering them until the husband set up a treat" (202), was no ordinary form of harassment. Like any other folk custom, it proceeded according to a specific set of culturally ingrained guidelines. Moreover, as some local informants' descriptions suggest, the serenades were of particular importance to the community at large, because they brought together a significant number of local people who otherwise might have been busy tending to their work-related tasks. Although the recently married couple was the primary "target" in a given serenade, the custom itself was communal in nature. It is no coincidence that the practice of serenading faded at exactly the same "moment" as other forms of regionally oriented folklife.

Serenades were thoroughly *regionalized* in the Sawmill Valley. Their proper celebration relied upon certain local accouterments. As participants approached the married couple's house, they made as much noise as possible. For this purpose, certain objects were indispensable; as Loyce Dunbar's description of one serenade she attended as a child suggests, sawyers' tools were especially useful:

> Of course my dad worked in a sawmill. Well, he had one of these huge, huge saws, . . . and in the center of it of course there had to be an opening where, I don't know, an iron bar or something went through it. My dad took that saw, and I don't know who went with us. . . . They took that saw, put the stick through it. And they marched up to the house. Of course there was lots of other things—tin pans being beat, horns blown, bells. . . . I can remember them whacking on that saw. Well, what a racket it made. We never took the saw home. We took it back down to the edge of the road. And that saw stayed there for years and years and years.

Notwithstanding that all the other features of a serenade tended to vary, the millsaw was ubiquitous. As one sawmill after the next ceased operations, beginning in the 1920s, extra saws must have been in plentiful supply. If they no longer could serve the region's waning lumbering industry, at least they could be put to use in its social rituals. The fact that this particular serenading party abandoned its saw at the side of the road suggests that the tool functioned more as a useful relic than as a piece of operable machinery. As Robert Ripley notes, the hammer-saw combination was better suited (if not louder) than any other piece of the serenaders' equipment: "They would have a wagon, and on the wagon were the side boards, and they'd put a stick across and hang a big millsaw . . . one of those big, circular saws. . . . And you'd get on each side with a hammer and they'd come down the road. You'd hear them when they started and they'd pound that hammer and there'd be a whole crowd behind them. That was a serenade." Because noise was the key to gathering a large crowd, serenading parties worked to improve their racket-making capabilities. As Willy Stone explains, running a pipe through the center of the saw was preferable to using a dowel, "'cause a pipe would carry the sound more than a piece of wood through it."

After gathering a crowd, the typical serenade party made its way to the home of the wedding couple. The group would stand out in front of the house until the bride and groom made an appearance. "You wanted to have plenty cigars and candy handy" if you were "hosting" such a party, says Robert Ripley.

For all its apparent festivity, a serenade did not warrant suspending the rules of gender-based or religious propriety. "Usually the bride and groom would come out and they'd give candy to the women and pass out cigars to the men," explains Vernon Aiken. "Once in a while, one would be against tobacco and so he . . . had a huge burlap bag full of peanuts." There is no mistaking the relationship between the valley's serenading customs and a veiled recognition that the wedding night was equivalent to the moment of sexual initiation. "Sometimes, if they could get into the house," Aiken recounts, the serenaders would "remake" or "short-sheet" the marriage bed. Pranksters would "put the sheet halfway down. When they [the bride and groom] went to get back in bed they'd strike the barricade." The emphasis was on creating as many frustrations for the married couple as possible.

Bride-stealing, in which friends or relatives of the bride took her away on a ride by horse and buggy or automobile for a short time, was calculated especially to upset the groom, as well as to reassert the community's proprietorship of young women. Vernon Aiken recalls one episode in particular: "When Andy and Rachel LaClaire got married . . . they had the serenade, off of Briggs Road. And some of the girls got Rachel on one side and got to talking to her. And they got her in a car and drove off with her. They didn't often do that, but once in a while they'd take the bride and take her off somewhere. And they'd be gone for half an hour or more. And then they'd bring her back. But I remember her husband was, he was kind of angry when they stole his wife on him. One of his brothers says, 'Oh,' he says, 'they'll be right back. Don't get stirred up.'" Despite its intention to amuse, bride-stealing rarely failed to upset the new couple. Like so many other age-old folk practices, it struck an important chord for both the newly married pair and the community at large.

For bride-stealers and newlyweds alike, the practice constituted a symbolic form of dalliance and served to enforce the community's stake in even the most intimate affairs of its members. From one viewpoint, the serenade was essentially a benign initiation ritual, a means by which the married couple's neighbors and relatives celebrated the bride's and the groom's attainment of full-fledged adulthood and membership in the community. For all their harmless intentions, however, the men and women who formed a serenading party were asserting a form of (symbolic) control over the newlyweds. Serenading customs expressed the Sawmill Valley's steadfast belief in the primacy of the village as the rightful arbiter of local social life. Those customs declined in conjunction with a concomitant decline of the village as the central factor in the construction of regional identity.

Not unlike more palpable elements of village folklife, such as one-room schoolhouses, local festivities were *institutions.* Indeed, in the Sawmill Valley, as many informants indicate, the Fourth of July elicited an actual rearrangement of village landscapes. Even those who wanted nothing to do with the holiday's rampant pranksterism had no choice but to accept the fact that, on the night before the Fourth, young people were given free rein to impose as much (controlled) chaos as they could upon the appearance of the villages. Robert Ripley explains that, on the night before the Fourth, "You never left any machinery or anything out or around, [or else] it would be up on the church lawn in the morning." Inevitably, even families who had taken precautions to hide their machinery would find it on the North Leverett church lawn, if not on the roof of the local store or somewhere in the Sawmill River. "Nothing ever happened to the people who" pulled such pranks, recalls Loyce Dunbar; some aspect of the local mentality welcomed this inversion of the usual order. As Joe W. LaClaire tells an interviewer, "nobody controlled" the young people who pulled Fourth of July pranks. Instead, "they just let them go."

Among the people who grew up in the Sawmill Valley during the first twenty years of the twentieth century, one target of Fourth of July pranks is remembered more vividly than any of the others. Even people who were too young to have seen it happen recall being told about the time when one North Leverett resident had his wagon taken from his house. "The boys got Dr. Fiske," says Loyce Dunbar. "He was a little short, plump man. He lived next door to us. And I don't know why they took his wagon. I don't know. Perhaps because it was near the millpond, I don't know. But they took it—of course, this is a story that was handed down to me—and the boys took it and dumped it in the millpond. I don't think it was ever taken out."

Evidently Dr. Fiske was an easier target than most, because other informants remember another episode. "One year they put old Dr. Fiske's buggy on top of the . . . [North Leverett] store," recalls Robert Ripley. I asked him how "they" managed to do such a thing. His answer does not quite explain the mechanics of the procedure, but it does indicate the custom's magnitude as a focus of social activity, as well as suggesting why it eventually disappeared from local practice:

> MH: How'd they get it up there?
> RR: I don't know. But it was up there in the morning. Of course there was

> probably twenty people around there, young folk all from Moores Corner and all around here. They'd go up, they would ring the church bell. They'd lock the church up so they couldn't ring the bell and they'd break the door. And they rung the bell 'til they cracked it. Well, they didn't ring it, they hit it with a hammer and cracked it. Well, anyway, as I say, quick as the automobiles come in they didn't have to look for entertainment for themselves. But, well, we've had mowing machines and horse rakes and everything else up there. If you couldn't find it the next day you went up to North Leverett. Wagons. And that was a big day for the young folks. The night before the Fourth.

Willy Stone provides a unique form of corroboration for Ripley's account. On one occasion, he was among the "young folks" who stole a Ripley sleigh. "One time we . . . got a sleigh down to Lucien Ripley's," Stone says, "and towed it up the road. It was a tar road then, and it left two beautiful lines of fire, going up the road. . . . We towed it all around town, because it was so pretty, them streaks of fire coming off of the runners."

Stealing a wagon was an activity that required more than a few individuals to orchestrate. As Willy Stone describes them, such large-scale pranks required full participation from just about all the young men in the region. In front of the North Leverett "church, the hall steps were made of wood, you know, they's all one piece. Well they'd take them and a bunch of men would put them up on the store roof, you know, on the porch roof of the store. And then, if they could, they'd get a buggy and put it right on the ridge pole of the store. You know, a gang could do those things. Half a dozen or eight or ten men, and then it was quite a job for the single man to get them down the next day. But usually the guys would come and get together and take them down for him. I remember that. They done it just for fun, and [to] stir people up a little." Like serenades, Fourth of July pranks involved a combination of limit-testing behavior and tacit approval by village elders. The young men who lifted a farmer's wagon onto the store roof "usually" could be counted upon to return the next day to help take it down.

For all the fun and cooperation that characterized many Fourth of July pranks, the custom could take some unpredictable and occasionally frightening turns. Many informants' recollections of pranks are marked by nostalgia for a now-departed age of innocence, when village residents all knew and interacted with one another on a friendly basis. Some of the stories that locals tell about Fourth of July pranks, however, suggest that, amid the amusement and community spirit, there existed at least a measure of coercion, if not outright persecution. When Fred Cole had his ears torn by village pranksters in Moores Corner, it is unlikely that he was a willing victim.

Sawmill Valley folk customs, such as serenades and Fourth of July pranks, illuminate a form of inequality inherent in, but also threatening to, the intricate patterns of village relations. For some members of the community, the "friendly" harassment that certain village practices brought to bear on families and individuals may have seemed harmless and good-natured. But for others, the sorts of celebratory activities that were necessary for the smooth functioning of regional folklife proved patently oppressive. Customs such as Fourth of July pranks can be interpreted as forms of containment, means by which young men's impulses to break the ordinary bounds of proper behavior could be indulged temporarily; as long as the unwritten "rules" were followed, no harm was done. But because pranks so often relied for successful completion upon raising their victims' ire, they often had the effect of further isolating individuals who already had been labeled "characters," testing the limits of their patience and forbearance.

As folklorist Barre Toelken writes in his book, *The Dynamics of Folklore,* many pranks are intended to establish a given group's proper boundaries, to set "outsiders" apart from "insiders," or at least to allow questionable "insiders" opportunities to prove their potential for "inside-ness." Toelken is discussing the pranks that seasoned loggers pull on greenhorns in the Pacific Northwest, but his remarks may be applied to pranks in general. Loggers' pranks must allow, at least hypothetically, for the existence of three groups: "The insiders who perform, the strangers who know little or nothing, and the local outsiders, the new workers who—by means of pranks—become insiders. Each of these audiences is essential: the very fact that the stranger knows nothing about the process helps to strengthen the esoteric sense of heightened participation in a special group. And the victim, to cease being a victim, must try and move as quickly from the outside audience category to the inside audience, thence to become a performer to other audiences" (114).

As applied to the Sawmill Valley and its Fourth of July pranks, such a description would cast as "insiders" the young men who stole wagons. "Strangers"—people who are not natives to the region—need exist only in theory, but their existence is vital because, even in its absence, it helps bolster the regional group's sense of identity by defining its outer limits. "Local outsiders," people like Fred Cole or Dr. Fiske, are the least reliable participants in local pranks. Unlike greenhorn loggers, some of the victims of Fourth of July pranks in the Sawmill Valley were neither able nor willing to conform to the village standard. Their permanent existence at the psychological center of the community's folklife—as the indispensable targets of its limit-defining pranks—emphasizes the essential permeability of the regional folk group. Certain locals, whether by choice or by circumstance, never made the transition from "outside" to "inside," despite the fact that they had spent all or most of their lives in the Sawmill Valley.

When she was telling me the story about Dr. Fiske's wagon being dropped in the North Leverett millpond, Loyce Dunbar asked if I had ever heard about the doctor's daughter, Miss Edith Fiske. Although a number of locals talk about the fun and games surrounding Dr. Fiske, none but Dunbar told me the story of another Fourth of July run-in, one which failed to come an easy resolution. Edith Fiske

> Used to be a schoolteacher. I don't know, to me, as I remember, I don't know, she was always nice to me. She used to take me swimming down at Buckmaster's Pond. . . . She was kind of quick-tempered, I guess. Her feathers got ruffled. Well, anyway, a bunch of boys were down in the road, midnight before the Fourth. I don't think they were doing anything, only hollering and yelling. I know I can remember hearing them tell she'd throw brooms at them. But anyway, she got mad this night and she got out the shotgun, she fired right straight into the middle of them. Why she never killed anybody I don't know. She . . . shot . . . the Grove boy. He lived up on Hemenway Road. And I think it was his knee. And he spent a long, long time in the hospital. His folks had brought it to court. Judge Ball was the judge at that time, and this is what I heard—that Judge Ball was a very close friend of Dr. Fiske, and Dr. Fiske was Edith's father, and nothing ever happened to Edith at all.

Based on this one account of the incident, it would be impossible to judge the entire community's reaction to Edith Fiske's having overstepped the bounds of "normal" Fourth of July practice. Even so, because Dunbar indicates that the story of the court case was one that she "heard," it seems safe to assume that the notion of a conspiracy between judge and doctor was a form of "hearsay," a product of communal speculation. Taken together with the fact that Dr. Fiske so often was the target of Fourth of July pranks, the account of the shotgun incident and the imputation of an alliance between a judge and a doctor suggests that class-based rivalry may have played a role in what targets were selected by "the boys," as well as the entire village. Although such rivalry certainly was not the only motivating force behind pranksterism, it is useful to note that even fun can have unseen purposes. In their effort to "stir people up," pranksters unwittingly revealed tensions lying below the surface of village life. The fact that Miss Fiske's case had to be heard in court, at a distance from the Sawmill Valley itself, suggests that the region no longer could contain animosities like those between "the boys" and the doctor's daughter.

Tucker Players and the "Money-making" Dance Hall

Residents of the valley did not always restrict their social activities to specific calendar events or days. Until automobiles began to offer them means of traveling to larger communities for their entertainment, many local young men and women of courting age participated in a form of folk play-party which they called "Tucker." For this type of entertainment, only a hall, a musician, and a certain amount of free time were required. Because Tucker parties could be incorporated into any number of community get-togethers, they took place on a fairly regular basis; those who attended them did not have to wait for special occasions.

In addition to the area's Tucker players, women and men who were less restricted by their church affiliations occasionally participated in actual dances, usually held in barns or occasionally in people's homes. Like the Tucker parties, these country dances typically were held at the end of various village gatherings—harvest suppers, holiday parties, and so on.

In the eyes of their participants, Tucker parties and country dances were ideal forms of community entertainment. They demonstrated the self-sufficiency inherent in the valley's social life, as well as the resourcefulness of local men and women who had turned geographical isolation to advantage. But in the years around 1915, when two enterprising valley men opened a commercial dance hall near North Leverett's main intersection, the Sawmill Valley's sense of autonomy as a social arena began to wane. To be sure, the dance hall's existence was by no means *responsible* for the gradual decline of region-specific play-parties and dances. In introducing an "outside" element into the local social life, however, it reflected a condition of regional permeability which was changing the Sawmill Valley's social and economic life.

The contrast between local memories of Tucker parties and of the North Leverett dance hall is one of the most intriguing features of the oral record of Sawmill Valley folklife. Tucker parties, which involved only local residents and strictly forbade liquor, epitomized regional innocence. Even those informants who were allowed to dance held Tucker parties in high regard as a wholesome form of male-female interaction and entertainment. Loyce Dunbar describes a typical game of Tucker and places it within an overall context of village social life:

> Oh they [Tucker parties] were a lot of fun. . . . Now they had them on both ends of the town. But they had different people to play different instruments. I think it, oh, Steve Maynard, I think used to play the fiddle for the Moores

> Corner Tucker players. And down here in North Leverett, Gene Glazier played the accordion. And we used to have oyster suppers, we used to have corned beef suppers. And probably baked beans. And of course the women were raising money for, I don't know what, probably the church. And so afterwards we'd play Tucker. Why, we thought it was so wonderful, you know. You probably have played or seen it done. You march around right and left and then somebody'd yell it. When you came to a girl that you wanted to lock arms with and march around the hall with, you yelled "Tucker!"[3] And then everybody had to pair up with the one that was opposite them.

For particularly religious players, Tucker was a perfect substitute for dancing. It featured the same music as the more conventional square dance, yet its rules were in keeping with even the Hard-shell Baptists' strict sense of propriety. Moreover, it reinforced the valley's sense of social autonomy and easily could be combined with church functions.

Local descriptions of Tucker parties liken them to any number of other dance and play-party patterns. According to Gertrude Carey, playing Tucker was "almost like [playing] the Virginia Reel." As Joe W. LaClaire describes it, Tucker was "a good deal like dropping the handkerchief." Evelyn Skerry compares Tucker to Portland Fancy, "where you're in . . . a circle . . . and you're marching around, two by two, and then you join hands and go counterclockwise, and grab hold of each one's hands." Whichever play-party or dance Tucker most resembled, players were quite self-consciously *not* dancers. "We didn't say 'dancing Tucker'; we'd say 'lets play Tucker,'" explains Loyce Dunbar.

Tucker "wasn't actually dancing," explains Ruby Hemenway. "Some of those very strict people would let their young people play Tucker, because it was only marching and it wasn't dancing."

Robert Ripley, who *was* "one of those very strict people," reiterates the distinction. When local people spoke about Tucker, or its equivalent, "Pound the Broom," "they didn't call that dancing. That's the only thing you could have up in the church hall in North Leverett. You could play Tucker and Pound the Broom, but you couldn't dance. I was brought up a Hard-shell Baptist and you didn't do those things." Even Hard-shell Baptists were allowed to participate in play-parties: "We used to play 'Pound the Broom.' It was the same thing [as Tucker]. You'd march around with couples. . . . And one in the middle. And he had a broom. Well, every time he'd pound the broom you got to shift partners, and that's the time to try and get one. Well, Tucker's the same thing. Every time you hollered 'Tucker!' you got to change partners. And that's the time you tried to get a partner. But they played by music, you know." Music was an important factor drawing people to the Tucker and Pound the Broom parties. Although none of the fiddlers and accordion players who orchestrated Tucker parties are still living, present-day informants remember them well. Whether they played for Tucker parties or for "real" dances, local musicians were in high demand in the days before radios and cars modified valley residents' social activities.

"Back in my grandfather's time," Marion Fleming explains, "they had dances at various houses. My grandfather [J. W. Watson] played fiddle, so he'd go 'fiddle for the dance,' as he put it in the diary."

Local fiddlers hired out to the families who hosted dances. "We had a neighbor who was a really good fiddler," recalls Marion Norwood, "Steve Maynard. And there were other ones in the neighborhood. I know they would go to people's houses that had the room . . . or even a hall possibly, and play for square dances and things like that."

Barns were popular dance venues. "I can remember up in Dudleyville . . . there was a huge, huge barn," recalls Clifford LaClaire. ". . . I don't know who owned it then, but there was a big barn up there and they used to have barn dances. I think that's where my father met my mother."

A few valley residents were in the habit of traveling a short distance out of town for one barn dance in particular. "Sometimes they would go up to Jennisons' in Wendell," recall Joe N. LaClaire and his sister Marion Norwood. According to Norwood, "They'd have usually at least two fiddlers and maybe a third one. And they met in a kind of a barn actually. And there was enough lights outside that some of them were outside. And they had a caller who called the numbers, and people really had a wonderful time, you know."

The key element in such dances was local resourcefulness. Musicians and dancers alike came from within the community. To judge from the oral record, music and dance styles tended to be uninformed by more popular urban forms. The overwhelming popularity of the fiddle well into the Jazz Age suggests that a distinctly rural style prevailed in valley entertainment.

Local dances' strictly regional orientation began to change in the years immediately preceding World War I, as the new North Leverett dance hall began to welcome often unruly guests from outside the valley. Robert Ripley describes the hall's inception: "Farley Glazier . . . used to have dances in his house, every winter. Just country dances. Just somebody'd come, play the fiddle, and they'd dance. And then he, that got so good he built a—there was an old tobacco shed down here, right above the shop, little shop over here. . . . There used to be a tobacco barn, quite a good-sized one. And they made it into a house and they put a stage in there and they had dances there every week for a while. . . . They had dances there quite often. They'd come from all over. . . . Of course I wasn't brought up to dance. Dance wasn't up the Baptists' line."

At least initially, local residents—most of whom were always in search of new sources of income—had few concerns regarding the new dance hall. If there was any symbolism in the conversion of a tobacco barn into a "money-making" dance hall, valley residents probably were too busy with their own economic struggles to take note of it.

For some local people, certainly, the dance hall was an exciting new source of entertainment. Loyce Dunbar, whose childhood home was no more than a quarter-mile from the dance hall, remembers going to it one night for a costume contest. Among other things, her story reveals that fiddle music had given way to a more contemporary style:

> The only time I ever went down there to a dance—at that time my father was working in the sawmill so he only would come home on weekends. And [my brother] Merle and I heard they were going to give a prize if you came in costume down there. The one that had the best costume. Must have been around Halloween, I don't know. So we both dressed up, got down there, and come to find out they weren't going to do the judging until midnight. Merle says: "I'm not going to wait any longer, I'm going home." He paddled up the road. . . . And Gene Glazier says to me, "Now if you want to get a prize you've got to get out there and dance the foxtrot." I never heard of a foxtrot. He says, "It's easy, I'll go out with you." He says, "Just make believe you're a fox and dance around like one."
>
> They gave me, I remember, a little box of chocolates. I was so tickled. . . . Boy, I was so glad to get home. I ran in the bedroom, showed my mother. She was in bed, of course. Showed her the chocolates I won. I don't think Merle won any prize. He didn't do any foxtrotting, I know that.

Dunbar is one of the few living local residents who describes an experience inside the dance hall. The two other informants who described the hall presented an outside view; they had been forbidden—or lacked the inclination—to venture near *any* dance, much less one that had a reputation for being raucous. "It weren't too many of the local people bothered to go there," explains Vernon Aiken, "because it was kind of a rough place."

From the local perspective, the dance hall was a "foreign" incursion into the heart of the region. The dance hall was an uproarious place, and its guests tended to be outsiders in search of a new, anonymous venue for dangerous behaviors. According to Vernon Aiken, "It was in Prohibition times, and fellows would go somewhere and buy moonshine. Then they'd come to the dances. And of course they'd tip a little too much and they'd get kind of rough. . . . They'd come from Millers Falls, Montague, Wendell. A few of the local boys, I guess, used to go there once in a while. But it was mostly people [who] wanted to get out of town where people didn't know them."

Apparently the combination of liquor, dancing, and thrill-seeking nonresidents doomed the dance hall venture to eventual degeneration. "They were getting drunk, knocking over the lamp," Loyce Dunbar remembers having heard; "they couldn't control them and there was much trouble." Farley Glazier and Ed Waterman, the men who built and ran the dance hall, apparently had allowed their desire for extra income to overrule responsibility to the regional group. In the hopes of making money by bringing an outside crowd into the valley, they had sacrificed their own, as well as a measure of the community's, integrity.

Money (or the inordinate desire for it) was a harbinger of trouble for a good many valley endeavors during the turn-of-the-century period. Loyce Dunbar supplies the following version of an anecdote indicating the connection between money and local unease. One night, after a particularly disruptive dance had come to its close and the usual midnight supper had been served, the proprietors "left the money in the kitchen in some kind of pouch, hanging up, and the back door of the kitchen was open and somebody took all of it."

The pouch, Robert Ripley explains, actually was "a leather satchel, [with] maybe fifty dollars in it." Farley Glazier had set about cleaning after the dancers "and he couldn't find his satchel with the money in it. Somebody stole it. 'By god,' Farley says, 'it won't do them no good. It's locked.'"

Vernon Aiken's version includes still more detail. Farley Glazier's wife "had . . . one of these old-fashioned handbags. It's got a little lock on the top and it's got a key. And somebody stole it. And old Farley told somebody, says, 'Just won't do them no good.' He says, 'It was locked and I just got the key.'"

Neither Robert Ripley nor Vernon Aiken ever had set foot in the dance hall, but as local residents both came by this one anecdote and its one line of remembered speech. Dunbar, whose "foxtrotting" experience comprised the extent of her direct involvement with the dance hall, also came by her description of the event in her capacity as a member of the regional group.

What about the event and Farley Glazier's remark could have been so compelling as to warrant its absorption into the local lore? Residents of the Sawmill Valley who for so long had prided themselves on their high degree of self-sufficiency and resourcefulness must have had misgivings about the presence of an intoxicated and generally unruly crowd in North Leverett. Farley Glazier's neighbors hardly could have failed to note that Glazier's efforts to earn extra income (at the region's expense) eventually had been foiled by his own inability to manage the chaos that he had invited into the valley. Overconfident of their ability to keep their enterprise under control, the dance-hall owners had not calculated the dangers inherent in loosening the bonds of a strict and mostly self-contained regional milieu. The desire for money had impelled Glazier and Waterman to open the dance hall in the first place. Evidently they had done quite well on the night of the satchel theft; but, perhaps because they were accustomed to a village social life based upon complete familiarity with one's neighbors, they were not careful enough to hide their cash. Like the region's often overprotective attitude toward its own identity, the case containing the cash was a sealed entity which, despite its apparent impregnability, was all too susceptible to being carried away altogether. Farley Glazier retained the key to his money bag, just as his neighbors held onto the trappings of self-sufficiency; but who could prevent the thief from ignoring the lock altogether and opening the bag by force?

Chapter 5

Question: What Happened to Regional Identity in the Sawmill Valley?

The modern-day Village Coop, at the center of Moores Corner, March 1999. Photograph by Janice Sorensen.

Answer: The Village Coop, among Other Things

Old-time residents of the Sawmill Valley differ in their interpretations of how and why their region made the final leap from relative self-sufficiency to inclusion within the larger cultural/geographical entity which, in this retrospective age geared to tourism, has come to be known as the *Pioneer* Valley. Some locals say that, by World War II, cultural life in the region had made an irreversible turn toward dissolution. While cars once been had common without entirely replacing horses, they now began to take the place of horses in every family, as well as in the valley's woodlots and fields. Moreover, the plowing of roads in the wintertime—which had been unthinkable in the days of sled use—began to make automobile traffic a year-round option. Automobiles, in turn, made it much easier for children to travel long distances to centrally located schools. Where once they had been educated in village-centered one-room schoolhouses, valley children, as of the early 1950s, were bused not only to the Leverett Elementary School in Leverett Center but also—as they reached their teens—to Amherst Regional High School. While once they had formed attachments primarily with their next-door neighbors, now, as a result of traveling to nearby villages and towns, they formed additional ties to children from other communities.

Gradually, the men and women of the Sawmill Valley began to think of themselves more as Leverettites or Montagueites than as residents of their particular villages. By the 1940s, travel from North Leverett and Moores Corner to Leverett and Montague Center no longer was restricted to Town Meeting night; instead, at least some locals engaged in such journeys on a daily basis. As more and more valley residents sought and found daytime employment in industrial towns such as Greenfield and Turners Falls, their farmsteads evolved into homes—places to which they returned from work in the evening and on weekends.

As industry itself began to wane in the Connecticut Valley, Sawmill Valley people found themselves serving yet another sort of economic master—higher education. The postwar expansion of the University of Massachusetts at Amherst touched the farthest reaches of rural Franklin County; a mere ten miles distant from the university, the Sawmill Valley quickly evolved into what some old-timers refer to as "a bedroom community for professors" (and lawyers and doctors). Even long-standing local families, who once never would have given academia the slightest thought as a source of employment, found themselves enmeshed in varied capacities in a university-oriented economy. Indeed, the largest employer in both Hampshire and Franklin counties is now the University of Massachusetts.

Today, dominated by the presence of the university and its attendant cultural forms, the entire Pioneer Valley continues to be territory where clashing worldviews compete for dominance. This is not to imply a simple squaring off of town and gown. Although cultural diversity certainly is more prominent in the demographics of the Connecticut River Valley than it was during the turn-of-the-century period, rural sections of the area remain predominantly white.

In the Sawmill Valley itself, change has come about in large part as a result of another sort of cultural shift. Inspired by the left-leaning "back-to-the-land" movement of the late 1960s and early 1970s, many young former urbanites and suburbanites have attempted in the Pioneer Valley and in the Sawmill Valley to recreate a form of communal, or village-oriented, existence. Ironically, their ideal is not so different from the lifestyle recalled by older locals.

Nowhere has this latest cultural twist been more apparent than at the center of Moores Corner, directly across North Leverett Road from the site of one of J. W. Watson's most ambitious enterprises. In 1875, Watson, former village "kingpin," opened a dry goods store right next to the Moores Corner schoolhouse. In its time, the store was such a prominent feature of local cultural life that, even though few of my informants ever had seen it (it burned down in 1909), many of them could describe it to me, based on accounts they'd heard from their parents. Despite the owner's stark, businesslike aura (Watson's aunt, who funded the construction, warned John Wesley against chatting with his patrons), so the story goes, the Moores Corner store evidently conducted a lively social as well as monetary commerce.

Another store took its place in 1918; thus, with a few interruptions, a store has been in existence in Moores Corner straight on into the present. Marion LaClaire Norwood, who ran the store for a time, describes its social function in the days when her mother was the proprietor: "It was very busy at one time. And I knew for many years the store was . . . supposed to close around five or six. . . . But if anybody needed something later, she'd always go down. . . . There was a big old woodstove in the middle of the floor, and, especially when the mail was coming in, they'd go down there and wait for their mail and sit around and talk."

These days, "they" continue to gather at the Moores Corner store, which now is called, alternatively, the Village Coop or the Leverett Shutesbury Coop. Instead of sitting around a woodstove, however, they sit in the "schmooze space" and eat BF's pizza and focaccia, or purchase their herbs, spices, and brown rice in bulk, or spin their kids on the low-tech merry-go-round in the broad yard out in front of the store and in front of the ruins of the old Asa Moore watermill.

The coming of the hippies, at least as it has been described to me by both old-timers and the hippies themselves, certainly was unheralded; in fact, it did not create much of a stir among the valley's eminently unflappable denizens. Fears of drug use and loose sexual behavior notwithstanding, many old-timers took a characteristically Yankee "wait-and-see" attitude. Many of the hippies, it soon became apparent, were more than willing to work, and work hard. Whether or not they were getting checks from mom and dad, they could be seen chopping their own firewood, building their own houses, and planting their own gardens. In a region whose keenest approval was awarded to those capable of taking care of themselves and the land around them, these newcomers obviously were to be taken seriously. Moreover, not only were they willing to do challenging physical labor, but a few also obviously had a propensity for business. This became apparent especially in the early 1980s, in the wake of the Shutesbury selectboard's decision to deny the local natural-foods buying club access to the town's community center.

Marion Norwood and Harry Norwood, the old-timer proprietors of the Moores Corner store, invited the cooperative to share the store's tiny, primitive storefront along the Sawmill River. The period during which the store was a shared entity has been described to me by both sets of occupants as stressful, crowded, and chaotic. A humorous highlight of this era, according to the Coop's founders, is referred to as "The Mayonnaise Wars," in which mainstream and natural-foods brands of mayonnaise vied, sometimes on an hourly basis, for the store's most visible display shelves.

Nonetheless, an alliance of respect (and convenience) was forged between old-timers and newcomers. The Coop's storefront was run by Dan Bennett, a drop-out Brandeis University philosophy professor and self-identified Marxist, and his partner, Julie Shively, who had been an active member of the antiwar movement at the nearby University of Massachusetts at Amherst. By the mid-1980s, as the Norwoods were approaching retirement, the Coop business was pulling in the lion's share of profits. By means of a more or less gradual and friendly transition, the LaClaire Store became the Village Coop.

A further transformation occurred in the early 1990s, when the Coop itself moved across the road to a much larger store, built with local money and participation. Old-timers were among the most active participants in this move, both as contributors and, perhaps more important, as laborers. Few of these long-time residents of the village shop at the Coop; their interest in and allegiance to the store apparently stems from their devotion to the *concept* of a village store—a locally run, rural outfit in a community which looks to surrounding towns for nearly all its business dealings. Evidently the old-timers take comfort in the store's historical legacy and in the fact that it offers a safe, local haven within a high-speed economy and social sphere, where locale often is rendered meaningless by franchises and highways.

The old-timers are not alone in privileging an invented past. Many of the newcomers (whose roots grow deeper as their children get older and their compost heaps become richer) are equally eager to replicate what they take to be a benevolent past, a sense of communal belonging which is tied to the land itself. Old-timers and newcomers alike have a vested interest in participating in what historian Michael Kammen calls "the American quest for consensus and stability" (14) in the face of perceived cultural dissolution and social decay. Each group commits acts of cultural invention which reflect its own particular ideological and economic interests.

Accordingly, the Village Coop answers many needs. It buys locally-grown produce from residents who are looking for a receptive market in troubled times. It sells cigarettes and ice cream, as well as tofu and medicinal herbs; it rents videos of both Hollywood blockbusters and experimental foreign films. For all its customers, in other words, the Coop provides not only goods and services, but ways to maintain cultural identity and comfort through commerce, consumption, and a shared sense of place. Like so many other "alternative" American institutions these days, the Village Coop tries its best to serve an increasingly diverse clientele, not only by pleasing as many different sorts of people as it can with its goods and services, but by promoting and adhering to a progressive inclusivity that in certain respects harks back to a time when ordinary activities like grocery shopping reinforced neighborliness and community.

In this respect, the Village Coop supports an updated but nonetheless consistent extension of turn-of-the-century regional identity. To the extent that it, too, promotes what Robert Dorman refers to as an "alternative route for Modernization" (25), the store is quite worthy of its location near the site of the old Watson store. Whatever his *motivations* might have been, the result of Watson's own endeavor was—for a time, at any rate—to promote the Sawmill Valley's agenda of self-reliance, to create a local outlet for trade. Across the generations, in other words, residents of the Sawmill Valley have sought to make their home region a more or less sheltered environment where, cognizant as they may be of outside events, they can experience a measure of (perceived) continuity with premodern and preindustrial village life.

In a sense, like "those who stayed behind" in Chelsea, Vermont, the residents of the Sawmill Valley—both at the turn of the century and now, as they approach the shift to a new millennium—have "experienced a sense of stability that elude[s] a good number of their contemporaries" (Barron 136). They have been afforded this apparent luxury as a result of several factors, not least of which has been the relative absence of cultural and economic conflict of the sort that characterizes not only most American cities but many rural areas as well. The residents of the Sawmill Valley at both ends of the twentieth century, for all their modernistic savvy and progressive ideology, have constituted a relatively homogeneous group, ethnically and culturally speaking. But the process of attaining that state of cultural homogeneity has been less simple than it appears.

Homogeneity, after all, can take shape only as a group of people distinguishes itself from other groups. It comes about through a largely silent process of sublimation, a *reactive* process. A homogeneous community can create itself only with an outside world against which to balance, or define, itself. And this balancing act, I have discovered, is no less interesting and indicative of the divergent sources of American culture than more overt cultural encounters are. It is always exciting when a research project such as this one yields results which are at variance with one's initial expectations.

When I began to conceptualize this study in 1990, one of the ingredients which seemed to me indispensable was cultural dissimilarity. Why should the folk region be any different from any number of other cultural matrices? Couldn't I take for granted that, since turn-of-the-century rural New England was populated by a relatively diverse set of ethnic groups, I would find signs of ethnic difference as well as inventive *defer-rence?* I knew, if nothing else, that in the Sawmill Valley French names were nearly as common as Yankee ones. As soon as I began interviewing the descendants of these Franco immigrants, I guessed, I would be able to tease out the elements of cultural diversity that inhere in regions. Franco Americans would tell me about their ancestors' adherence to French Canadian customs. Anglo-Americans would provide me with evidence of their original cultural allegiances. I would be challenged by the exciting task of unraveling the disparate strands.

I was wrong. I did interview descendants of French Canadian and Irish immigrants, as well as Anglos, in the Sawmill Valley. None of these people denied their respective heritages, but none betrayed any overt allegiances to ethnic origin, either. As for French Canadian customs, legend motifs, or any other outward signs of ethnic particularity, I came away empty-handed. I do not doubt that some rural regions of the United States do retain overt signs of ethnic dissimilarity. In the border regions of the United States, especially in the Southwest but also along the line separating Quebec from Maine, New Hampshire, and Vermont, examples of ethnic and linguistic dissimilarities continue to thrive. But the Sawmill Valley was never a site of tumultuous interethnic exchanges or coexistences. During the period 1890 to 1920, it *responded* to cultural dissimilarities and, occasionally, even incorporated them. The development of regional identity in the Sawmill Valley was not the result of Franco-American or Irish folk customs and beliefs having been interwoven with Anglo ones. Rather than retaining old customs and worldviews, the men and women who came to the Sawmill Valley in the years between its initial settlement in the late 1700s through the 1920s reinvented themselves, regardless of their origins, as natives of the region. The valley's few indicators of ethnic dissimilarity were sublimated in a regionalizing process by which "newcomers" evolved to become Yankees.

This process of reinvention involved no easy consensus. Certain questions bear asking. Why *didn't* Franco "newcomers" to the Sawmill Valley retain their Catholicism or their French language? Why were so many individual residents of the valley marginalized and accorded "town character" status? How is it that women, who by all accounts worked just as hard as men, appear to have been minor players in the development and cultivation of a specifically regional lore within the valley? The answers to such questions are by no means simple or uniform, but all of them center on a process by which one basis for identity (ethnicity or gender, for example) is supplanted by a more dominant perspective—namely, that of region. While the

Sawmill Valley's residents were by no means sealed off from neighboring regions, they managed nonetheless to ward off any sort of overt cultural admixture by inventing a version of themselves as socially and economically conservative Yankee holdovers. The main indication of cultural dynamism in the Sawmill Valley was local residents' *resistance* to change, their adherence to certain largely imaginative constructs—rootedness in the landscapes of the past, for example, and masculine self-sufficiency.

Banal stereotypes about essentialist multiculturalism are not supported by close study of places like the Sawmill Valley. Indeed, editorial-page commentators who draw alarmist comparisons between ethnic strife in the former Soviet Bloc and the allegedly increasing level of "Balkanization" in America might do well to visit with the elderly residents of America's many Sawmill Valleys. Such visits might help people distinguish one form of cultural strife from another. America certainly has experienced more than its share of interracial and interethnic bloodshed. But the processes by which a great many ethnic groups have been exposed to one another—at least in the rural Northeast—in many cases have involved less outright violence and oppression than cycles of pressure, sublimation, and assimilation. In her 1998 address to the American Studies Association's annual meeting, Janice Radway offers some useful insight on this matter. Recent scholarship in the field has "made a critical theoretical break with earlier [static] formulations of identity," she observes. "Sometimes (but not always) informed by post-structuralist understandings of the ways in which subjectivities are constructed, this work has detached the question of difference from various bodily, cultural, and geographical essentialisms and has begun to explore the complex intersecting ways in which people are embedded with multiple, conflicted discourses, practices, and institutions" (9). In other words, cultural encounters in modern America occur on multiple levels, and within these encounters bounded forms of identity are of much less importance than various acts of collusion, mixing-and-matching, and self-creation. That this book arrives at a similarly de-essentialized conclusion is the result of deliberate thinking, but the relative homogeneity of my subject valley, too, played a guiding role. In the Sawmill Valley, the relationships that Radway refers to as "intricate interdependencies" (11) were invisible largely because regional culture took shape in response to events and people on the valley's margins. Nonetheless, inasmuch as modernity forced locals to reinvent their culture by comparing themselves to neighbors seen and unseen, homogeneity became merely a superficial condition of their existence.

Acts of invention lie at the heart of any expression of cultural identity, from the dangerous notions of purity that motivate "ethnic cleansing" to the relatively benign impulses behind regionalization. What separates the men and women of the Sawmill Valley and other areas of rural New England from their less peaceable counterparts elsewhere seems to be an outgrowth of their adherence to an ethic which only gives the appearance of simplicity. For all their economic deprivations and self-styled humility, the settlers of this picturesque but hardscrabble valley made a deliberate decision not only to accept their lot in life, but to do so with full knowledge of what they were relinquishing in the process. In so doing, they may have deferred the violent acts of invention that still divide so many of the world's people.

To be sure, partisans of all manner of bloody causes have committed countless atrocities in the name of a homeland; allegiance to place in and of itself never has been a guarantor of virtue or peaceableness. In every nation in the world, zealots anchor their claims to legitimacy in various backward-looking ideologies. Such-and-such a people has a historical claim to the land; God Himself mandates another people's rigid maintenance of borders. Nationalism is built upon nostalgia. But nationalism is also a direct outgrowth of, and especially a troubled reaction to, modernity.

In the Sawmill Valley at the turn of the century, love of the land did offer locals a form of past-oriented legitimacy; whenever the men and women of Moores Corner or North Leverett glanced up at the remote heights of Brushy Mountain, they were looking at the heroic preserve of their worthy ancestors. But the folk traditions of the Sawmill Valley were no less strident in recognizing the facts of life in a changed and changing world than they were in their adherence to the standards of an invented past.

Each chapter of this book has addressed the regional group's inherent double consciousness, and such ambivalence is exactly what most militant forms of nationalism attempt to avoid. Indeed, the distinguishing feature of the Brushy Mountain tradition—to take the most obvious example of history- and hero-worship in the Sawmill Valley repertoire—is the mountain's wilderness, its core unpredictability. For every nostalgic memory of tree-shorn landscapes or anti-industrial lifters of heavy machines, the lore of the valley's farms and woodlots offers an anecdote like Robert Ripley's account of his neighbor's laconic acceptance of Chestnut Hill's stony outcrops or Vernon Aiken's story about Henry Mercier's defiance of the town welfare board. Likewise, local outsiders like Fred Cole and Baker Whipple prevented even the most isolationist of valley residents from achieving anything approaching full-fledged conformity; town characters offered evidence of the regional standard's inherent instability and susceptibility to internal fragmentation. Yankee stick-to-it-iveness notwithstanding, the regional culture of the Sawmill Valley—and, by extension, regional cultures in other rural areas of New England—was too heavily invested in the psychological and economic conditions of twentieth-century life to be wholeheartedly reactionary or intolerant of change. The valley's culture provides an illustration of a distinctively future-oriented and American form of tradition—one that is, as Simon Bronner describes it, "appropriate to a mobile, modernized society" (479).

Unsentimental devotion to the local landscape offered residents of the Sawmill Valley a means of coming to terms with modernity without entirely yielding up their determination to uphold what they took to be the exacting standards of their pioneering predecessors. Having relinquished their boldest claims to self-sufficiency, the men and women who inhabited the land between Brushy Mountain and Chestnut Hill gained another, perhaps more valuable, form of legitimacy: the right to participate in (as opposed to simply observe) the inevitable transformation of their world. In what I suspect was typical New England fashion, they carefully withheld their enthusiasm. Like Loyce Dunbar's grandfather on his visit to Springfield, they claimed—on the basis of their rootedness in the land—not to "know much of anything" of the surrounding world. Ironically, it was that same sense of belonging to place which caused them to tell stories that prove otherwise.

Appendix
About the Informants

Charlotte Glazier Abbott was born in East Leverett in 1935. Like all other children in the area, she attended a one-room schoolhouse through the eighth grade. In her teenage years, she went to Amherst Regional High School and New Salem Academy, which she remembers as having offered a significant change from the relative simplicity of the village schools. Abbott is a long-time resident of Moores Corner, living directly across Rattlesnake Gutter Road from the Moores Corner cemetery, where many of her ancestors are buried. She works as an assistant to the Leverett school nurse and is active in local church activities.

I first heard about *Vernon Aiken* from two other informants, both of whom promised that he would be a most informative and entertaining person to interview. "Vernon mimics people's voices when he tells stories," they told me, and I discovered that those people were right. His wife Katie Aiken told me that many times in her life, hearing a neighbor's voice in another part of the house, she had been surprised to find that the "neighbor" actually was her own husband holding forth in front of one audience or another. Vernon Aiken learned to tell stories when he was growing up, helping his father run a dairy and a log-hauling business. He must have been an especially good listener; anytime he begins a sentence "My Dad told me," one can't help expecting to hear a fascinating (and often a humorous) story. Aiken was born in 1912, in the same North Leverett house where he and his wife now live.

Clifford Blinn was born 1917 in Moores Corner and lives right next to the old Dexter Moore Mill at the corner of Dudleyville and North Leverett roads. He attended the Moores Corner schoolhouse and spent a good many years as a woodcutter before he began commuting to work at the Greenfield Tap and Die factory. Like most of his neighbors, he grew up on a small farm but also "worked out" from a relatively young age. Louise Minks of the Leverett Historical Society referred me to him, and he and I first met at the Leverett Senior Lunch, which he helps to prepare every week. Mr. Blinn currently is assembling a collection of old photographs of the North Leverett–Moores Corner area.

I first heard about *Gertrude Maynard Carey* from her cousin, the late Mary Ward Keniston, who was a North Leverett resident. Carey was born in 1907 and grew up in Moores Corner, where she helped her parents run the village store. She moved to Turners Falls, Massachusetts, in her preteen years but returned to the Sawmill Valley when she married into the Carey family. When I interviewed her, she was living just a few yards from Lake Wyola, in Shutesbury. She died in 1996, at the age of eighty-nine. Quite late in life, she served her community as a church organist. She was an avid Boston Red Sox fan and insisted on having me call her "Grandma Carey." I was always glad to oblige.

I was referred to *Loyce Glazier Dunbar* by her long-time friend, Professor Audrey Duckert of the University of Massachusetts at Amherst. She was born on February 29, 1908, in North Leverett, which means that, despite her eighty-nine years, she is a mere twenty-two birthdays old. Although she left the Sawmill Valley in the mid-1920s, when her father bought a house at the southern foot of Rattlesnake Gutter, she always has been a resident of the town of Leverett. Having grown up listening to all manner of stories, not only from her father, Maurice Glazier, but also from her aunt, Ruby Hemenway, Dunbar is an authority on Sawmill Valley lore, not to mention a wonderful storyteller. She spent a number of years as a schoolteacher in the town of Leverett and is fondly remembered by all her pupils. I first interviewed Dunbar at the home of her niece, Charlotte Glazier Abbott (see above) but since have visited with her on a number of occasions at her present home on Amherst Road in Leverett.

Bill Fleming was recommended to me by Charlotte Abbott, who lives about half a mile from him. Although he had given me relatively detailed directions, it still took me about forty-five minutes riding my bicycle around in the snow to find his house, which is known locally as "the old Watson place." Unlike most other older dwellings in the Sawmill Valley, the Flemings' house is about a quarter-mile uphill from the nearest road. Born in 1911 in Riveredge, New Jersey, Bill Fleming came to the Sawmill Valley in the 1940s after marrying into the Watson clan. He picked up a great deal of local lore by listening to his mother-in-law's stories, as well as those of his fellow woodcutters, "Uncles" Henry Towne and

Clifford Blinn. Bill spins a good yarn, too, and is especially fond of teasing listeners with intermittent "stretches of the blanket." When my wife Janice Sorensen and I recently visited him and his wife Marian in order to take their picture, he was just settling down after having spent several hours in his yard chopping cordwood with an electric saw.

Although *Marion Watson Fleming* did not spend her childhood years in the Sawmill Valley (she was born in Abbington, Massachusetts, in 1916), she grew up hearing all manner of valley lore from her mother, Verdie Watson, and her grandfather, the locally renowned J. W. Watson, both of whom *had* been born in the region. Marion Fleming spent many of her childhood summers at the Watson house, helping out on the family farm. When she married Bill Fleming, she led him up from New Jersey to her ancestral house, where they eventually settled. The couple opened the place to summer guests but also maintained a working farm on the eastern slope of Brushy Mountain. Mrs. Fleming is an accomplished craftswoman, and entire rooms of the Watson house are devoted to her elaborate miniatures.

Lionel Girard grew up in Turners Falls, Massachusetts, where he was born in 1907. I first heard about him from Michael Nobel Kline, who had interviewed him for the Pioneer Valley Folklore Society's Western Massachusetts Folklife Project. Because I was interested in finding out about the French Canadians who lived on the periphery of the Sawmill Valley, I was eager to meet Girard. In addition to having grown up in Turners Falls' sizable French Canadian neighborhood, Girard has been a knowledgeable and articulate community scholar. He is a founder and past president of the Montague Historical Society, as well as author of a number of historical pamphlets. Among other things, Girard told me about ethnic street gangs that—from a child's point of view, at any rate—ruled Turners Falls during the second and third decades of the twentieth century and set it apart from its surrounding rural communities. In 1945, Girard moved to Montague Center, where he still lives. When I interviewed him in 1992 and 1993, he was working five days a week for Franklin County Home Care. Recently he has survived a series of strokes but continues to live at home and maintain an active family life.

Although I never had the good fortune to meet her, I feel that I have come to know *Ruby Hemenway* by listening to taped interviews that Audrey Duckert conducted with her, as well as by reading her newspaper columns for the

Greenfield Recorder. Born in 1884, Hemenway lived until the age of 103. She died after establishing herself as the nation's oldest newspaper columnist, having begun writing her column when she was in her nineties. She attended Montague Center High School and the Teachers' College in North Adams. She was not only an authority on Sawmill Valley history and customs, but also a captivating storyteller and, by all accounts, one of the region's best loved and most appreciated cultural treasures.

Anyone who is interested in finding out about Moores Corners' charcoal kilns ends up being referred to *Wayne Howard,* who once ran them. Born in 1921 in North Leverett, Howard "grew up in charcoal," having begun helping his father burn the kilns and sell the charcoal before he reached his teens. Because his family also ran a considerable diary farm, Howard grew up "in cows" as well, learning at a young age to pretend that he didn't know how to milk them. He and his brother Ethan Howard ran the charcoal business well into the 1960s, when, according to local lore, environmentalists put them out of business. At one time, Wayne Howard was the fire chief of Leverett, and the local historical society has a number of photographs of him driving the idiosyncratic town engine. He now lives just a couple of blocks from the University of Massachusetts in Amherst, but he still travels regularly to North Leverett and Moores Corner. Recently he has been tracing the history of the Sawmill Valley's earliest sawmills.

Clarissa Truesdell LaClaire lives on my favorite road in Leverett—Jackson Hill. Born in 1908 in Wendell, Massachusetts, Clarissa LaClaire is a preacher's daughter, "the fourth in line of ten children." LaClaire came to know nearly all her neighbors at a young age, since she often accompanied her clergyman father on his visits to parishioners throughout the Sawmill Valley and beyond it into Leverett Center. She spent most of her adult years as a schoolteacher in Leverett and other towns, so she can recall the one-room schoolhouses from both student's and teacher's points of view. She continues to participate in church functions and attends the Leverett Senior Lunches on a regular basis. Her husband was Clifford LaClaire.

When I first called *Clifford LaClaire,* he told me that he might be too busy remodeling his house to participate in an interview. I called him back two weeks later, somewhat concerned that he was going to be an unenthusiastic, if not a reluctant, informant. Despite the fact that both he and his wife had colds on the day of our interview, the two went out of their way to welcome me into their home and supply me with an hour and a half's worth of valley stories; my initial fears proved entirely unfounded. Clifford LaClaire was born in Wendell, Massachusetts, in 1915. At a very young age he moved to Dudleyville, where he was brought up by his Quebeçois grandfather, "Old Joe" LaClaire. Clifford LaClaire spent most of his working years as a woodcutter. He died in 1994.

Joe N. LaClaire was born in 1922 and grew up in Moores Corner. His parents, Joe W. LaClaire and Harriet Bourne LaClaire, were well-known raconteurs in their own time, and their legacy lives on in his accounts of early-twentieth-century life in the Sawmill Valley. In addition to the work he did as a woodsman, Joe N. LaClaire spent a considerable portion of his adult life working at the University of Massachusetts at Amherst. He lives directly across from the Village Coop, which he was instrumental in helping to build back in 1990.

David Mercier was born in 1917 in North Leverett and spent most of his adult life as a woodcutter. He also devoted quite a bit of time to hunting in the wilder stretches of the Sawmill Valley. When I chanced to meet him at Willy and Mary Stone's house in Montague Center, he told us a number of stories about his adventures stalking wildcats in Rattlesnake Gutter with "Boy" [Ethan Jr.] Howard. More than any of my other informants, Mercier seemed to enjoy exploring the local wilderness just for the sake of exploring it. He passed away in 1996.

Louise Minks of the Leverett Historical Society told me about *Marion LaClaire Norwood* very shortly after I began interviewing people. Norwood was born 1920 in Moores Corner. Because her parents—Joe W. LaClaire and Harriet Bourne LaClaire—were prolific storytellers, Norwood grew up completely surrounded by local lore. Moreover, in many years as the daughter and sometime assistant of the Moores Corner postmaster (her mother, who served in this post from 1918 to 1967), Norwood had the opportunity to encounter nearly all valley residents on a daily basis. For ten years after the post office closed, she and her late husband, Harry Norwood, ran a store in the same building. Having retired, she devotes a good deal of her time to genealogical research on the LaClaire and Bourne families. She now lives at the foot of Taylor Hill in Montague Center.

Robert Ripley is a person who became a genuine legend during his lifetime. Born in 1900 on Chestnut Hill in Montague, Ripley lived to the age of ninety-three and was active until the very second he died. Approximately one year after I met him for the first time, Ripley passed away—in the act of directing the Moores Corner Church choir. During his ninety-three years, he worked as a farmer, woodcutter, and maple sugar producer. In fact, Montague Center celebrates its annual "Sugar on Snow" dinner with what is locally known as "Ripley's Gold." Ripley also was an energetic participant in community affairs of all sorts, including the North Leverett Baptist Church's Sunday School. In the early 1990s, he and folklorist Michael Nobel Kline hosted a group of former street-gang members who were participating in a video therapy program through a local halfway house.

Mary Williams Stone was born 1925 in North Leverett and grew up on a small farm. Like most other local girls, she started to work at a young age, helping her mother with the younger children. After she married Willy Stone, she worked for a short time as a storekeeper; the Stones once operated a filling station in North Leverett. Mary Stone always has been a participant in activities at the North Leverett Baptist Church, teaching Sunday School and helping to operate the church's Vacation Bible School. She also has worked from time to time in home care for local elders.

Although *Wilton (Willy) Stone* was born in Guilford, Vermont, he has lived in the Sawmill Valley for most of his life. He was born in 1919 and moved to the valley in 1923. The Stone farm was located "up in the brush," about a mile from North Leverett on Chestnut Hill, within the town limits of Montague. Over the years he worked as a woodsman and a storekeeper and now is retired. Willy Stone lives in Montague Center, but, because valley people still pay scant attention to town boundaries, that doesn't keep him from attending the Leverett Senior Lunch every Friday.

Notes

Introduction

1. This is a question that at least one historian has asked before about rural New England communities after the Civil War. The very title of Hal Barron's 1984 study of farming in Chelsea, Vermont (*Those Who Stayed Behind*) conveys an interest in rural resistance, if that is the right word, to urbanization and industrial expansion.

2. A number of cogent articulations of this "new" version of the folk region exist. Mary Hufford's introduction to the American Folklife Center's *One Space, Many Places: Folklife and Land Use in New Jersey's Pinelands National Preserve* (1986) contains an extended exploration of the ways in which ethnic and regional identity converge and diverge in the vernacular region. "Tending the Commons," Hufford's recent article in the *Folklife Center Newsletter* (1998), deals with ramp-eating among Appalachian women and applies a microcosmic approach to the various cultural meanings that emerge from a study of this particular foodway and its role as a subtle—or not so subtle, when taste and smell are taken into account—gesture of regional defiance. In *Sense of Place: American Regional Cultures,* ed. Barbara Allen and Thomas Schlereth (1990), Allen's introduction compresses almost a century's worth of regional folklore study into a tidy, serviceable unit. Schlereth's concluding essay provides still more insight into the various meanings that folklorists and cultural geographers have attached to the vernacular region. Clarence Mondale's 1989 survey article offers a similar synthesis of recent approaches to regional studies. A 1987 essay by Jim Wayne Miller brings a regional perspective to bear on contemporary American literature. Kent Ryden's *Mapping the Invisible Landscape* (1995), in addition to a lyrical chapter on the sense of place as applied to the folklore of the Coeur D'Alene mining district in Idaho, contains a useful essay on regionalism, sense of place, and consciousness in American folklore studies. Finally, an interesting inversion of the rural-urban regional equation can be found in Richard Dorson's study of the Calumet region of northwestern Indiana, *Land of the Millrats* (1981). Dorson suggests that some of the same principles that folklorists have applied to studying rural folk regions can and should be applied in urban and industrial contexts.

3. Stowe's *Oldtown Folks* (1869) provides a particularly cogent illustration of such eloquent plain-spokenness in the character of Sam Lawson, the "village do-nothing."

4. See the legend about buried money on Brushy Mountain (chapter 1) as a classic example of a "purely" folkloric set of accounts.

5. For an example of such materials, see Vernon Aiken's description of a family of French Canadian woodchoppers who lived and worked in the Sawmill Valley for a short period around the turn of the century. It can be found in chapter 2.

6. An example might be the occasional use of the pronoun "to" as an alternative form of "at"—i.e., Willy Stone's reference to an event that occurred "up to the Hemenway place."

Chapter 1

1. Interestingly, Robert Ripley was the only one of my informants who drew an actual connection between Rattlesnake Gutter and rattlesnakes. Even his account of the name's origin was speculative, however: "They named it that 'cause there's rattlesnakes there. I don't know if they ever seen any, . . . but my guess is maybe there was some there."

Chapter 3

1. Loyce Dunbar tells the following story about a man who *did* suffer the humiliation of being consigned to the Town Farm: "Used to be a Poor Farm over on the Cave Hill. I can remember hearing my aunt tell about this old man, he had no relatives, he had no money. And so . . . she said she could remember . . . he [was] going by in the back of this buckboard. They were taking him to the Poor Farm. He said he didn't want to ride behind any oxen to the Poor Farm, he wanted to ride behind a horse. And she said they took him there with horses."

2. Other examples of valley residents who struggled in order to meet the demands of self-sufficiency, despite physical and mental handicaps, can be found in the chapter 4's treatment of village eccentrics.

3. In the words of Lawrence Levine, "the magnification of the self" was a means by which the tall-tale heroes of the American frontier sought to overpower "insecurities produced by forces greater than themselves"—wilderness, inclement weather, etc. (104).

4. Clifford LaClaire attests to Carey's unique ability to assess the size of a day's timber harvest: "Walter Carey, they tell me, he had no education. But he could add up lumber on a truck, and tell you how many thousand feet you had on a truck. . . . I used to work for Walter and I used to pass him lumber and he'd be on the truck and he'd get way above the cab and he'd tell us, tell me, 'That's enough. We got on three thousand feet of lumber now.' So I don't know how he figured it out, but he evidently figured it out one way or another."

Chapter 4

1. As far as I have been able to determine, the Sawmill Valley's most noted eccentrics were all males. This may be because one of the primary criteria for "eccentric" status within the regional group was solitariness, and even women who were unmarried or widowed usually were looked after in some capacity by their families. Solitary men found

their way into the valley, often enough, because they had been attracted by its work prospects, by its woodlots and sawmills. Some of the so-called "drifters" to whom Marion Norwood, Vernon Aiken, and Loyce Dunbar refer ended up as town characters.

2. The folk custom of "serenading" newly married couples is—or was until recently—in any number of American regions. According to Mitford M. Mathews' *Americanisms,* the "serenade," as people in the Sawmill Valley and other areas of rural New England refer to it, is termed a "shivaree" in the Mississippi Valley, a "belling" in western Pennsylvania, a "skimmleton" in the Hudson Valley, and a "horning" in Rhode Island (233).

3. When I asked informants if they knew anything about the name "Tucker," I came away with some befuddled but inventive answers. Loyce Dunbar: "Perhaps when they was all tuckered out they'd yell 'Tucker!' I have no idea." Vernon Aiken: "There might have been somebody by that name, that did the dance. But I don't know."

Works Cited

Primary Sources

All the interviews conducted by Michael Hoberman are archived on audiocassette at the Northeast Archives of Folklore and Oral History, Maine Folklife Center, Univ. of Maine at Orono.

Abbott, Charlotte Glazier; and Dunbar, Loyce Glazier. Interview by Michael Hoberman. 28 Mar. 1992.

Aiken, Vernon. Interview by Michael Hoberman. 27 Mar. 1992.

———. Interview by Michael Hoberman. 25 June 1992.

Blinn, Clifford. Interview by Michael Hoberman. 20 Feb. 1992.

Briggs, Forrest. "Brushy Mountain History, 1780 to 1880." Pamphlet. Leverett Historical Society.

———. Recorded interview by the Leverett Historical Society. May 1984.

———. Transcription of interview by Louise Minks and Lois Feldman, with Wallace Briggs. 23 Nov. 1984. Leverett Historical Society.

Carey, Gertrude Maynard. Interview by Michael Hoberman. 17 June 1992.

Clark, Edie. "The Oldest Newspaper Columnist on Earth." *Yankee,* Jan. 1984, pp. 102–14.

Dunbar, Loyce Glazier. Interview by Michael Hoberman. 25 June 1992.

Fleming, Bill; and Fleming, Marion Watson. Interview by Michael Hoberman. 17 Mar. 1992.

Girard, Lionel. Interview by Michael Hoberman. 5 Feb. 1992.

———. Interview by Michael Hoberman. 18 June 1992.

Glazier, Maurice; and Hemenway, Ruby. Recorded interview by Audrey Duckert. 17 Oct. 1966. Private collection of interviewer.

———. Recorded interview by Audrey Duckert. 3 Apr. 1967. Private collection of interviewer.

Hemenway, Ruby. Recorded interview by the Leverett Historical Society. 6 Apr. 1984. Leverett Historical Society.

———. Recorded interview by Audrey Duckert. 15 May 1967. Private collection of interviewer.

Hemenway, Ruby; LaClaire, Joseph W.; and LaClaire, Harriet Bourne. Recorded interview by Audrey Duckert. May 1967. Private collection of Marion LaClaire Norwood.

Historic and Archaeological Resources of the Connecticut Valley. Boston: Massachusetts Historical Commission, 1984.

Howard, Wayne. Interview by Michael Hoberman. 10 Feb. 1992.

Keniston, Mary Ward. Interview by Michael Hoberman. 10 June 1992.
LaClaire, Clifford; and LaClaire, Clarissa Truesdell. Interview by Michael Hoberman. 6 Mar. 1992.
LaClaire, Joseph N. Interview by Michael Hoberman. 9 June 1996.
Norwood, Marion LaClaire. Interview by Michael Hoberman. 28 Feb. 1992.
Ripley, Robert. Interview by Michael Hoberman. 3 Feb. 1992.
———. Interview by Michael Hoberman. 18 June 1992.
———. Recorded interview by Michael Kline. 28 Jan. 1991. Northeast Archives of Folklore and Oral History.
———. Recorded interview by Michael Kline. 1992. Northeast Archives of Folklore and Oral History.
Skerry, Evelyn. Recorded interview by the Leverett Historical Society. 10 Feb. 1984. Leverett Historical Society.
Stone, Wilton; Stone, Mary Williams; and Mercier, David. Interview by Michael Hoberman. 16 Mar. 1992.
Stone, Wilton; and Stone, Mary Williams. Interview by Michael Hoberman. 15 Dec. 1992.

Secondary Sources

Abrahams, Roger. "After New Perspectives: Folklore Study in the Late Twentieth Century." *Western Folklore* 52 (1993): 379–400.
Allen, Barbara. "Regional Folklore." In *American Folklore: An Encyclopedia,* ed. Jan Harold Brunvand. New York: Garland, 1996.
Allen, Barbara. "Regional Studies in American Folklore Scholarship." In *Sense of Place: American Regional Cultures,* ed. Barbara Allen and Thomas Schlereth. Lexington: Univ. Press of Kentucky, 1990.
American Folklife Center. *One Space, Many Places: Folklife and Land Use in New Jersey's Pinelands National Preserve.* Washington, D.C.: Smithsonian Institution, 1986.
Anderson, Benedict. *Imagined Communities: Reflections on the Origin and Spread of Nationalism.* London: Verso, 1983.
Ayers. Edward L., and Onuf, Peter S. "Introduction." In *All Over the Map: Rethinking American Regions,* ed. Edward L. Ayers et al. Baltimore, Md.: Johns Hopkins Univ. Press, 1996.
Barron, Hal. *Those Who Stayed Behind: Rural Society in Nineteenth-Century New England.* Cambridge, England: Cambridge Univ. Press, 1984.
Ben-Amos, Dan, ed. *Folklore Genres.* Austin: Univ. of Texas Press, 1976.
Berman, Marshall. *All That Is Solid Melts into Air.* New York: Viking Penguin, 1988.
Blejwas, Stanislaus. "The Inherited and the Disinherited: The Polish Peasant Farmer in New England Literature." *Connecticut Review* 14, no. 2 (Fall 1992): 49–88.
———. "Puritans and Poles: The New England Literary Image of the Polish Peasant Farmer." *Polish-American Studies* 42 (Autumn 1985): 46–75.
Bluestein, Gene. *Poplore.* Amherst: Univ. of Massachusetts Press, 1994.

Bodnar, John. *The Transplanted: A History of Urban Immigrants in America.* Bloomington: Indiana Univ. Press, 1985.

Botkin, B. A. *A Treasury of New England Folklore.* New York: Crown Publishers, 1947.

Brault, Gerard. *The French-Canadian Heritage in New England.* Hanover, N.H.: Univ. Press of New England, 1986.

Bronner, Simon. *Following Tradition: Folklore in the Discourse of American Culture.* Logan: Utah State Univ. Press, 1998.

Brown, Dona. *Inventing New England: Regional Tourism in the Nineteenth Century.* Washington, D.C.: Smithsonian Institution, 1995.

Brunvand, Jan Harold. *The Study of American Folklore: An Introduction.* New York: W. W. Norton, 1968.

Daniels, Roger. *Coming to America: A History of Immigration and Ethnicity in American Life.* New York: Harper Collins, 1990.

Cunningham, Roger. *Apples on the Flood: The Southern Mountain Experience.* Knoxville: Univ. of Tennessee Press, 1987.

Davidson, Levette. "'Gassy' Thompson—and Others: Stories of Local Characters." *Folklore Quarterly* 5 (1946): 339–49.

Dolby, Sandra K. "Essential Contributions of a Folkloric Perspective to American Studies." *Journal of Folklore Research* 33, no. 1 (Nov. 1996): 58–63.

Dorman, Robert L. *Revolt of the Provinces: The Regionalist Movement in America, 1920–1945.* Chapel Hill: Univ. of North Carolina Press, 1993.

Dorson, Richard. *America in Legend.* New York: Pantheon, 1973.

———. *American Folklore.* Chicago: Univ. of Chicago Press, 1960.

——— *Buying the Wind: Regional Folklore in the United States.* Chicago: Univ. of Chicago Press, 1964.

———, ed. *Folklore: Selected Essays.* Bloomington: Indiana Univ. Press, 1972.

———, ed. *Folklore and Folklife: An Introduction.* Chicago: Univ. of Chicago Press, 1972.

———, ed. *Handbook of American Folklore.* Bloomington: Indiana Univ. Press, 1983.

———. *Jonathan Draws the Long Bow: New England Popular Tales and Legends.* New York: Russell and Russell, 1947.

———. *Land of the Millrats.* Cambridge, Mass.: Harvard Univ. Press, 1981.

Douglas, Ann. "The Literature of Impoverishment." *Women's Studies* 1 (1972): 3–45.

Dunaway, David K.; and Baum, Willa K. *Oral History: An Interdisciplinary Anthology.* Nashville, Tenn.: American Association for State and Local History, 1984.

Dundes, Alan. *Folklore Matters.* Knoxville: Univ. of Tennessee Press, 1989.

Dundes, Alan; and Pagter, Carl. *Work Hard and You Shall Be Rewarded.* Bloomington: Indiana Univ. Press, 1978.

Gardner, Emelyn. *Folklore from the Schoharie Hills.* Ann Arbor: Univ. of Michigan Press, 1937.

Garrison, J. Ritchie. *Landscape and Material Life in Franklin County, Massachusetts, 1770–1860.* Knoxville: Univ. of Tennessee Press, 1991.

Gladsky, Thomas. "The Immigrant on the Land: Polish Farmers and New England Novelists." *New England Quarterly* 51, no. 3 (Sept. 1988): 429–38.

Glassie, Henry. *Patterns in the Material Folk Culture of the Eastern United States.* Philadelphia: Univ. of Pennsylvania Press, 1968.

Halpert, Herbert. "American Regional Folklore." *Journal of American Folklore* 60 (1947): 355–66.

Hand, Wayland, ed. *American Folk Legend.* Berkeley: Univ. of California Press, 1969.

Hobsbawm, Eric. *The Invention of Tradition.* Cambridge, Mass.: Cambridge Univ. Press, 1983.

Hufford, Mary, ed. *Conserving Culture: A New Discourse on Heritage.* Urbana: Univ. of Illinois Press, 1994.

———. "Tending the Commons: Ramp Suppers, Biodiversity, and the Integrity of 'The Mountains.'" *Folklife Center News* 20, no. 4 (Fall 1998): 3–11.

Hubka, Thomas. *Big House, Little House, Back House, Barn.* Hanover, N.H.: Univ. Press of New England, 1983.

Hurley, Gerard T. "Buried Treasure Tales in America." *Western Folklore* 10 (1951): 197–216.

Jones, Suzi. "Regionalization: A Rhetorical Strategy." *Journal of the Folklore Institute* 13 (1976): 105–21.

Juillard, Etienne. "The Region: An Essay of Definition." In *Man, Space and the Environment,* ed. Paul Ward English and Robert C. Mayfield, 429–41. Oxford, England: Oxford Univ. Press, 1972.

Kammen, Michael. *The Mystic Chords of Memory.* New York: Knopf, 1991.

Leverett Bicentennial Committee. *A History of Leverett, Massachusetts, 1774–1974.* Northampton, Mass.: Gazette Printing Co., 1974.

Levine, Lawrence. *Black Culture, Black Consciousness.* New York: Oxford Univ. Press, 1977.

Lightfoot William. "Regional Folkloristics." In *Handbook of American Folklore,* ed. Richard Dorson. Bloomington: Indiana Univ. Press, 1983.

Limerick, Patricia Nelson, "Region and Reason." In *All Over the Map: Rethinking American Regions,* ed. Edward L. Ayers et al., 83–107. Baltimore, Md.: Johns Hopkins Univ. Press, 1996.

Lockridge, Kenneth. *A New England Town: The First Hundred Years.* New York: W. W. Norton, 1970.

Mathews, Mitford. *Americanisms.* Chicago: Univ. of Chicago Press, 1951.

Massachusetts Historical Commission. *Historic and Archaeological Resources of the Connecticut Valley.* Boston: Office of the Massachusetts Secretary of State, 1984.

Mechling, Jay. "If They Can Build a Square Tomato: Notes Toward a Holistic Approach to Regional Studies." *Prospects* 4 (1979): 59–77.

———. "On Sharing Folklore and American Identity in a Multicultural Society." *Western Folklore* 52 (1993): 271–89.

Meinig, D. W., ed. *The Interpretation of Ordinary Landscapes.* New York: Oxford Univ. Press, 1979.

Merchant, Carolyn. *Ecological Revolutions: Nature, Gender and Science in New England.* Chapel Hill: Univ. of North Carolina Press, 1989.

Miller, Jim Wayne. "Anytime the Ground Is Uneven: The Outlook for Regional Studies and What To Look Out For." In *Geography and Literature,* ed. Jim Wayne Miller, 1–20. Syracuse, New York: Syracuse Univ. Press, 1987.

Mondale, Clarence. "Concepts and Trends in Regional Studies." *American Studies International* 27, no. 1 (Apr. 1989): 13–37.

Montell, William Lynwood. 1983. Rpt. with New Foreword. *Don't Go Up Kettle Creek: The Verbal Legacy of the Upper Cumberland.* Knoxville: Univ. of Tennessee Press, 2000.

———. *The Saga of Coe Ridge: A Study in Oral History.* Knoxville: Univ. of Tennessee Press, 1970.

Mullen, Patrick. "The Folk Idea of Unlimited Good in American Buried Treasure Legends." *Journal of the Folklore Institute* 15 (1978): 209–20.

Nicolaisen, W. F. H. "The Folk and the Region." *New York Folklore* 2 (1976): 143–49.

———. "Folklore and Geography." *New York Folklore Quarterly* 29 (1973): 3–20.

Nissenbaum, Stephen. "New England as Region and Nation." In *All Over the Map: Rethinking American Regions,* ed. Edward L. Ayers et al. Baltimore, Md.: Johns Hopkins Univ. Press, 1996.

Onuf, Peter S. "Federalism, Republicanism, and the Origins of American Sectionalism." In *All Over the Map: Rethinking American Regions,* ed. Edward L. Ayers et al. Baltimore, Md.: Johns Hopkins Univ. Press, 1996.

Oring, Elliot. *Folk Groups and Folklore Genres.* Logan: Utah State Univ. Press, 1986.

Pressey, E. P. *History of Montague* (1910). Turners Falls, Mass.: Pioneer Litho, 1987.

Radway, Janice. "What's in a Name? Presidential Address to the American Studies Association, 20 Nov. 1998." *American Quarterly* 51, no. 1 (Mar. 1999): 1–32.

Rourke, Constance. *American Humor.* New York: Harcourt Brace Jovanovich, 1931.

Russell, Howard S. *A Long, Deep Furrow: Three Centuries of Farming in New England.* Hanover, N.H.: Univ. Press of New England, 1982.

Ryden, Kent. *Mapping the Invisible Landscape.* Iowa City: Univ. of Iowa Press, 1995.

Sollors, Werner. *The Invention of Ethnicity.* New York: Oxford Univ. Press, 1989.

———. "Region." *Prospects* 4 (1979): 442–45.

Stahl, Sandra K. D. "The Local Character Anecdote." *Genre* 8 (1975): 283–302.

Stilgoe, John. *Common Landscape of America, 1580–1845.* New Haven, Conn.: Yale Univ. Press, 1982.

Stowe, Harriet Beecher. *Oldtown Folks.* 1869. Rpt. New Brunswick, N.J.: Rutgers Univ. Press, 1987.

Toelken, Barrie. *The Dynamics of Folklore.* Boston: Houghton Mifflin Co., 1979.

Tuan, Yi Fu. *Space and Place: The Perspective of Experience.* Minneapolis: Univ. of Minnesota Press, 1977.

Tye, Diane. "Local Character Anecdotes: A Nova Scotia Case Study." *Western Folklore* 48 (1989): 181–99.

Whisnant, David. *All That Is Native and Fine: The Politics of Culture in an American Region.* Chapel Hill: Univ. of North Carolina Press, 1983.

Zelinsky, Wilbur. *Cultural Geography of the United States.* Englewood Cliffs, N.J.: Prentice-Hall, 1973.

Index

Yankee Moderns was designed and typeset on a Macintosh computer system using PageMaker software. The text and chapter openings are set in Garamond. This book was designed by Ellen Beeler, typeset by Kimberly Scarbrough, and manufactured by Thomson-Shore, Inc. The recycled paper used in this book is designed for an effective life of at least three hundred years.